War & Society

War & Society

Miguel A. Centeno
Elaine Enriquez

polity

The right of Miguel A. Centeno and Elaine Enriquez to be identified as Authors of this Work has been asserted in accordance with the UK Copyright, Designs and Patents Act 1988.

First published in 2016 by Polity Press

Polity Press
65 Bridge Street
Cambridge CB2 1UR, UK

Polity Press
350 Main Street
Malden, MA 02148, USA

ISBN-13: 978-0-7456-4579-7 (hardback)
ISBN-13: 978-0-7456-4580-3 (paperback)

A catalogue record for this book is available from the British Library.

Library of Congress Cataloging-in-Publication Data

Names: Centeno, Miguel Angel, 1957- author. | Enriquez, Elaine, author.
Title: War & society / Miguel A. Centeno, Elaine Enriquez.
Other titles: War and society
Description: Cambridge, UK ; Malden, MA : Polity, 2016. | Series: Polity
  political sociology series | Includes bibliographical references and index.
Identifiers: LCCN 2015029522| ISBN 9780745645797 (hardback) | ISBN
  9780745645803 (paperback)
Subjects: LCSH: War and society. | War--Causes. | BISAC: POLITICAL SCIENCE /
  Peace.
Classification: LCC HM554 .C46 2016 | DDC 303.6/6--dc23 LC record available at
  http://lccn.loc.gov/2015029522

Typeset in 11 on 13 pt Sabon by
Servis Filmsetting Ltd, Stockport, Cheshire
Printed and bound in Great Britain by CPI Group (UK) Ltd, Croydon

For further information on Polity, visit our website: politybooks.com

Contents

Acknowledgments

We have many people to thank for their contributions to the development of this book. Our gratitude goes out to Randall Collins and Siniša Malešević, who each gave invaluable feedback on early material. We also would like to thank two anonymous reviewers who provided thorough readings and productive critique of the manuscript. Their responses improved the book considerably. Jonathan Skerrett has gone beyond the call of duty in his patience and support as an editor. Thanks are also due to the myriad students and assistants-in-instruction of the Princeton University course on which this book is based, The Western Way of War.

Miguel Centeno has far too many people to thank and fears that any listing will unjustly exclude too many. Students, colleagues, staff, family, and friends have lived for years under the specter of the "war book." I hope they find the result worth their patience and good will (but reading not required!). Three women helped raise me and taught me most of what I know: Ana Maria Gutierrez, Marta Souza, and Amalia Dahl – I owe them all everything.

In addition to those listed above, Elaine Enriquez would like personally to thank Lauren Lynch, who graciously provided space and time to complete this manuscript, and whose hospitality and patience were unending. I dedicate this book to the many people in my life who have served in the military and with whom I have had countless invigorating discussions – Joann Enriquez and Christopher-Ian Reichel among them.

Introduction

This book is the culmination of over a decade and a half of teaching the course The Western Way of War at Princeton University. The course, as does this book, analyzes the development of warfare in the Western world – Europe, the Americas (primarily the United States), and, to some extent, Japan. Other societies are touched upon, but for the most part this book is a survey of wars and conflicts in these parts of the world. It uses the historical comparative method to glean sociological insights about the nature of warfare and how it reflects and shapes social dynamics and institutions.

Hundreds of undergraduate students have heard these arguments, read the books referenced, and contributed to the thought-provoking discussion that the topic deserves. It is a pleasure to put those years of claims and evidence into book form for other students of war and history, academic and lay alike. We do so in the hope that this work encourages a re-awakening of interest in war on the part of sociology.[1]

After a discussion of the nature of war and its origin, we have organized the book around two separate claims. The first is that the history of human warfare is one of increasing size, complexity, and organization over the *longue durée*. Most certainly the first coordinated efforts at violence were little more than collections of individuals – men fighting for a common cause that was temporary and circumscribed. Whatever the source of hostilities, whether scarcity of resources or the need to defend a settlement, these conflicts were limited in scale.

Introduction

As group conflicts developed, it was still the actions of prominent characters – fighters like the valiant warriors Achilles and
Hector and leaders like Alexander the Great – which affected the
turn of warfare. Warriors were called to fight, and outcomes could
depend on the actions of a few.

Eventually, through a mutually reinforcing relationship of
conflict, capital, and politics, war developed into actions between
nation states involving armies. Particularly in Europe, we see the
development of a series of armies, from mercenary to standing,
at the service of a single political entity. These wars of armies
would, in turn, be an important foundation for nationalism and
statecraft.

The increasing scope and complexity of conflict would continue
until history would see veritable wars of societies. European colonialism would forever alter the trajectories of civilizations, from
Latin America to Africa to the Pacific. Warfare on a scale here-
tofore unknown would follow the turn of the twentieth century
and would involve the very real threat of total annihilation.
Industrialized genocide would become a fact of the human chroni-
cle, and utter destruction would touch the lives of the European
peninsula and beyond – not once, but twice.

This, however, brings us to our second claim and organizing
principle. Parallel to this historical arc of increasing scale and complexity of conflict, the nature of war has proven to be at all times
paradoxical. Its essence is brutal, destructive, and chaotic. Yet war
also demands the very best of its participants – heroism, bravery,
and inventiveness. It has often been enacted for the greater good,
for the betterment of a society, and to protect and extend life. And,
incredibly, through its drive for greater lethality, it has been an
engine of stunning creation.

The increased numbers of men fighting over greater and greater
distances would see the development of a number of state institutions and technological innovations. Census, taxation, citizenship,
and the technologies of destruction and communication would all
be a result of constant battle. Modern communication systems,
including the Internet and global positioning systems, are the
direct products of the practice of warfare. And participation in

war, ironically, has led many to a better life than they would have otherwise had, socially and economically.

World War II is without question the apotheosis of the massification of war that we trace throughout this book. And now that we are already more than half a century beyond its closure, we conclude the book looking to the future of war. We argue that, particularly as a function of the proliferation of nuclear weapons, the nature of war has changed. The empires of Europe came to an end, often violently, in part because the politics and morality of post-war Europe simply could not sustain such forced colonization and occupation. Guerrilla warfare and insurgency are now the hallmarks of conflict in the world, although there are still certainly the threats of large land wars. But attendant with the development of fantastic technologies of war has come a dramatic change in military composition, particularly in the West. We argue that these three developments – the end of empire, insurgency, and a dramatic shift in military service – are what characterize this new future of war in the world.

The literature of war is vast – so vast as to be daunting to all but the most dedicated pupil. We sincerely hope that this volume allows the reader some appreciation of all that makes the subject so fascinating to so many people – its drama, its pathos, and its brilliance. This book may answer some questions, but the greatest of them all – what means war? – may never be satisfied.

1

The Nature of War

What is war? It is foremost a social fact. War is a reflection and consequence of social structure, group norms, and relations. As such, war can be studied using the very same principles and methods that social science has used to understand other social phenomena, whether marriage or market exchanges. War may be a traumatic and gory social fact, but we cannot allow the horror of it to obscure the underlying principles behind it and its very real political and social consequences. Moreover, war is a critical force in shaping those very structures from which it stems, such as the state, as well as related institutions such as citizenship and class.

In the past one hundred years, the toll from armed conflict has been so high and the pain caused by it been so great that distinguished political and philosophical thinkers have made important arguments about its inherent insanity and the need for its prohibition.[1] There is no question that war is chaotic – the very roots of the word in several European languages denote confusion.[2] Yet, a central theme of this book is that to dismiss war as irrational, stupid, horrific, and evil is to accomplish very little. We write this in full awareness of the myriad costs of war – social, fiscal, and ethical. In the twentieth century, over 150 million people died as a result of war (Clodfelter 2008). To these we may add more hundreds of millions whose bodies were disfigured or whose homes were destroyed during war; a significant percentage of all those who lived in the past century saw their lives shattered by war.[3] It should come as no surprise then that, beginning with the late nineteenth century, accelerating after the First World War, and culminating with the opposition to nuclear Armageddon after 1945, some of the wisest voices of the planet have called for an end to war.

War is a social fact, and we must appreciate that war is responsible for some of our highest achievements and deepest held values as a society. The organization required to conduct war is intimately tied to the organization of statecraft. The technologies of destruction have often come from and been translated into technologies of development and production. The highest awards in the military celebrate honor, courage, and selflessness – values we hold to be positive and life affirming. Further, despite the antibellic clamor of the past century, there is arguably a much longer literature extolling war as the righteous acts of the chosen.

It is also important to study war in a contemporary world dominated by market pricing as the basis of social relationships.[4] The relative peace in the developed world of the past few decades has made market dynamics and behavior the central template for much of social science at individual and group levels. Yet war and conflict represent a form of social interaction considerably older than truck and barter. While economic and rational-actor models may help explain why groups fight (even as these models have explanatory limits), they become much less useful in explaining what happens in battle. Appreciating the power of hatred, aggression, discipline, and bonding as complements to optimization in human behavior is an important task for any sociological perspective.

Violence and Aggression

War is about violence. This is one reason why the use of the word "war" to describe a broad array of political campaigns and policy efforts is so often contentious. Efforts to stymie the flow of drugs, to end poverty, or to assure adequate energy supplies are not wars. Wars involve physical assaults on human beings. The instruments of war are weapons designed to damage, mutilate, and destroy the bodies of enemies. War is about inflicting as much pain as is necessary to other human beings until the point that they cease to exist or are willing to accept another's absolute authority over them. In turn, war is also about enduring as much pain as opponents may hurl so as to outlast them in the path to victory.

While wars are necessarily violent, or at least involve the threat of violence, there are many forms of violent behavior we should distinguish from warfare. To begin, we need to discriminate between what we might call hostile or impulsive and instrumental forms of aggression (McEllistrem 2004). Aggression or violence that is hostile and impulsive is associated with anger and emotion. It is aggression or violence that is out of control and originates in rage or madness; it is violence as an end in itself. This form of aggression is closely linked with biochemical processes as well as with reactions to particular environmental stimuli. Thus, impulsive aggression is often associated with either some form of intoxication or some abnormal chemical state or with the immediate sensation of fear or danger. This form of violence is also associated with low levels of socialization. This is the violence of the socially marginal: football hooligans, drunken louts, or plain old thugs.

We do often see this type of violence in war, and certainly it is difficult to avoid it in the midst of battle, where the emotional states of combatants will be primed for aggressive behavior. Thus, war may be partly defined as the social and political space in which this kind of aggression is allowed and encouraged. The very same acts that might condemn a young man to jail when at home, might earn him a medal in battle. But war as a social fact is not about and cannot depend on the individual acting out of aggressive impulses. It is a product of coordinated efforts and motivations.

War is a function of what has been called "coalitionary aggression" (D. L. Smith 2007). That is, wars involve aggression not of some completely independent individuals but of groups of people united in some way to act in concert. In contemporary wars, the numbers involved can be in the tens of millions. Can we really say that the millions of men who fought for control over Flanders from the sixteenth through the twentieth centuries were uniformly suited for and comfortable with violent behavior? What about the multitudes supporting them or waiting for their moment on the battlefield?

War involves a very different form of aggression: instrumental or premeditated. This is violence as a tool in the pursuit of some other end. If the first type of violence is associated with the classical conditioning of innate reflexes, this form is about operant conditioning driven by expectation of a desired re-enforcement (McEllistrem 2004). It is associated with the most socialized and most valued members of a society: those willing to make the ultimate sacrifice on behalf of their social unit.

What makes war sociologically fascinating is that it makes horrible brutality part of a rational course of action for huge numbers of people – people who would otherwise not act out in particularly lethal ways. Understood as a social phenomenon, war is about how human beings are made to do the impossible and bear the unbearable. The whole point of studying war sociologically is to find out how this happens.

War as Organized Violence

With this distinction in mind, we can come to better comprehend what Clausewitz ([1832] 1984) means when he refers to war as "an act of force to compel our enemy to do our will. . . . [A] true political instrument, a continuation of political intercourse, carried on with other means" (75, 87). This idea of war as a political instrument has been very productive in the academic world, and much has been written in political science and international relations about the ways political entities use and manage violence and conflict. Part of what makes war an excellent candidate for sociological study is the way in which it is an example of micro-level motivations and activity (soldiers, officers), meso-level coordination and strategies (group training, particular engagements and wars), and macro-level political coordination and intent.

The purpose of war as organized coercion is often latent – that is, underlying, but this is true of the logic of most social behavior, whether it be patterns of discrimination or courtship practices.

Similar to the social organization of tribes, educational institutions, or business corporations, wars are too complex a form of behavior and coordination to be spontaneous. The sociological perspective helps us to see the latent organizational purposes and to uncover the ways that these three levels – the individual (micro), the intermediate (meso), and the large scale (macro) – combine to create outcomes that are greater than the simple aggregation of individual efforts.

If we are to distinguish between war and simple violence, another key difference is the numbers involved. To merit the name of a war or war-like conflict, the acts of violence to which we are referring must involve a significant number of people. In standard social scientific analysis, the threshold for deaths necessary to call a violent conflict a war is one thousand (Small and Singer 1982). This is a purely arbitrary number and reflects the technological capacity of contemporary wars. Certainly conflicts between ancient Greek poleis could be classified as war even if it is unlikely that more than a few hundred men might have perished during a particular struggle.

Also central to our notion of war is that these individuals not be randomly associated. Somehow they must belong to whatever organized political groups are in an armed struggle. War is a form of aggression between groups that can be institutionally distinguished from each other (Bull [1977] 2012, 178). In contemporary times, this means states or groups that aspire to statehood, but in prior centuries the units involved could be as small as cities or even (with some caution) tribal entities.

The organization of war also requires a significant degree of social cooperation on at least three meso- to macro-sociological levels – the intra-group interactions and organization, the inter-group or society level, and coordination and organization at the institutional level. These levels of organization create observable social facts that are far greater than the aggregate of the individuals they comprise, and, in fact, often outlast those specific people involved in their initial interactions, creating long-lasting social artifacts.

First, organization is required within the groups in conflict in order to assure that enough of their partisans not only show up to fight, but also come willing (or coerced) to do so. They must also arrive with the relevant materiel needed to make the battle possible. A second and more interesting form of cooperation is that which occurs *between* the warring parties. In many battles, negotiations have preceded the encounter in order to assure the participation of all groups at a particular moment and place. Even when this explicit cooperation does not take place, both sides share a significant number of expectations and norms that make the battle possible.[5] On the broadest level, war also requires the cooperation of members of a global or even regional political system. American political scientist Quincy Wright emphasized that war involves the "sanctioned use of lethal weapons" and that it is a "form of conflict involving a high degree of legal equality" (1964, 7). A state of war requires that the combatants recognize each other as such. This does not necessarily imply mutual agreement to fight, but it does mean that the groups battling recognize their mutual existence as institutionalized bodies. At this third level of social cooperation, war as a classification of violence implies that the aggression observed and measured has a certain degree of political legitimacy. As Norbert Elias ([1939] 2000) argued, in our daily lives violence is taboo and punished, but we expect states to be constantly ready to inflict carnage on possible competitors.

A Paradox of War: Organization and Anarchy

War is a paradoxical form of violence in that it requires a great degree of cooperation and coordination prior to the actual outburst. Before war can occur, individuals must unite as a group in order to fight yet another. Consider, for example, one of the earliest literary testaments of war and one filled with the madness, rage, and carnage associated with it. The *Iliad* is full of combat and its descriptions of what happens to those who lose are quite explicit. Yet, before any blow is struck, before the rages of Achilles (first at Agamemnon, then at Hector), consider the social effort expended in building the ships, coordinating allies, organizing embarkations, and the order necessary to maintain a camp for nine years. The earliest part of the narrative has little to do with Troy and much more about the problems of hierarchy, exchange, authority, honor, and duty that beset all social groups.

War thus reflects what could be called our animal instincts in that it can turn us into beasts – insatiable but with buckets of blood. But it is also a very human creation requiring the resolution of collective action problems, the creation of rationales and beliefs, and the planning of complex actions. The question of what war is must address both aspects. This dual face of war is often portrayed as a contrast between the ideas of seventeenth-century English philosopher Thomas Hobbes and eighteenth-century Genevan philosopher Jean-Jacques Rousseau. For the former, war is inevitable in that the natural state of humans is aggression and this is only controlled through the development of hierarchical and authoritative institutions. In this way "society" – and in particular the social and political institution of the state ("Leviathan") – is what makes us behave less like the beasts we might be and more like the civilized humans we can become. For Rousseau, however, our natural state is a peaceful one and it is the development of these very same institutions, such as private property, that produces aggression.

The debate has been going on for years, from elevated philosophical and scholarly salons, to arguments over beer and coffee in bars and dorm rooms. We want to suggest that the answer, if such a definitive word can be used, is to consider how both Hobbes and Rousseau are right and wrong. Rousseau is right in that war would be impossible without some form of political authority. This is not because such institutions pervert our better natures, but because they make organized violence possible. Without the rudiments of a command structure, war dissolves into nothing more than the simultaneous, barely instrumental, acts of aggression and individual struggles for survival. Hobbes is correct in that the imposition of the monopoly over the means of violence[6] is a first step toward peace (at least within the Leviathan), but he neglects the potential, and likely, competition and violence between rival leviathans.

In the next section we explore this fundamental question of whether violence and war are inherent to human nature or a human construct by examining four major questions about the nature of war. This requires us to examine archeological and anthropological evidence, socio-biological arguments, as well as questions of gender and culture.

War as a Human Construct

Was the first contact between *Homo sapiens* unknown to one another fraught with violence? Have we been fighting each other since we began collectively organizing? We can never know exactly what humans were doing at the beginning of our existence. We can, however, use archeological and anthropological evidence to estimate whether we "invented" warfare and, if so, at what point. In order to organize the empirical evidence available, we have broken down this debate into four questions: (a) Is war unique to humans? (b) Is war natural or instinctual? (c) Is it a particularly male phenomenon and (d) Is it universal across humanity?

Is Human War Unique?

One strategy in attempting to define the nature of war is to compare human behavior with that of animals, specifically with that of other primates. The rationale behind such a research strategy is to determine the extent to which war is a form of biological fact that we share with other creatures. The consensus of research on these topics is that (a) humans are certainly not the only species that shows aggression against its own, (b) coordinated aggression by groups is also not unique to humans, and (c) other animals engage in aggressive behavior that looks remarkably like ours, including war-like behavior.

Humans do not have a monopoly over individual aggression and violence (Huntingford 1989). The number of species that exhibit these behaviors is very large. Many species' individuals respond to frustration, fear, or danger with displays of aggression and many fight members of their own species in competition for resources and mates. Most attention has been paid to violence among non-human primates and particularly chimpanzees. The evidence indicates that some chimpanzees can be extremely violent with each other and that they use aggression as a way of establishing, challenging, and defending hierarchies within groups (Wrangham and Glowacki 2012).

Coordinated behavior may be observed in many species, particularly while hunting, and the link between hunting and war has an illustrious intellectual history (Ehrenreich 1997). We are developing more evidence of coordination in aggression against members of the same species or within immediate groups, including wolves and primates (Wrangham 1999). But the most impressive non-human organized violent effort is that by several species of ants (Moffett 2010). These exhibit complex tactics and strategies and appear to be able to change these in light of new events or contexts. They even have complex shows of aggression and elaborate outcomes to wars including slavery.

What may best distinguish human violent behavior from that of animals is that we are the only species that is reflexive about its own capacity for violence. We have a considerable archive of moral condemnations of violence and also just as large a stack of literary and philosophical justifications and invocations of it. Especially when considering instrumental violence, we ponder alternatives and circumstances. Arguably we are the only species that plans and executes mass killing, while being quite aware of what we are doing. But this begs the question: how much of a choice do we have?

Instinctive Brutes

Konrad Lorenz, a twentieth-century Austrian ethologist, famously maintained that aggression was instinctively bred into us and that we ran the danger of using the very cognition we developed in our own destruction: ". . . the Prometheus who learned to preserve fire used it to roast his brothers" (Lorenz 1966, 231). More recently, Potts and Hayden (2008) have made the case of an evolutionary predisposition toward violence. To what extent is aggression and war-like behavior instinctual and inescapable?

There is considerable evidence that aggression in part is a natural, adaptive response to certain situations and stimuli (Nelson 2006). Attack behavior, for example, appears to result from the stimulation of the hypothalamus. Aggressive behavior can be induced by increases in male sex hormones, especially testosterone. A great deal of work has been done on the regulation of aggression by neurotransmitters. Continuing research is attempting to establish whether pathologically violent people share physiological or genetic characteristics that help explain their behavior.

One interesting new indication is that violent or brutal individuals may not be programmed for such behavior, but actually lack the equivalent programming for empathy (Baron-Cohen 2011). "Dehumanized perception," which may facilitate violence and brutality, is not just the province of a few, but may be elicited in broader groups with particular signals (L. T. Harris and Fiske 2006; L. T. Harris and Fiske 2011). But there is equal evidence that we have instincts for cooperation and for affection. That human beings are hard-wired for behaviors is clear; but it should also be obvious that the on/off switches of these are not deterministically pre-set.

Perhaps the best way of thinking of the relationship between our physical makeup and war is that part of the brain is programmed to respond to some circumstances aggressively, but that this does not control every one of our actions. We are not the perfect utopian pacifists of some dreams, but nor are we the predatory sharks of our worst nightmares. Perhaps the best way to understand the complex relationship between nature, society, and war is by focusing on the relationship between it and sex.

War, Sex, and Gender[7]

War has been nearly the exclusive domain of men. Males make up more than 99 percent of global military forces throughout history, and even today, with the increasing participation of women in the military, global forces are still 97 percent male (J. S. Goldstein

2001, 10). But why is this the case? Are males biologically more prone to fighting, or are they taught to do so?

There is a history of controversial arguments about gendered violence and warfare originating in biology and psychology,[8] much of which rests in and echoes arguments described in the previous section. While the fields are distinct, they both argue that "nature" is the source of drives, tendencies, and behaviors that respond in particular ways to environments, leading to the social organization of life, including violence and war, that we see today.

Sociobiology, the study of the biological basis of social life, argues that the male of mammalian species has an innate predisposition to aggressiveness, violence, and physicality, all leading toward a particular gendered practice of warfare. Sociobiologists highlight that males of mammalian, and particularly human, species are on average bigger, stronger, and have considerably more testosterone than females. Greater testosterone levels are associated with competitive, aggressive, and violent behavior, although there is also evidence that competitive activities themselves can precede testosterone production as well (Mazur 2005; Mehta and Josephs 2007). E. O. Wilson, the founder of sociobiology, has argued that males have a functional role in protecting the group, and are thus primed to act as soldiers, whereas females are innately passive and less aggressive (E. O. Wilson [1975] 2000).

A related field, evolutionary psychology, argues that society as it exists is the product of cognitive developments toward the evolutionary necessity of reproduction. The field was founded by John Tooby and Leda Comides, and their work (Tooby and Cosmides 1988, 2010) argues that males have been biologically and cognitively selected to be stronger, more aggressive, and adopt a "male combat identity" (2010, 196–7). An interesting suggestion from evolutionary psychology notes the relatively low value of males to females in the process of reproduction. In order to survive for more than one generation, a human group needs many females, but relatively few males (Daly and Wilson 1994). The resulting competition rewards the most aggressive males who, as in some non-human primate species, can establish their monopoly over reproduction. These genetic selections have, over the millennia, produced the stereotypical "violent male."[9]

While there are biological and psychological arguments for the gendered nature of war, the strongest arguments for the gendered nature of war come from culturalist explanations (Malešević 2010; J. S. Goldstein 2001). Military service is overtly associated with masculinity and the onset of manhood (rituals for acceptance as a warrior and as an adult male are often the same), while femininity is associated with submission to and support of the warrior. In some ways, women serve as the enforcers of the masculinity of war. Women are meant to gaze at soldiers and see them (in Virginia Wolf's phrase) "at twice their natural size" (Marshall [1947] 2000). Mothers and lovers have historically urged their men not only to take their weapons to battle, but also to either carry them back in triumph or lie upon them in death and defeat. Joanna Bourke speaks of women "buckling men's psychological armor" (1999, 303).

Even the most prominent exceptions to the male monopoly in many ways support it or help justify it. The ancient Greek historian Herodotus has his Amazons claiming, "To draw the bow, to hurl a javelin, to bestride a horse, these are our arts; of womanly employments we know nothing" (Herodotus 1997, 177). What is interesting here is that the Amazons do not dispute a gendered division of violent labor, but claim exemption from it, even practicing self-mutilation in order to be more masculine. This has been the historical pattern with female participation in war: allowed because of special circumstances, obtaining an honorary male status, but not challenging the underlying sexual specialization.

Examples of "real life" Amazons further underscore this pattern. During the eighteenth and nineteenth centuries the Dahomey, a kingdom in present-day Benin, had an all-female military corps. They were segregated, as male military corps often are, trained intensively, and displayed ferocity in war. They did not, however, upset or transform the male hierarchy of power or expected gender norms of their culture. They would call cowardly male soldiers "women" and "sissies," re-enforcing the association of weakness and fear with traditional women (Malešević 2010;

15

Edgerton 2000). Similarly, during World War II, Soviet female soldiers proved to be particularly ruthless and efficient at war, but they did not disrupt the gender hierarchy, rather being seen as outside of the norm (Malešević 2010; Cottam 1983).

Generally the likelihood of women participating in battle increases when they are on the side of a radical social change, when they belong to a marginal group, or when they find themselves geographically or politically distant from the center of social power. That is, the more transgressive the group may be, the higher the likelihood of females fighting for it. Thus, frontierswomen in a variety of settings can ignore the taboo on armed females, particularly if they are fighting an enemy recognized as even more alien than an armed woman – e.g. natives in the colonial hinterlands. Similarly, guerilla armies in the twentieth century have often prominently featured female combatants. Despite these exceptions, in the twenty-first century, female participation remains rare. Even the heralded Israeli experiment, female military participation, stops short of combat (J. S. Goldstein 2001, 86), as do current US regulations. Of course, in some settings the distance between combat and support roles can be reduced to almost nothing.

The evolutionary functionality (if there ever was any) of the biological basis of the gendered nature of war disappeared long ago, and the different roles have been maintained through cultural and social expectations. Whatever its origins, once the male monopoly was established, cultural reproduction would assure that this division of labor would be perpetuated and appear "natural." But why would males want to "own" war? While the costs of battle are obvious and women may be supposed to be spared these, they are also kept from the privileges associated with participating in them. The monopolization of violent labor may have its costs for men, but it also assured or supported their exclusive access to political and economic authority. The link between military service and citizenship or property ownership, for example, has been historically rooted, as you will read about in Chapter 5. Even today, one path to citizenship – with its rights to legitimate political and economic participation – is through military participation.

The Nature of War

The broader nature of war may parallel the same arguments made regarding the sexual division of military labor. Yes, it is based on some inherent physiological conditions and predispositions: humans are capable of violence and it may even make evolutionary sense for us to have a threshold of danger or fear which elicits aggression in self-defense. Yet, war is too varied and too complex to be derived from individual cognitive or biological responses. War is a creation, not just of our genes, but also of our societies. The social cohesion, coordination, and political and economic production required for war have nothing to do with individual propensity for aggression or the physical dimensions of a person – particularly when we compare body types across history and cultures – and have more to do with the social organization of power and politics, more of which is discussed in Chapters 3 and 4.

Universality of War

Has war occurred everywhere and in every era? This is a critical question because if the answer is yes, we can be relatively certain that, in the words of William James, nineteenth-century philosopher and brother of Henry James, "our ancestors have bred pugnacity into our bone and marrow, and thousands of years of peace won't breed it out of us" ([1910] 1995, 19). If, on the other hand, we find significant historical or geographical pockets of peace, then we can identify the conditions that seem to produce warfare as well as its absence, and even construct a space in which this form of violence will be impossible.

The argument for the temporal and geographic universality of war has been best made by Lawrence Keeley (1996) and supported by the work of Steven LeBlanc (2003). According to this broad and deep scholarly accounting, there does not appear to be a time period or global region, or even a level of civilization immune from war. According to Keeley, the minute *Homo sapiens* appear on the scene, definitive evidence of homicidal violence becomes more common. He attests that there is simply no evidence that warfare in small-scale societies was more rare or a less-serious undertaking than among more "civilized" societies. We may not even make the argument that contemporary war is more violent than its pre-historic antecedents. According to Keeley, the killing ratio of "primitive" war appears to be the same or higher than in "modern" war.

This position of the historical pervasiveness of war, however, is contested. Scholars including Douglas Fry (2007; Fry and Söderberg 2013) and Brian Ferguson (2003; 2008) strongly disagree with Keeley. For them the critical moment is the Neolithic Revolution of roughly 10,000 to 8,000 BCE, when sedentary life became possible thanks to agriculture, and when we also see first evidence of permanent settlements. For these authors, the evidence cited by Keeley reflects the existence of inter-personal violence,[10] but it does not provide confirmation for the existence of their more demanding definition of war – which we largely parallel here. For example, in looking at pre-Neolithic depiction of inter-personal violence, they note that it is restricted to a few individuals and does not indicate the presence of mass groups in conflict. War, they suggest, is a product of the creation and the aggregation of a stored surplus which is only possible with the Neolithic era.

This argument is supported by the work of Guilaine and Zammit (2005). They suggest that both Neanderthals and Cro-Magnons were clearly capable of violence, but that this tended to be fairly individualistic and not necessarily approaching the organization required by war. The key turning point for them is the Mesolithic (roughly 12,000 to 10,000 BCE). They emphasize two sites from roughly this time period: the first are the famous paintings in Ares del Meastre (roughly halfway between Barcelona and Valencia). These paintings clearly depict a number of individuals working in unison and fighting another group doing the same. The second site is the burial site in Djebel Sahaba in Northern Sudan where the remains of at least fifty-nine individuals have been found, most of which exhibit damage from some kind of human wielded weapons. These authors suggest that at least some of these conflicts are linked to increasing competition for control of land and water (the latter the subject of perhaps the oldest "war speech" we posses in the *Epic of Gilgamesh*), as well as the first indications of social inequality and competition for control. The Mesolithic thus serves as the prehistoric bridge to the "invention" of agriculture following 10,000 BCE and the subsequent creation of permanent settlements. Obviously, the dating of these periods and subsequent first indications of war varies by region (Ferguson 2008), but the key insight is that warfare as we have defined it seems closely associated with the establishment of more sedentary living arrangements.[11] The same linkage between social complexity and new forms of conflict may be seen in Mesoamerica (Hassig 1992).

The evidence in this debate is tricky and may be a perfect example of how hard it is to confirm falsifiable statements in social science. First, archeological evidence only reveals what is found. Archeological analysis may be an extreme example of looking for lost or dropped items only below the street lamp – not because they are more likely to be there, but because that is the only place where we can see them. We may never know if many incidents of organized violence preceded the Mesolithic – we simply have not found evidence of them. What we do know is that certainly from that point onward (with different dates for different regions), warfare appeared practically everywhere. More contemporary anthropological evidence can be read in conflicting ways as well. The behavior of the famous Yanomamo of Venezuela can and has been read as evidence of their inherent violent natures as well as the more benign nature of humanity (Ferguson 2003).

The positive correlation between social complexity and war making is quite strong among anthropological studies (Fry 2007; Eckhardt 1990). If civilization is about the process of orderly aggregation of humans and synchronization of needs and hierarchies, then war may not only be conducive to it, but it may be the ultimate expression of it. Certainly the apparent coincidence of the appearance of organized violence and the very first agriculturally fed permanent settlements suggest that war and civilization are anything but antagonistic. Similarly, the apparent rise in violence accompanying increases in social, political, and economic complexity during the Neolithic Era also supports some sort of relationship between social, economic, and political complexity and war. The very victory of agricultural civilization, which is at the core of our contemporary life (Massey 2005), may have been as a result of war. While previously most had considered that the craft and science of agriculture was diffused peacefully from a few centers, increasing evidence points to a process of conquest and colonization by our farming ancestors. It is also possible that the greater likelihood of conflict further encouraged urban concentrations and the development of walls, thereby further privileging the central role of cities in social life.

The conclusion we can come to from the evidence available is that while inter-personal violence may be a part of our physical and cognitive composition, the more complex process which we call war is not.[12] This may be small comfort in that it indicates that we have the potential for aggression, but obviously we also have the potential for cooperation and for caring for some aggregate group, even so much as to kill or die for it. War may actually be a marriage of both aspects of our nature. On the one hand, we can work together and come to share a set of beliefs and loyalties. On the other, in doing so, we may transfer the aggression from within the group to outside it – and in the process perhaps solidify the ties that bind us to our immediate neighbors.

War may thus be seen as representing a bridge between our biologically programmed behavior and our more historically bound culture. At some point in time, institutions arose that were able to repress intra-group aggression and direct it toward outside threats. This involved two basic social processes. First it required a political hierarchy of some sort that could impose the internal control and coercion needed to manage aggression. Second, it also required the creation of a hierarchy of identity whereby the obligations to the collective overrode individual preservation or duty to immediate kin. This same process also required the creation of enough of a collective identity to distinguish those against whom aggression was prohibited and those against whom it was encouraged. Throughout the following chapters of this book, we will discuss the manner in which war builds order on a variety of levels – individual, group, and societal – but for now we may begin with a perhaps extreme position that war and civilization are actually not opposed, but quite entangled.

The Causes of War

If we don't have to, why do we have wars? If the answer to "why war?" is not some form of individual or innate blood lust, then we have to ask why organized, instrumental, and rational groups persist in engaging in this behavior. We should first understand that, despite all the years of study and of debate, there is no consensus regarding the answer to this question (Levy 1998). For our purposes, we are less interested in the analyses provided by the disciplines of social science and by history regarding the causes of particular wars or the variation in periods of peace and war. Rather, we are interested in the general explanatory schemes for war as a social act. We may identify three broad schools of explanations for both specific wars and for the social fact of war itself. The first focuses on material explanations, the second lays responsibility on cultural predispositions, and the third blames psychological phenomena.

Fighting over Resources

It is undeniable that war is often about controlling some form of scarce resource. We can frequently reduce the origin of a war to competition over some asset or material producing conflict between two or more groups. A market rationale would argue that war comes about when some group decides that the costs of violence outweigh the cost to be incurred in engaging in it. Some have suggested that the failure to discover significant signs of organized violence in the Paleolithic era may be because the population density was so low as to make struggles over resources deleterious (Guilaine and Zammit 2005, 33). Once there were enough humans to be able to come into contact over a disputed good, organized violence was likely. The list of resources over which societies may fight is considerable; thus we will concentrate on two that appear to be historically common (and rather interesting): genetic diversity and territory.

Conflicts and war can be a critical step for the simple demographic re-production of a society. In order to survive, all relatively small groups need to search for exogenous genetic resources. Genetic diversity is a necessity for healthy group repro-duction – and it is a functional reason for the near-universal incest taboo. One way of obtaining exogenous genetic resources is to raid and kidnap people from other groups. In most cases, given the a priori establishment of a male monopoly over violence, this involves raiding for young women. Disputes about females or raids in order to obtain new sources of female population are very common in the anthropological literature. Male war captives may also be used to replenish a population that has been depleted through war or other means. Alternatively, wars may actually be a very functional way of dealing with an excess of a particular sort of demographic resource: young males demanding a greater share in the distribution of collective goods.

More familiar to contemporary readers, fights over territory are perhaps the most common dynamic in explaining a significant instance of wars. In the broad history of the West, author Robert O'Connell (1995) sees the organized violence of war originating in the competition between new settlements and the still populous nomads in the first several millennia of the Neolithic era and well into the Iron Age. From this perspective, the creation of seden-tary civilization produced a higher likelihood of conflict than had existed when all were essentially foragers. The presence of permanent settlements required established territories that were the domain of some people and not others. These settlements also presented an almost irresistible target containing stored food. Any reading of the oldest surviving literature from a variety of cultures will find the theme of conflict between settled people and nomads fairly common.

The creation of permanently settled groups also signals the start of the potential for the organized and often expensive enter-prise that is war. The agricultural revolution not only produced a key motive for war (territory), but also its means, by enabling groups to produce enough surpluses to allow significant number of members not to participate in farming but instead to specialize in a variety of non-food production activities such as art, govern-ance, and knowledge creation (Massey 2005). This also made possible the specialization in violence – the creation of a class of people dedicated to protection and hostility. Settlements also coincided with – indeed may have necessitated – the construction of walls and defense ramparts, the destruction of which is such a common trope in the ancient literature on war, from Jericho to Troy. Finally, such surplus also perhaps permits the elaboration of exclusive senses of identity and supporting ideologies that are so important for war. As the wealth of these groups increase, not only do they represent more tempting targets for marauding bands, but their parallel growth in power fuels ambitions to dominate other similar centers.

This competition for others' wealth in whatever form is as common throughout history as to not require much elaboration. Yet, as important as the competition for resources may be, we have to go further to explain the emotional impact of war and its cultural resonance. The competition for resources may be at the heart of the rational origins of war, and it is certainly the basis for economic and political studies of international conflict, but the willingness of millennia of soldiers to sacrifice themselves for the collective good cannot be totally explained by a purely economic or resource-oriented explanation. Wars have been waged out of spite, for justice, and for honor. We must search for the roots of war in the human soul as well as in the human brain.

Blame It on Culture

Culturalist explanations have long been used to explain variations across societies, but there has been an explosion of them over the past twenty years. The core idea of this perspective is that some societies are simply more prone to engaging in wars, and that some groups are inevitably going to fight each other. These explanations can be as equally deterministic as the biological or psychological explanations of warfare, substituting a view of the essential characteristics of some societies and cultures for individual characteristics.

One prominent example of this type of explanation was the literature on the Balkan wars of the 1990s, which sought to emphasize the long-standing enmity that supposedly existed between the groups sharing that part of the world (R. D. Kaplan 1993). The media used a similar story to explain the Rwandan genocide. In another variant, some groups are simply thought to think of the world more violently or have political or religious aggression taught to them from a young age; for example, the far too common attribution of violence done by Muslims to a supposedly "jihadist" orientation in Islam.

One obvious problem with such accounts is that they are usually used to explain the behavior of either perceived enemies or societies that the observers have declared as "beyond the pale" of civilized behavior. Thus the "tribal savages" of "darkest Africa" (Jarosz 1992) are condemned to fight each other by their primitive natures, the emotionally immature clans and ethnicities of the Balkans (R. D. Kaplan 1993) have no choice but to relive their history, and the "evil" and authoritarian nature of Islam (Kappeler and Kappeler 2004) is confirmed with each suicide bomber. Yet, an external observer new to human history might well observe that the greatest pouring of blood has often come at the hands of the "most civilized." Western Europe certainly has a much bloodier history than the Great Lakes region of Africa. Similarly, students of comparative religion might blanch at the violence encouraged by the Old Testament and question the extent to which Christianity has a weaker commitment to "holy war" than does Islam. Those who contend that a history of violence is a sentence of perpetual warfare might also wonder what happened to the great bellic power of the seventeenth century, Sweden, or how the previously sought-after Swiss mercenaries became peaceful bankers and watchmakers.

Further, culturalist explanations are especially popular for forms of violence that observers find particularly brutish or bloody. They are much more often used to explain the aggression by a terrorist or by a machete-wielding teenager, but rarely against the bombardier raining death from thousands of feet above ground.

Culturalist perspectives assume that violence is a constant in a society and that views do not shift. Yet there is no evidence that either is true. Relations between Serbs and Croats have changed and adapted over the centuries. The hatred between Hutus and Tutsis is difficult to discern prior to the institutionalization of such identities in the twentieth century and the subsequent distribution of post-colonial spoils. The potential or probability of violence is much higher in contemporary San Salvador than in downtown Stockholm, but there is little to say that this has to do with a timeless and pervasive cultural outlook of each location.

A much more useful take on the culture of war might begin with Jeremy Black's notion of "bellicosity" (1998). By this Black means a more time-specific set of attitudes or mentalities. This can include a popular or elite willingness to accept violence as an inevitable part of inter-societal relations or a greater legitimacy of certain martial institutions. It accepts the possibility of manipulation and that a set of cultural assumptions and repertoires can be used by some to create an atmosphere where violence is more acceptable or even justified. From this perspective, wars happen not because cultures push us toward them, but because cultural prohibitions against violence are lowered and identification of the threat leads to an acceptance of it.

Us and Them

A third explanation for the causes of war comes from social psychology, particularly the writings of Henri Tajfel, a twentieth-century British social psychologist. His work, developed in response to the Second World War, helps us understand how collectives come to perspectives and actions and how these then lead to organized violence. In particular, he studied how people come to form ingroups and outgroups and how they behaved once formed (Tajfel 1974, 1981, 1982). His work was specifically motivated by the question of how ordinary people could commit genocide and war on a mass scale.

It is important to identify the group psychologies that help shape individual behavior. Intergroup conflict is not produced by some collective aggregation of individual violent tendencies, but results from social processes that originate in the very act of our coming together to form communities. There is some evidence that we read physical differences as signals allowing us to distinguish between different groups and that this behavior may be linked to the very process of cohesion within "like" groups (Gil-White 2001). We appear to find some universal qualities to groups, but particularly the "ingroup bias" through which we perceive those whom we define as belonging to "our group" much more positively than those we define as "outsiders." This is not only found throughout history and across global geography, but also replicated in laboratory experiments.

Groups are inherently competitive because individuals are motivated to achieve or maintain a positive social identity. Essentially, we want to feel that a group to which we belong is superior. There is some evidence, for example, that there is a relationship between feeling good about your "ingroup" and less positive about those outside it. It seems that hating others might help us love ourselves. Thus aggression toward others and the creation of external threats and "holy" crusades serve to create social cohesion. The scape-goat phenomenon (whereby a group seeks unity through the alienation of and aggression against an outsider) is a function of group psychology.

In this sense, war is not necessarily the opponent of civilization or collective social life, but its handmaiden. If we choose to celebrate the creation of an "us" as the basic social act of humanity, then we may have no choice but to accept the creation of a "them." Many aspects of realist theory in political science follow from this division – the reason we have wars is that we lack a single power strong enough to make us behave as one. In the words of Philip Gourevitch, genocide may serve as an exercise in community building (1998, 88). Note that the differences between one group and its mortal antagonist need not be significant to begin with and that some of the crueler wars have been an expression of the "narcissism of small differences" (Jacoby 2011).

An important sub-set of what we are calling psychological theories emphasizes not the qualities of individuals, but the dynamics of the manner in which they interact. Randall Collins (2008) claims that violence is a set of pathways that circumvent the barrier of tension and fear, pathways being the social techniques for controlling emotions by which some people sometimes commit violence, even though tension and fear tend to prevent it. One of the most interesting observations from Collins' study is that violence is not contagious – I am not necessarily more likely to hit someone because you have hit him. The exception is when antagonistic groups are defined a priori; the key step in violence is not necessarily the first punch, but in identifying someone as "different" or as part of a group representing a threat.

The emphasis on interaction is at the heart of many social scientific theories of war. Experiments using reiterative games and theories of balance of power or transitions essentially hold that war has to be understood not as the product of single agent's desire or strategy, but as the product of the actions and expectations of the groups involved. A variation on the interaction perspective is that suggested by Keeley: many wars are "neighborhood effects" caused by the presence of a particularly aggressive group. This would indicate that it is not necessary for all involved in a conflict to be aggressive; rather the (still unexplained) presence of "bad apples" will transform the entire barrel.

Explaining War

It is something of an occupational hazard in the academy to search for parsimonious explanations of complex behavior, often resulting in deterministic accounts. Nevertheless, we present these different materialist, cultural, and psychological causes of war as important explications of why societies have engaged in large-scale violence.

Thucydides claimed that people went to war for honor, fear, and interest. Each of these has their cultural, material, and psychological components. Honor, for example, is partly a cultural creation, a mechanism of defense, and a psychological response. It functions both on an individual basis as well as on a collective one. Fear has its rational and irrational components, while the judgment of interest is not immune to social and cultural influences. Consider, for example, the cycles of revenge which have historically played such a prominent role in war. A culturalist explanation might focus on the force of a set of values requiring blood payment for any perceived wrong or slight. Revenge may also be sensitive to cultural standards of expected and acceptable respect. It may also be a perfectly rational response to a competitive world where the outstanding threat of retaliation serves to protect one's resources from potentially dangerous neighbors. The difference between the nuclear strategy of mutually assured destruction and vendetta cultures emphasizing "an eye for an eye" may be more of degree than of kind.

In a recent book, Samuel Bowles and Herbert Gintis (2011) identify a fascinating paradox in human history: "the tension between the relentless logic of self-interested behavior and the ubiquity of collective action" (6). Human beings are unique in that cooperation extends beyond immediate genealogical kin, and may include those who, by any stretch of the imagination, remain strangers. It may be that war as organized violence is the key to this apparent contradiction. We first note that in practically every case societies with higher levels of aggregation tend to have advantages over those with lower levels (Flannery and Marcus 2012). Those groups that were able to organize themselves in a violent competition for resources in periods of dramatic environmental change or increasing population density (Christian 2004) would have a distinct advantage over those that remain atomized. Following the logic of "group selection" reintroduced by recent authors such as Boehm (Boehm 2012; Boehm 2000) and Wilson (E. O. Wilson [1975] 2000), we might speak of war as a learned behavior that selected for those groups that were able to practice it in the most efficient manner possible. Once organized violence was unleashed into an environment, only those who adapted could and would survive. Certainly the standard suspects of the prehistoric origins of war (sedentary social development, population density, competition for resources) all seem to share the characteristic of a local concentration of human beings. These same concentrations allow both the development of collective notions of shared identities, and the socialization of cultures of opposition to strangers. In a sad reversal of 1960s utopianism, "coming together" may not be the recipe for peace, but just the opposite.

In more general terms, we may link war with social concentration. What we observe over the past 10,000 years is not necessarily the decline of violence, as some have argued (Pinker 2011; Morris 2014), but its aggregation. Violence is not necessarily declining, but rather becoming ever more organized and affecting ever-larger groups with ever-greater amounts of killing power. Stephen Pinker may be right in that we kill each other much less randomly than we used to, but the twentieth century would indicate that when we set out to do so, our capacity for violence is ever larger.

So are we condemned to war by our social nature? This would seem just as deterministic as, and no more hopeful than, a genetic destiny, but it is not. First, through using an historical comparative approach we will see that different societies practice different forms of war, and different styles of conflict produce different societies. Recognizing and exploring the link between war and social structure allows us to begin identifying which aspects of our communal lives encourage organized conflict and which do not, and how conflict not only reflected social reality, but also helped shape it.

2

War of the Warrior

We begin our analysis of the social foundations of war by examining the experience of the individual soldier. The behavior of warriors, armies, and societies is shaped and defined by each other, and thus we look to understanding the ways in which the individual warrior experiences war, the sociological puzzle of why anyone would engage in such destructive activity, and how societies have solved that puzzle to create soldiers.

What does the warrior do and what does his[1] world look like? It is impossible to understand war as a social phenomenon without at least some appreciation of what it entails. Only when we realize the true horror of war, can we come to appreciate the sociological wonder of its existence. How could something so awful be so relatively commonplace? How have so many millions of normal, ordinary men been convinced and/or coerced to engage effectively in something so obviously dangerous? At the heart of war, there is the need to do something "which would be impossible for men to do in cold blood" (Tsouras 2005, 48). How do they do it?

Before doing so, we should appreciate that while battle is central to images of war, it is not its primary condition. It may, in fact, be the exception. For long periods in the history of war, the art of generalship involved successfully avoiding battle. In the nuclear age of the last half of the twentieth century, such evasion became the central point of strategy. Even within armies actively engaged in a war, combat was relatively rare. The Napoleonic armies, for example, only had about two hundred days of pitched battle in two decades of campaigning, and some 60 to 80 percent of the soldiers were effective at any point in time. During World War II, only 40 percent of American servicemen actually served in combat units in the European theater, and in Vietnam the "tooth-to-tail" ratio of combat and support personnel was argued to be as high as 1:11 (McGrath 2007).[2] Serving time in the military has, since its inception, involved many hours of boredom interposed with moments of panic. Yet it is those rare moments that define the experience and that are at the core of our sociological challenge in explaining it.

The Horror of Battle

Battle usually occurs on a plain large enough to allow the maneuver of anywhere from hundreds to hundreds of thousands of men. While considerable horrific combat has taken place in either mountainous terrain or in jungles and deep forests, the classic battle of almost every military tradition takes place in open areas. These spaces allow for the complex and organized movements that are central to all militaries. It is this organization of bodies of people that is one of the sociological foundations of war.

What does it feel like to be in battle?[3] A survey of the immense amount of scholarly, literary, and popular writing on war would indicate the overall importance of two emotions: confusion and loneliness. The combination of these two defines the special terror of battle. Consider the challenge of facing the threat of danger, sometimes ominously random, coming from an uncertain environment and without much social or moral support. This is the experience of all warriors.

Confusion comes from the fact that, for most of history, most individuals in a battle have no idea of where they might be or what role they are meant to play in the larger drama of the battle. Well into the twentieth century, average soldiers would not have had access to maps, nor would they have been able to read them. Often soldiers may not even know where they are in time, as the flow of days and exhaustion mix into a blur.[4] Even today's most advanced soldiers, with their GPS apparatus and their constant feedback from command, may feel lost within an urban warren, or dislocated by the flow of battle. Almost all accounts of battle emphasize the haze and cacophony associated with it. Whether the eyes are blinded by the dust raised by thousands of sandaled feet or by the smoke from thousands of shells, the individual warrior will find himself caught in a man-made hell of confusion. Danger lurks everywhere, but is often invisible.

The loneliness of battle is terrifying. There is an observed tendency for warriors to bunch together and to provide some sort of emotional re-enforcement through each other's company. (This is actually a very dangerous position following the development of artillery.) Yet, there is no getting away from the basic existential loneliness of possible death. The particularity and uniqueness of one's own death, arguably the loneliest experience of our lives, makes the horror around the warrior ever more frightening. The intensity of relationships forged in battle is partly a function of this powerful feeling of alienation and need.

To this psychological trauma we can of course add the obvious observation that battle is an extremely unpleasant and uncomfortable physical experience. Churchill's famous list of "blood, toil, tears, and sweat" (1940) might more accurately also include mud, vomit, urine, and feces. A letter from a young lieutenant in World War I offers this description of a battlefield:

> . . . Leprous earth, scattered with the swollen and blackened corpses of hundreds of young men. The appalling stench of rotting carrion . . . Mud like porridge . . . Swarms of flies and bluebottles clustering on bits of offal . . . men with bowels dropping out, lungs shot away, with blinded, smashed faces, or limbs blown into space. Men screaming and gibbering. (quoted in Fussell 1991, 36)

There are also massive amounts of acrid smoke, deafening noise, and, perhaps most universally, sheer exhaustion. Battle usually occurs after men have had to walk or been transported in uncomfortable circumstances over very long distances. Moreover, they have done so while usually carrying large amounts of materiel – from sixty pounds that was standard for a Roman legionnaire to the one hundred pounds (130 pounds including food) carried by American GIs landing on World War II beaches. Over the past two decades, the US military has also added body armor and the extra gear sometimes required by the threat of biological and chemical weapons. Sleep deprivation has been a constant of battle from time immemorial and has arguably become much worse as the length of time involved in combat or in readiness thereof has increased. An old trick from World War I can give us an indication of the challenge: men were taught to place bits of tobacco in the eye in order to stay awake.[5]

We should also recall that the normal conveniences of hygiene are usually not available anywhere near the battlefield and that most men have been living in an unaccustomed state of filth and personal shame. The quantity and quality of food and water also degenerate as we get closer to frontlines. The popularity of horsemeat in armies through the twentieth century gives us one indication. In contemporary wars fought by the armies of wealthy countries, the food situation may have become more secure with the provision of items such as meals-ready-to-eat (MRE), but the experience remains unpleasant.

To all of the horrors described above, we of course have to add the great probability of pain (Glasser 2006). There is first the psychological anguish and vicarious horror of seeing bodies in conditions never before encountered. Battlefields are often covered with limbs and pieces of human flesh that can shock even the most hardened sensibility. "In war, as in air accidents, 'insides' are much more visible than it is normally well to imagine. To soldiers they are deplorably familiar" (Fussell 1989a, 271). With the development of more effective ammunition came new horrors: soldiers describe the experience of having parts of comrades' bodies or innards cover them. Injury from bones projected from shot or exploded bodies were fairly common during World War I. The violation of human bodies that occurs in battle appears to be one of the strongest memories of anyone who has been involved in them and one of the most terrifying aspects. The actual pain suffered from wounds is literally indescribable. This emotional distance between those who have experienced it and the vast majority of us marks one of the foundational gulfs between those who have been soldiers and those who have not. In part because of the physical assault of pain, perhaps the most important task for anyone assisting the wounded is to mitigate the symptoms of shock through which the body begins to shut down in the face of unbearable stress.

We should note that in many battles, one's chances of surviving are better than even[6] and that is an important variable in defining the relationship between different social structures and the practices of war. The "killing efficiency" of any army is a reflection of the training of its soldiers, the type and quality of equipment, and the underlying strategic logic behind military action. While most of the focus regarding the casualties of war has quite understandably been on death, we may need to pay much more attention to wounding and the fear thereof.

Since the mid-nineteenth century the ratio of wounds to death has increased dramatically. In World War I the ratio of deaths to wounded was 1:1.75, in World War II it was 1:1.65, and in Vietnam there were 2.6 wounded for every death (Goldberg 2014). To compare, in Afghanistan (Operation Enduring Freedom, 2001 to present) and Iraq (Operation Iraqi Freedom, 2003–11) the ratios are 8.38 and 7.17 wounded for every death ("Casualty Status" 2015). The social consequences of having a significant part of the population either physically incapacitated or bearing the psychological scars of battle have not been adequately explored.

All of these circumstances help explain why the overriding emotion associated with battlefield is fear. It is certainly a much more common phenomenon than our popular imagination or romanticized views of war would like to accept. The very pervasiveness of fear should indicate that we cannot understand war as a simple expression of aggression. Rather, we have to analyze it as a phenomenon whereby social institutions push millions into situations they would under all normal circumstances avoid.

One response to this fear is to escape the situation or alter the circumstances. Significant numbers of men have historically not gone "over the top" into battle. From time immemorial, leaders have been concerned with desertion and have selected battle sites and routes in order to minimize the losses to it. Obviously, many who did desert did so for a variety of reasons other than fear, but the prospect of death and mutilation no doubt played a role in such disappearances.

The level of desertion is an excellent indicator of the social legitimacy of a conflict as well as a measure of the institutional capacity of the military to enforce its rules. There has been a clear decline in the percentage of organized armies that escape their obligations, as both the ideological justification of wars and the coercive capacity of armies have increased. Desertion remains a good measure of societal support in our contemporary times, however, with, for example, the US military in World War II experiencing a fraction of what it did in Vietnam. Another version of non-participation may include the phenomenon first identified by S. L. A. Marshall in his studies of World War II (S. L. A. Marshall [1947] 2000), and which indicated that a significant group of US soldiers did not fire their weapons in combat. While these findings have been highly disputed, there is considerable evidence that "battle passivity" is fairly common (Grossman 1995).

Arriving at the battle, the vast majority of soldiers might still exhibit fear. The reported symptoms from memoirs, literary accounts, and scientific studies are fairly consistent in their descriptions. Fear usually manifests itself as apprehension and restlessness. Soldiers report a violent pounding of the heart as well as sinking feelings in the stomach, uncontrollable trembling, cold sweat, and vomiting. A significant number of men in battle experience involuntary bowel and bladder movements, thereby adding personal shame to the fear. Extreme silence or inappropriately manic behavior is also quite common. The vast majority of accounts describe a diminished awareness of sound and a heightened visual clarity – a tunnel effect, as it were. Many report extreme disassociation from reality.

Across geography and history, people tend to be afraid of similar things, but these change depending on the amount of experience with fighting. For those going into battle for the first time, fear of being found a coward is the most common. This appears to change after the initial battle experience, when soldiers worry less about their reputation and express more apprehension about the actual physical danger. Among these fears, that of death is perhaps not as great as the dread of pain and physical mutilation. Groin injuries receive the most attention and elicit the most horror.

Death in war has many forms. Consider this scene described by Richard Holmes (1986), quoting a veteran of Passchendale:

> From the darkness on all sides came the groans and wails of wounded men; faint, long, sobbing means of agony, and despairing shrieks. It was too horribly obvious to me that dozens of men with serious wounds must have crawled for safety into shell holes, and now the water was easing above them and, powerless to move, they were slowly drowning. (186–7)

Unfamiliar weapons or ways of killing also seem to have their terror. Whether British soldiers afraid of Zulu assegais, Spanish conquistadores fearful of Aztec sacrifice, Vietcong irregulars shocked by B-52s, or American GIs horrified by IEDs, new forms of death seem to strike a significant chord. There is also an associated fear of mutilation after death and many militaries have made a point of not leaving comrades behind or of instilling hatred by describing reported violations.

In general, the biggest source of fear is the uncertainty of the battle experience. The battlefield may be the extreme example of where humans absolutely lose control over their individual lives. This sense of powerlessness seems to be at the core of much battle fear. This is one reason why decisiveness is so important in military leadership. Soldiers will look for an order even if its implications are more dangerous than not receiving any; a battle may be one of those times when a wrong decision is better than none.

The terror of battle may be somewhat abated or controlled by the apparent unreality of it all. Given that the battlefield will be an extremely new and alien experience for most warriors, it is not surprising that many report an overall sensation of unreality. Many accounts describe a sense of distance from the battle. For contemporary soldiers, the sense of being in a film (even an unpleasant one) is very common. In the words of a US soldier in Vietnam, quoted by Michael Herr: "I hate this movie" (1991, 203). For American soldiers in Iraq, the line between combat and videogames appears at times to have blurred.

Is it any surprise then that soldiers are famous for their consumption of alcohol or whatever narcotic substance may be available? Getting soldiers ready for battle has often involved some form of intoxication. Where previously this might have involved a proverbial shot of liquor, a magic mushroom, or a mug of octli, the twentieth century has seen a more precise approach with issues of Benzedrine or more sophisticated pharmaceuticals. Independently, soldiers seek the solace of intoxication, as practically every fictional and historical account makes clear. We should note, however, that such images can be embroidered and that the supposed intoxication of soldiers or an army has often been exaggerated (Kuzmarov 2009).

Because of this degree of trauma, no human being can exist in a permanent state of combat. There is a limited window during which warriors are useful. While men new to battle need time to learn the informal skills needed for survival, those kept in combat of one form or another for too long quickly lose their effectiveness. Too much awareness of the consequences of failure and too much wearing down of soul and body make for a useless soldier. All soldiers have breaking points and a surprising number of incidents of "cowardice" (Walsh 2014) come from the breaking of the spirit or from the mind literally losing contact with a reality too horrible or too overpowering to bear.

We can think of the effective life or "productivity" of a warrior as a sort of inverse U-curve (Grossman and Christensen 2008). This applies both to the immediate physical conditions and to the longer-term utilization of soldiers. From the point of view of immediate performance, there is a "golden range" of physical stimulation that appears ideal for battle, but too much can decrease effectiveness. A heartbeat of between 115 and 145 seems ideal as it provides the physical foundation for appropriate action without either leading to manic behavior or to collapse. For encounters of short duration between individual warriors, however, short bursts of frenzy may be ideal. In the longer time horizon, soldiers new to the battle need time to be effective, but continued battle exposure for more than sixty to ninety days leads to physical and psychological exhaustion. Much longer-term exposure, such as in modern war, or in sieges, may permanently hamper lives. The multiple deployments of American GIs in the "permanent battle" zones of Iraq and Afghanistan are broadly blamed for the increase in suicides and general decline in mental health among veterans of these wars (Williams 2012).

While fear, alienation, terror, and panic are subjective, it is critical to understand that these are also social phenomena and that they must be placed in context. For example, how responding to the need for respite has been a problem for all modern armies for whom battle is a perpetual state. Keeping soldiers at the front is not a viable solution. Giving them periodic rests, however, may actually increase the horror of battle for those who have re-familiarized themselves with civilian life. Trying to import normal life into the battle zone (a la Col. Kilgore in *Apocalypse Now*) may also merely serve to highlight the horror of the situation. Limiting the exposure to a set period of time (as did the US military in Vietnam) will come at the cost of unit cohesion and a different kind of dysfunctionality. These issues serve to highlight the organizational and social challenges facing any armed force. These are social units that consistently face much greater pressures than any others and whose failure has arguably the greatest consequences.

Similarly, with some due appreciation for the variability of individual psychologies, we should not speak of cowardly or courageous men, but rather of circumstances and conditions under which more or fewer battle participants will behave in particular ways. Given the horrors and fears described above, no armed force could ever count on perfect compliance based on individual commitment to "bravery."[7] Conversely, the collapse of armed units at particular points in time cannot be ascribed to a larger than normal number of cowards within it.

The above section details the severe conditions of war, specifically of battle, on the individual soldier. The above characterization is one of soldiers as passive inhabitants of particularly terrible conditions. What follows examines how it is that soldiers and their collectives come to act out in cruel and horrifying ways.

Brutality

Given that battle is about violence, the notion of brutality in war is unsurprising. War is a particularly brutalizing experience on the individual and collective, and we must acknowledge the brutality that individuals and the collective enacts in its course. We must put violence in a context if we are to understand both the macro-level transformations in war and the individual-level variations in behavior within it. There are clear differences, for example, across time and space in the kinds and degrees of violence applied. We need to understand the conditions under which particular thresholds of violence, cruelty, and abuse are surpassed. We also need to become much more aware of the context in which these thresholds are defined and applied.

On the broadest comparative schema, there are two contradictory trends observable over the past several millennia of war. On the one hand, the use of wanton and explicit viciousness or malice has lost much of the legitimacy it once possessed. In the twentieth century, particularly in the aftermath of World War II, long accepted practices regarding the treatment of opponents and noncombatants have become more restricted and those who violate particular standards are more quickly and broadly condemned. On the other hand, the degree of violence and destruction applied in war has increased exponentially and the acceptance of what are euphemistically called "collateral damages" has also increased. The levels of physical devastation of urban areas and numbers of civilian and combatant deaths that have become possible through bombing have dramatically transformed the violence of war. We may have created stricter norms, but have also come more readily to accept greater destruction. The difference is that the violence has become more bureaucratized, but it has not diminished. We will review these trends further in Chapters 3 and 4, and here we focus on lower levels of aggregation.

We do find significant differences in war behavior across closer distances of time and space. Two examples should suffice. Within the American Civil War, all accounts agree that battlefield behavior and attitudes toward enemies changed between the initial period of conflict in 1861–2 and the last half of 1864 and 1865 (Keegan 2009; Grant [1885] 1999). Another prominent case concerns the behavior of the Wehrmacht depending on where, when, and whom it fought (Evans 2009; Burleigh 2011). What these cases tell us is that we cannot think of violence as a constant of war, but rather a variable that depends very much on the broad historical and social context in which it is fought.

Are wars made by madmen, or do wars simply make men mad (Rhodes 1999)? The answer seems to be a bit of both. With regards to the latter, there is no question that even if wars do not drive people to insanity (which they often do), they certainly provide a context for mad behavior to become normal or accepted. All of us live with constraints on our emotions and actions, but in war many of these are loosened. For some individuals, this process might lead to the release of psychotic tendencies that would have remained hidden or under control in other circumstances (Fenichel 1945). For the vast majority, war also allows for the release of rages and the acceptance of actions far removed from ordinary life. Many veterans of conflict report that this loss of inhibition can be exhilarating and that the emotional appeal of being in control over violence and the lives of others is considerable.

For some behavioral extremes, we need better to understand the process of "running amok."[8] With due acceptance of a certain percentage of psychotic personalities, most cases seem to arise from the physical and psychological stresses discussed above. That is, aggression seems to generate itself and may even be socially contagious. There also appear to be some forms of what we might call aggressive momentum where, once begun, it is difficult and not impossible to stop or slow the progression of violence. Randall Collins' (2008) concept of "forward panic" captures this phenomenon and uses it to explain incidents of group violence from police charges to infantry battle. Collins explains,

> A forward panic is a zone in time where the emotional impulses are overwhelming, above all because they are shared by everyone: by one's supporters and fellow attackers, and in a reciprocal way, by the passive victims. (121)

For example, it has been found that surrendering to a charging armed force is particularly difficult, as it requires opponents to stop momentarily and instantaneously transform their categorization of a dangerous enemy to a prisoner who is to remain unharmed.

There appears to be a strong correlation between the distribution of atrocities and the recent combat experiences of units and individuals (Grossman 1995). Youth and inexperience may also be factors. Atrocities may also be a somewhat rational response to a perceived permanent state of fear, and this is particularly the case in campaigns where battle lines and the identities of combatants are both fuzzy and disputed. The evidence seems to indicate that some kinds of duties tend to produce a more callous and violent response from soldiers. The experience of the IDF in the West Bank and the US Army in Iraq clearly demonstrates that even in well-disciplined armies, with significant regulations, and a commitment to humane principles, prolonged exposure to certain tasks may lead to dehumanization of the relevant population and an accompanying increase in the likelihood of "brutal" behavior (Phillips 2010; "Breaking the Silence," n.d.).

There is also the moral inversion of moral codes that occur in war. Consider one example among many that could be used. In Exodus 20:13 of the Bible, God commands "thou shall not kill." Yet a relatively short time later, in the book of Joshua, the same God seems to approve as the Israelites enter Jericho and "they utterly destroyed all that was in the city, both man and woman, both young and old, and ox, and sheep, and ass, with the edge of the sword" (Joshua 6:21). The transformation of moral norms and practices can lead to broader ethical crises for individual warriors and perhaps to the very dissolution of any demarcations of appropriate behavior. This confusion can occur not just on an individual level, but also on that of groups, further encouraging forms of behavior.

The major problem of understanding atrocities on both analytical and judicial/philosophical is the assignment of responsibility (Walzer 2009; McMahan 2009; Hersh 2000). Can individuals be held responsible for obeying bad orders, for responding to an insane situation with madness, for not resisting social pressures too much for anyone to bear? The contemporary US military justice system includes possible and likely contradictions. On the one hand, it requires obedience of lawful orders. On the other, it prohibits and threatens to punish cruelty and maltreatment of those under soldiers' orders (e.g. prisoners) as well as a long list of ordinary crimes including murder. Consider the confusion of battle discussed above and think about the position of any individual soldier in the midst of battle, pondering the balance between obedience, survival, and ethics.[9]

In this light, we also need to realize that war crimes or atrocities may be part of official policy. For certain armies and in certain theaters, mass killing or other forms of violence may not be an individual exception, but an explicit part of strategy. Often this is a form of what we may call "instrumental brutality" meant to cow and sow fear in the enemy. Even standard military rhetoric is quite bloodthirsty and encourages violence against those whom it is fighting, with little room for moral cautions and subtleties. When making judgments regarding military strategies we need to be sensitive to the contexts in which they are devised and the relevant moral codes that they are supposedly breaking. Is it, for example, worse to kill unarmed civilians through random shooting or through random bombing? Arguments about intentionality are often used to justify one kind of violence over another, but to the victims the mindset of perpetrators may not be so relevant.

There are clear patterns that we can define in the probability of both individual and collective violence. Most clearly, we are more likely to see excessive violence, atrocities,[10] or brutality when the lines dividing the two sides are (in roughly increasing order): ideological, religious, and racial. That is, the more alien or threatening the enemy, the more likely that whatever bounds of behavior may be normal in war will be crossed. It is critical to note that this distance does not need to be "real" or recognizable to an outsider, but that it is the perceived gulf between the "us" and the "them" that makes all the difference. Thus, Black Union soldiers were treated extremely harshly if captured by Confederates, the Wehrmacht could treat British or American opponents with a very different attitude than it used against the Russians, and American troops had very different attitudes toward the Germans than to the Japanese in World War II. Collins (2008) notes that cruelty and barbarity can be forms of a kind of boundary management – they both reflect and mark who is inside and who is outside the violent group (119–20). Collins notes that in many religions there is simultaneous call of charity, forgiveness, and love to coreligionists and a call for hatred and rejection for those outside of the faith. Similarly in war, we may observe self-sacrifice and love for comrades accompanying forms of inhuman cruelty toward those deigned the enemy.

The importance of social context is obvious in looking at perhaps the two cases of atrocity most familiar to an American audience: My Lai in 1968 and Rwanda in 1994. These are sadly not the only ones we could study, but they both are examples of excess violence that appears to have no instrumental reason. Yet, understood from a sociological perspective, they both appear less instances of individual human depravity (although that may come into play) and more the creation of their social context.

On March 16, 1968, Charlie Company of the 11th brigade of the American Division, consisting of 105 soldiers, walked into the hamlet of My Lai.[11] The area was seen as dominated by the Viet Cong and the North Vietnamese Army, both of which had surprised the Americans during the recent Tet Offensive. Over the next two hours several hundred civilians were killed, many women were raped, bodies were mutilated (sometimes with a carved "C Company"), and most prisoners were executed. Over the next twenty-four hours, C Company also participated in documented destruction of villages, mistreatment of prisoners, and possibly other unjustifiable deaths. The response to the discovery of these events often depended on how one viewed the war. Similarly, the response to the conviction of Lieutenant Calley as the person most responsible, mirrored broad social attitudes about class and personal responsibility (Milam 2009). But subsequent myriad studies indicate that the brutality was more a product of exhaustion, apprehension, absence of clear orders, and the too common dehumanization of the victims. In this case, brutality did not serve any instrumental purpose as a war-time strategy, and its roots could best be traced to the absence of any organizational purpose.

A very different case occurred twenty-six years later, between April 6 and mid-July 1994, when at least 500,000 and possibly up to one million people were killed in Rwanda as part of an ethnic-cleansing campaign (Prunier 1995). Most of the victims were Tutsi, while the killing was largely in the hands of Hutus. Most of the killing was done in close quarters with small firearms, machetes, and axes, and many of the victims and perpetrators knew each other. Rapes, mutilations, and desecrations often accompanied the killings. In much of the early coverage of the massacre, the focus was on the individual brutality of the (implicitly barbarian) "tribal Africans" (Chari 2010). In fact, while bloodlust certainly was a factor, the killings were planned and abetted by a sophisticated organizational structure – there was little spontaneity. Perhaps more disturbing for many in Europe and the US, the genocidal regime had close alliances with the French government, then led by the Socialist François Mitterrand. There is considerable evidence that the French played a significant role in the continuing race construction and differentiation of Hutu–Tutsi conflict through their obsession with keeping Rwanda politically dependent (Prunier 1995).

In both of these instances, individual responsibility has been sought, but, as in many such incidents, it is impossible to explain what happened in an organizational or social vacuum. Accounts of both events emphasize the extent to which the violence was either planned well in advance and was anything but spontaneous, or was partly caused by organizational and social dynamics including pressure to perform militarily or confusing signals regarding acceptable action. The point is not to devolve individual responsibility, but again to understand this form of violence within a broader social setting.

The juxtaposition of the horrors described above and the vast number of people who have participated in battle and return as heroes must be at the heart of the sociological analysis of war. How do we account for the fact that men not only tend to show up and stay in battle, but also engage in tremendous acts of self-sacrifice – acts that are far too common and well documented to be the acts of superheroes? Under practically every imaginable circumstance it would be rational for men either to flee or avoid battle in some way. Yet, while desertion and non-participation occur, the majority of those in a military encounter will at least remain in their posts. How do societies induce this particular form of collective behavior?

One might argue that remaining in battle is an expression of a socio-biological instinct that uses individual sacrifice for the good of a kinship group in the name of genetic survival (E. O. Wilson [1975] 2000). Such explanations may make sense for relatively small groups, but not for the units of thousands that are common to war for several millennia. Similarly, warriors might believe that they will not be killed, or that the benefits of participation outweigh the possible costs. But this begs the question of how they have come to think this way.

The answer lies in the institutions created to foster this kind of thinking. These are the institutions that, in Albert Einstein's words, are responsible for "heroism on command" (Frank [1947] 2002, 158) on which war depends. The following section details the values that are used by society to create soldiers and the institutions which instill them.

Making Warriors

Given that the vast majority of human beings are neither idealized warriors nor blood-lusting madmen, how can we understand the fact that, for millennia, large numbers have not only obeyed orders that would place them in danger, but also engaged in forms of violence that would normally be considered unthinkable? Heroes might withstand the horror of battle, but how do we account for such collective emotions among men who may not fit the image of an ideal warrior or hero?[12]

One possible answer is that many appear to enjoy war. Here we are not speaking of marginally psychotic personalities or of "adrenaline junkies," but of "ordinary men" who seemed to relish the particular conditions of armed conflict (Marlantes 2011). Lt. Gen. James Mattis may have spoken for many across the ages when he described being a Marine in Afghanistan: "Actually it's quite fun to fight them, you know. It's a hell of a hoot" (Scahill 2008; "General: It's 'Fun to Shoot Some People'" 2005).

What does the joy of battle consist of? There is always the appeal of "the glory that never dies" that Achilles chooses over a long life. Such attractions tend to be significant in warrior societies; for mass armies their appeal may be insignificant. There is also the retrospective relief of survival. Soldiers report that the end of a battle was one of the happiest moments of their lives. The very intensity of combat, requiring extreme concentration and cooperation with a close group, also provides a rare form of joy. Battle and war in general will likely be the most emotionally powerful experience in the lives of warriors (perhaps the most common term used to describe battle experience is "vivid"). The concept of happiness or contentment being found in "being in the present" may find one of its most extreme versions in battle, where warriors have no choice but to focus on the "here and now" if they are to survive; what Robert Graves called "life's discovered transitoriness" (Hollander 1999, 188). Battle and its intensity may also mark an important break from the tedium of daily life. The temporary glory and importance given to actions may represent for many a rare moment of dignity and self-respect.

Another answer to our question of how society gets soldiers to fight is that many warriors had no choice but to fight or die. Coercion has a long history in warfare, and some military tactics have been designed so as to enforce implicitly and explicitly the discipline of fighting and facing danger. So, for example, untrustworthy troops might be placed between groups of veterans, assuring some form of compliance. From earliest times, we also have accounts of special units, whose only job was to make sure that the front lines stayed there. Cavalry units on the flanks of infantry could serve such roles, as might special guard regiments, whose loyalty was more assured through a variety of inducements. In contemporary times, the Soviet forces in World War II extensively used "blocking detachments," who manned exits from the battle zone; while in the waning days of the war, the German army instituted draconian rules regarding desertion. In the American army, meanwhile, a significant part of MP duties was to ensure that those stationed in the front stayed there.

The effectiveness of coercion in part depends on the nature of the battle. Relatively small set-piece combat can easily be mentored. As the size of the battlefield, the length of engagement, and the complexity of battle increase, the possibility of constant and active vigilance is reduced. Combat requiring autonomous action by small units over a large territory will frustrate coercive discipline. Moreover, coerced troops will usually be much less reliable than those genuinely committed to battle through some mechanism or other. The quality and depth of motivation of troops may make an invaluable contribution to victory.

In general, we may observe another interesting inverse U-shaped historical trend in the effectiveness of coercion. In relatively simple encounters where individual combat is central, motivation is vital and coercion difficult. As we increase levels of aggregation and the complexity of collective action, the possibilities of coercion expand. As war becomes more sophisticated and military formations less rigid, however, the effectiveness of coercion declines again.

Despite the critical importance of coercion, at the heart of the social phenomenon of war is an institution that transforms individuals with fears of and ethical objections to killing into elements of a collective whole designed to withstand horrific pain and to inflict it on others. What is the basis of this cohesion? We can divide the answer into two parts. The first consists of a set of values taught and privileged by military forces. The second involves a much more fundamental transformation of individuals through the creation of discipline and obedience.

Military Values

While we need to be cautious with assigning too much importance to an esprit de corps, morale plays an incalculable role in determining the success of any armed force. It has been cited, for example, for the surprising victories of many an armed force, from the Spartan delay of the Persians at Thermopylae to the amazing performance by the Wehrmacht against overwhelming odds in 1944 and 1945 (Kershaw 2008). Conversely, poor morale has been blamed for the performance of both US and South Vietnamese forces in the 1960s and 1970s (see various articles in *Reporting Vietnam, Part Two: American Journalism 1969–1975* 1998).

What are the values that underlie military morale? These are the collective social sentiments that help convince so many to participate in activities so few will find attractive.[13] Among these deserving special attention are: camaraderie, leadership, faith, honor, and courage.

Camaraderie

Small fighting groups are what Stephen Crane called "mysterious fraternities born out of smoke and danger of death" (Crane 1998, 31). Throughout history and across geography, descriptions of fighting emphasize the importance of friendship and the semi-erotic bond that unites men in battle. The same survey cited earlier by S. L. A. Marshall ([1947] 2000) found that obligations to the immediate fighting group (as well as thoughts of those at home) were the most powerful reasons cited for fighting. It is important to realize that the significance and appeal of battle camaraderie may be exaggerated through its depictions in myth and fiction, but its very ubiquity in fiction, classic and contemporary, written and filmed, would indicate that there is some reality to the ideal.

War-time is often remembered as the period of life when men had their most intense friendships, and, for many veterans, their memory of military service is often a collage of remembrances of and affection for those with whom they served. This bonding could take intimate forms, as with the Theban Sacred Band of fourth-century BCE Greece, where lovers fought side-by-side. The logic behind such an organization was clear. In Plato's words, "who would desert his beloved or fail him in the hour of danger?" (2012, 147). The same logic applies for non-erotic love. The notion of a special bond linking the men in what has come to be called a squad is universal. Certainly, the most pride and loyalty of individual warriors seems to be toward the small unit with whom he has established personal bonds. A soldier may not necessarily wish to prove his country or polis is best, but he might be more motivated by showing off the special skills and bravery of his unit.[14]

The organizational significance of the squad and its dynamics cannot be exaggerated. Squad cohesion is the foundation of any armed force and without it the collective delivery of violence for which armed forces are designed is ineffective. If the squad can hold together, there is a much greater probability that the organizational aggregates above it will as well. If it falls apart, the larger unit certainly will not hold. The centrality of this, the smallest unit of any military, is one reason why non-commissioned officers are so critical. They serve as the focal point around which the squad coheres while also providing the training and leadership necessary for action.

In the end, small unit cohesion seems to be the basis of soldierly behavior. All armies allow for some form of breakdown into units small enough that they can be seen as a social group with intricate and close links to each other. What we might call the "moral code of the buddy," with its rules of mutual loyalty and reciprocity, is at the heart of the combat experience. In the words of William Manchester,

> . . . men, I now know, do not fight for flag or country, for the Marine Corps or glory or any other abstraction. They fight for one another.

Any man in combat who lacks comrades who will die for him, or for whom he is willing to die, is not a man at all. He is truly damned. (quoted in Holmes 1986, 300)

This may be one of the greatest paradoxes of war: a social phenomenon based on violent competition and hatred may, in turn, actually rely on deeper notions of love than most men are allowed to express in their respective cultures.

Leadership

Leadership and its rights and obligations are a second fundamental military value. While warrior societies do posses a certain democratic ethos, even the most basic organized armies are inherently hierarchical. Even among groups of ostensibly equal warriors, some will be assigned positions of command during battle in reflection of their skills or experience. The importance of a command structure increases with complexity, but there appears to be something about military action that both requires and fosters leadership (Keegan 1988; Davis 2013).

First, there is the question of quickness of action. Unlike most large-scale social phenomena, military encounters take place in extremely constricted periods of time requiring very fast decision-making. They also require clarity of command and a code of obedience. It is precisely this coordination of individual efforts into a cohesive collective one that is socially fascinating about combat. These make the function of a military leader quite understandable, but we should also consider the psychological needs of men in battle and the cultural characteristics of successful leaders.

Precisely because they require such an intense form of commitment, participation in battle may require the inspiration associated with personal charisma. According to social theorist George Homans (1950), the leader is the one who "on the whole, best lives up to the standard of behavior that the group values" (169). This is very similar to the sense of charisma that the great German sociologist Max Weber (M. Weber [1919b] 1946; M. Weber [1922] 1978) theorized about. He argued that one aspect of charisma is that it is the personification of the best qualities of the group in a single individual. It is a special "state of grace" that bestows upon the leader an aura of group personification. Thus military leaders may provide a focal point in which the notions of honor or duty discussed below may be concentrated. They set a standard of soldierly behavior that allows them to forget their rational interests.

Contemporary armies cannot rely on the random appearance of charisma and devote a great deal of time and effort in creating the leadership qualities they will need. Many might scoff at the concept of teaching leadership, but precisely because the military must depend on many ordinary men to do extraordinary things, it has to institutionalize and standardize some form of training in order to produce the results needed. Candidates in the US army's reserve officer training corps (ROTC) program, for example, are constantly being prepared for leadership, culminating in a summer long "Warrior Forge" before their junior year. Here they are trained and evaluated on an extremely precise set of 'Leadership Performance Indicators" that provide feedback on minutely specific skills on an almost hourly basis. Accounts from military academies describe the same form of meticulous and unrelenting measurement and instruction (Mullaney 2009; Lipsky 2003; Murphy 2008).

Faith

Belief in a set of principles for which a war is being fought (and requiring sacrifice) is a third critical military value and may be the ideological equivalent of charismatic leadership in that it provides both a rationale for action and, perhaps, a sense of protection. These beliefs assure the warrior that not only is one's cause right, but that some higher authority (God, gods, destiny) will protect the righteous (Armstrong 2014). Recalling the importance of confusion in the experience of battle, faith provides an internal solace of certainty among the chaos.

Faith can take the form of simple superstition or it can be more in the form of traditional religious experience. Whatever the form, it is undeniable that the experience of battle tends to awaken a need for or an awareness of spirituality. The old line that there are "no atheists in the foxhole" may not be far from the truth. Alternatively, fighting men may comfort themselves with an embrace of nihilism and an acceptance of the inevitability of the random death.

Too traumatic a battle experience, or one considered illegitimate or requiring the breaking of too many moral taboos, may lead to a loss of faith or the questioning of values and norms. Anti-patriotism resulting from an apparently "wasted" military effort, or an apparently unnecessary war can be a political cancer on institutional cohesion. In cases, such as post-World War I Britain and France, or during the Vietnam era in the US, it can lead to a questioning of notions such as national allegiance and loyalty.

The general finding among all sources is that patriotism or nationalism may account for some initial enthusiasm for war and may even lead to improved enlistment. Nevertheless, there is little indication that men fight or die for patriotic reasons. Line soldiers do not like overly patriotic actions or speeches and strongly dislike those who are symbols of such but who are not doing the fighting. According to William Manchester, for example, John Wayne was quite hated among veterans who had fought in the Pacific (1987). There are exceptions, of course, reflecting particular societies and histories, and it is important to note that such ideological motivation may be critical for elite troops.

Rather than a set of abstract values, perhaps the most effective faith an armed force can develop is a belief in itself. All armies use some set of symbols and rituals in order to assure compliance and to underline authority. Individual soldiers may complain about what Paul Fussell calls military "chickenshit" (1989a), but it is precisely this marionette game of spit and polish that may keep dispirited armies together or allow a group of men to face horrible danger. This is a faith in their bearing as soldiers. This faith is in a set of values that have particular resonance in all military communities: honor and courage.

Honor

Honor is the necessary foundation of any military system (Hampson 1973; French 2003). Honor may be based on individual qualities or through membership in a group. The reputation in question may be that of a single warrior or of the collective – the squad, regiment, or country. Specific components of honor will depend on the time and place, but we can identify three critical components or aspects: feelings, behavior, and reputation.

First, we can define honor as the absence of self-reproach. To maintain one's honor is to be certain that one has kept allegiance to what is due or right and an unquestioning obligation to live by these rules. Note that the actual content of the rules may vary widely, but among military professionals, adherence to the code of honor provides an ideological link across a wide variety of cultures and behaviors. This can be disrupted if the definitions vary too widely (e.g. what is an honorable way to treat civilians), but honor remains the military lingua franca.

Honor is the polar opposite of irony. It takes itself very seriously and does not allow for sarcasm. One of the more interesting divides between military and civilians is the former's observation of and respect for self-serious rituals and conventions which often appear absurd or even funny to those outside of the fraternity. Adherence to these forms in the face of ridicule or opposition in turn can become yet another basis for honor.

Honor is also about the real and physical manifestations of actions required by these sentiments. Honor demands that behavior match intentions perfectly. One cannot merely wish to be honorable, nor is simply trying sufficient. One must always successfully behave as honor would dictate, regardless of the circumstances and consequences. Honor does not allow for judgment calls and certainly not for moral relativism. Military personnel are often accused of having too much of a Manichean perspective, where right and wrong are clearly articulated and where there is little or no gray zone. This is very much a product of an honor system that cannot allow for the articulation of escape clauses or ambiguities. Honor demands unquestioning compliance with a set of commandments and these might require sacrifice. We might even define honor by that possible requirement of sacrifice; obedience without sacrifice is not an expression of honor.

This sense of obedience permeates the literary and historical analysis of military honor, for it creates ethical dilemmas for its proponents. The concept of sacred oaths is quite old. For example, our word "sacrament," with its religious tones of a commitment between mortals and a divinity, comes from the Latin *sacramentum*, the oath of allegiance taken by Roman legionnaires, beginning with Augustus. Oaths to "bad" kings still must be obeyed, for example. The real quandaries are when orders might, in and of themselves, require behavior not otherwise considered honorable (e.g. killing of civilians). For some exponents of honor, only the ultimate sacrifice of death presents a solution to such dilemmas.

Finally, honor is a sentiment that must always be affirmed by others. While to do good anonymously or to suffer undeserved shame stoically may be honorable, honor is usually associated with praise, recognition, or deference. This is particularly important within the closed societies of warriors. A soldier's reputation among fellow soldiers is often the central ethical guidepost for many. Honor is what men on the battlefield seek from their fellow comrades. It may involve acceptance of pain and sacrifice without complaint or simply the fear of public shame. Sophocles' sentiment that it is better to not live at all than to live disgraced is universally found among military guilds.

Honor, therefore, cannot exist in social isolation, but requires an audience to give it, assure it, or threaten to take it away. In one form, this recognition might be understood as glory, the need or pursuit of exclamations of honor. This is most associated with a Homeric warrior ethic where one's standing and rank in a group of warriors is foremost. A very different sense of honor is associated with self-respect and is more Socratic in that it encompasses a notion of being true to one's self. These two forms of honor are often taught together, but they can also come into conflict – a classic trope in the literature on warriors.

Honor is central to notions of military sacrifice, whether as motivation for or to the mystification thereof. Notions of honor are at the very core of (often exaggerated) stoicism that characterizes so many warrior cultures (Sherman 2005). Notions of honor serve as the cultural glue that holds these huge conglomerations of men together and allows them bear the unbearable. It should come as no surprise, then, that armies expend considerable time and effort in instilling notions of honor. Similarly, societies with a significant warrior function or component will make honor a central part of notions of masculinity. Young men are explicitly told that they have left normal life behind and have now entered a brotherhood to the honor of which they must devote their lives. These abstract bonds are in turn maintained by the much more concrete relationships on an individual level.

Courage

Courage is also central to any military code (W. I. Miller 2000). To understand it, we must first distinguish it from bravery: In the words of an eighteenth-century French aristocrat: "bravery is in the blood, but courage is in the soul. Bravery is instinctive . . . courage is a virtue" (quoted in Stephenson 2012, 106). Bravery is associated with reckless behavior or a willingness to accept risks, often accompanied by a disregard for consequences. Such a state often has much to do with biochemical reaction or the stimulus of fighting. It may be associated with "berserkers," Norse warriors who, partly thanks to ingestion of alcohol or other drugs, would enter battle with a special fury. This type of behavior is associated with the non-rational forms of aggression described in Chapter 1.

Courage is something completely different: it is an intrinsically human quality in that it implies consciousness of danger and a willingness to deal with adversity. It is in many ways defined by fear and could not exist without it. The courageous person is afraid, but displays courage in resisting the fear. Courage is a form of self-control and is based on a conscious effort to manage our animal instincts for self-preservation (Clendinnen 1985). Courage was classically associated with intelligence as it represents a compromise between rashness and over-caution.

Empirically, the distribution of courage remains a significant mystery. If we can speak of fear and the instinct for self-preservation as universal and perhaps even a biological constant, the ability to control it is a product of a time and a place. Why do some individuals have more of this quality than others? Attempts to create any kind of predictive model appear to have failed. We do have more information regarding collective efforts and the central capacity for endurance. We might better ask, why do some societies tend to produce more of these individuals than might be normal in particular eras and when confronted with particular enemies? One of the many unexplored questions in the sociology of war is the systemic analysis of how courage arises as a social phenomenon. One clue, however, may be in the notion of duty and discipline.

Duty and Discipline

Linking the creation of a military faith, the reciprocity of camaraderie, the notion of honor, and the core of courage is the sense of obligation known as duty. Duty is about submission of one's own will or preferences to those of another or to a collective. It is a binding force that links warriors to those next to whom they fight and to the collectives that they represent. These values are in many ways the antithesis of the classic warrior ethos of an Achilles hungry for glory. Rather they are the much later development of a sense of collective obligation as at the heart of the warrior much more closely associated with Aeneas. In order to better understand the role it plays in the military ethos, we have to explore its associated notion of discipline.

Discipline is an old word which originates in notions of learning and being a pupil. European medieval discipline added elements of punishment, training, and most importantly the enforcement of obedience to a prescribed pattern of behavior centered on self-control. All these contribute to the modern notion of discipline as defined by Weber (1946a):

The content of discipline is nothing but the consistently rationalized, methodically trained and exact execution of the received order in which all personal criticism is unconditionally suspended and the actor is unswervingly and exclusively set for carrying out the command. (253)

This obedience must be uniform and based on habitual routinized drill rather than heroic ecstasy or personal devotion. This is the core behavioral focus on which the ethical values described above revolve.

This notion of discipline is not just inherent to military life, but, some would argue, represents the core of what we consider modernity. For the twentieth-century French philosopher and social historian Michel Foucault, the notion of discipline is transformed in the eighteenth century, when obedience becomes characterized by an automatic response that essentially skips the stage of conscious understanding ([1975] 1995). The development of such obedience requires the creation of a society of surveillance. It is a new form of power which is "individualizing" and "totalizing." It is totalizing in that it is impossible to escape it and it is involved in all aspects of life. It is individualizing in that at its core is the ability to monitor, and to correct individual control.

Modern forms of discipline break down pre-existing social collective into individual components and then reorganize these into a new, more efficient unity. This new form of discipline involves the transition from coercive force to one that we might call "therapeutic." It involves the replacement of threats of coercion with a form of internalized self-control. This new form of discipline, if originating in some training or surveillance, comes to rely more on self-monitoring than some external watcher. It involves the elevation of a social super-ego to dominance. Norbert Elias, a twentieth-century German sociologist, perceived the same process and spoke of discipline as a "moderation of spontaneous emotions" depending on individuals "regulating behavior with the upmost exactitude" ([1939] 2000, 236).

Military collectives have been in the forefront of constructing this kind of discipline. Consider that once the armed force was no longer representing an organic social unit (such as a family or a small clan), but a larger, more abstract whole, the need arose for a cohesive principle that would bind warriors together and allow them to function as a single unit. This binding has become progressively more sophisticated over time. In fact, according to Weber, the very origin of what we now see as modern discipline may be found in the ancient Greek phalanx. He argues that the nascent military discipline of the phalanx and the Roman legion gave them the transformative advantage over more "heroic" rivals.

The notion of obedience or discipline as used here helps to further understand the distinction between the specifically instrumental form of aggression that characterizes war, from the more instinctive forms of aggression associated with other forms of violence discussed in Chapter 1. The submission to the will of others, the compliance with a larger or aggregate logic than that of the individual, coheres the collective unit of armed force and is absolutely antithetical to the individual warrior hero.

Transforming that free individual into a useful and effective member of the collective whole has been a predominant theme throughout history. In the classic Western tradition what are the struggles of Adam and Eve, Abraham and Isaac, and Antigone and Creon, if not about resistance to obedience? Yet note that, with few exceptions, the moral of such tales is that obedience must be established and respected, no matter the pain or loss caused. While obedience may be the "bane of all genius, virtue, and freedom,"[15] it is also at the heart of collective action, and certainly of any military feat past the minimalist of sophistication. At the heart of obedience is the submission of the individual to an organizational mindset.

How do societies create such obedience? For many years, scholars attempted to associate a propensity for obedience with particular societies or forms of socialization. Over the past few decades, we have come to appreciate that the contexts in which obedience can be instilled can be of much shorter duration. The combination of some legitimacy, absolution of responsibility, and some sense of intimidation can create patterns of obedience nearly instantaneously. This was most spectacularly shown in the infamous psychology experiments run by Stanley Milgram at Yale University (Milgram 1974; Lutsky 1995). Much as Tajfel was responding to his experience in World War II, Milgram sought to understand how the millions of Germans complicit in the Holocaust could have participated in such atrocity. In his experiments, subjects ("teachers") were directed by the experimenters to punish "learners" (also an experimenter, unknown by the subject) depending on their responses to a set of questions. While the experimenters had thought that only a few of the subjects would be willing to go along with the procedure, much less reach the highest levels of punishment, Milgram found that almost all obeyed initial commands and more than 60 percent followed the orders to the very highest level of electric shock despite evidence that these shocks were causing harm to the learner.

Throughout history, armed forces have attempted variations on these patterns of learning and submission involving the inculcation of obedience to a hierarchical command structure. To do so, militaries have often created what Foucault describes as institutions that "induce in the inmate a state of conscious and permanent visibility that assures the automatic functioning of power" (Foucault [1975] 1995, 201). Such institutions American sociologist Erving Goffman has called "total institutions" (1961). According to Goffman, total institutions are situations in which people are separated from broader society and work, recreate, and sleep with only other members of the isolated group. Prisons are the most common example used, but Goffman also lists monasteries, psychiatric asylums, and armies as other obvious examples. Indeed, militaries are groups of warriors who temporarily or permanently close themselves off from the other parts of society and share many of these institutional qualities.

The basic training which contemporary recruits receive in modern armies is the latest expression of these efforts (Franke 2000; Ricks 1997a; Siddle 1995). At the heart of basic training is a psychological manipulation much more important than any set of military skills acquired. These periods of isolation from the rest of the world seek to change the way recruits think, making obedience and discipline no longer simple means but ends in themselves. The stages involved in the process are fairly standard. First, the beliefs and behaviors which the recruits bring to training are destroyed. Then alternative identities, role models, and behaviors are constructed, in which the values described above are extolled above all others. Young warriors or new recruits learn to obey instantly orders from above and to relish the membership in the select group that they represent.

In this chapter we have reviewed the individual experience of war and battle, which is typically that of boredom and waiting punctuated by extreme physical, psychological, and emotional trauma. We asked, how do individuals come to tolerate, even volunteer, for such extraordinary activity? We argue that specific traits, particularly military values of faith, courage, duty, discipline, and obedience, are inculcated in individuals in order to induce them into fighting, and perhaps suffering mutilation or death, on behalf of their country. In the following chapter we analyze the product of these values and virtues, but in an aggregated form.

3

War of Armies

In the first chapter, we argued that to understand war we need to think of it as a collective, social phenomenon. That is, we cannot properly study war if we overly emphasize the aggression that takes place on individual levels. In the second chapter, we did, however, focus on the individual warrior and asked how any significant number of people could ever be induced to participate in such horrific violence. In this chapter, we will ask a related, but different question: how are the collectives that are involved in war managed? We have seen one answer in the previous chapter though our attention to notions of duty based on obedience and discipline. In this chapter we will make use of these notions, but add to them two important aspects: the development of new forms of social organization and new technologies and how these interacted to produce the twentieth century's world of wars.

Fighting among individuals is fundamentally different from fighting among groups. The former rewards individual virtues that give the warrior a higher probability of winning – for example, strength and skill. The latter must translate the same attributes to the collective level through the elaboration of hierarchical institutional structures and the imposition of discipline. These two forms of fighting also involve different technologies, as the weapons that may be decisive in hand-to-hand battle may be insignificant when used by thousands. Most important is the level of social organization required to achieve this translation of coercive skill. Consider the movements an individual might engage in while playing a fairly simple game of basketball or soccer: backward and forward flows, side and fake movements followed by surprising runs. Now consider the managerial difficulty of achieving this same level of movement, but from a mass of one thousand men, or ten thousand.

We may best understand the progress of war over the millennia as characterized by the increasing complexity of these movements, requiring greater organizational sophistication, and the imposition of more elaborate forms of discipline, all leading to increasing lethality. These requirements change everything from the type of warrior formed by society to the form of political organization required to do so. Each shift has been accompanied by revolutionary changes in operations, logistics, technology, and social support (Chaliand 1994; Archer Jones 2001; Archer et al. 2002; Lacey and Murray 2013).

All of these aspects are parts of a central dilemma since the dawn of organized social life and of particular salience for militaries: how to aggregate humans in such a way as to make the whole encompassed and created by their integration greater than the sum of their parts. This is the central goal of military organization, from the simple tactical level to the most complex strategic plan: the aggregation of instruments of violence and the people who use them, and optimizing their use. The sociology of militaries seeks to explain how the amalgamation of sometimes hundreds of thousands of individuals can be managed and controlled so as to enable the new collective ensemble to focus on the immediate policy objective: the channeling of violence against an enemy.

Origins of Battle

In the first chapter, we discussed the Mesolithic cave paintings in Morella la Villa in Spain, depicting small groups of men engaged in what looks like armed conflict. The next extant depictions of battle come several thousand years later. From the third millennium BCE we have works such as the Standard of Ur and the Stele of the Vultures. Both of these depict men in battle, but with significant differences from the cave drawings. First, the number of warriors depicted has grown; second, they are more clearly organized into something we would recognize as "drill formation;" third, there is a clear hierarchy of command; and fourth, the bodies of the conquered make clear what the consequences of the battle are.

In between these representations something critically important happened. Unfortunately, the sequence of events leading from the encounter depicted in the cave in Spain to the triumphant march of Eannatum of Lagash is largely hidden from us (Trigger 2003). How did social units move from the disorganized and often ritualistic encounters between a few individuals to the deadly encounters of massed infantry? We do not know. We should, however, consider routes that were not chosen on the road to battle. For many societies, war involved the exchange of a ritualistic set of insults that left few, if any, physically hurt. More common was the practice, well established in many cultures until quite recently, of conflicts being decided by champions.[1] A third alternative would be a combination of the heroic warfare of champions with aspects of guerilla warfare today: conflict resolved through sporadic fighting between small groups. Instead, war evolved in most societies – becoming globally dominant by the nineteenth century – in a very peculiar way: masses of men would meet and seek to hurt the other side enough so as to either subjugate or even obliterate opposition. Just as there is nothing "natural" about war (as opposed to violence), there is nothing natural about the manner in which we battle. War as a social phenomenon is the product of historical path dependency and political, economic, and institutional orders.

How did the pattern of mass battle come to dominate the globe for centuries? We cannot trace its pre-historic origins with any precision, but we can observe other social developments that appeared to occur in tandem. As explained in Chapter 1, the development of organized violence is closely linked to greater sedentism and the rise of a notion of territoriality. As the complexity of the violence grew, it seems logical that it was accompanied, if not preceded by, the imposition of hierarchical authority and social inequality (Boix 2015). Prior to any evidence of war, we do have indications of urban settlements developed enough to merit the label city. While these differ in key characteristics, such as presence of walls, they seem to share a privileging of places within them where an elite might live.[2] The rise of this elite to power and its concomitant ability to command large numbers of men is at the very heart of the development of the modern state.

Whatever the causal order, it is imperative to appreciate the critical link between the new form of fighting and the institutions of social cohesion. It is important to appreciate the complexity and difficulty involved in producing the formations depicted in the Mesopotamian art described above. Consider the organizational challenges involved in creating any social collective we might recognize as an army: hundreds – if not thousands – of men must be brought together, their armament must be at least secured (if not provided), and enough training must take place so as to assure some minimum level of performance. Once in the battlefield, the warriors must, over the course of several hours, move in organized unison, all the time withstanding and delivering great amounts of violence.

Armies could only exist linked to elaborate forms of social order. The social basis of this type of warfare appears to have been relatively similar around the world. While cognizant of critical differences across these societies, all were characterized by class inequalities, dependency on a mass of agricultural producers, and having political authorities or states that were largely dedicated to war making (Boix 2015). It is not clear whether the states were created in order to make war or war arose because of the development of competing states, but that there is a relationship between phenomenon and institution was clearly established (Tilly 1985, 1992). The balance between use of the military to counter external threats and its use to maintain a domestic status quo is also unclear, but both roles were significant.

These developments appeared to have happened independently, although not simultaneously, in every major agrarian civilization of the ancient world, beginning around 3500 BCE[3] (Trigger 2003; Keegan 1993; Ferrill 1985; Herwig et al. 2003). Within geographical regions, the new forms of war may have developed in one or two centers and then spread. The destructive advantage enjoyed by those societies that made this organizational leap would have been significant and assured some form of dispersion either through conquest or learning. Consider, for a moment, the effect within any ancient geopolitical zone of the entry of a political group that not only exponentially increased its fighting power through aggregation and cohesion, but also rejected ritualistic combat in favor of destruction. Once one group discovered this form of fighting, others would have the limited choices of escape, enslavement, or emulation.

Our earliest detailed depictions of battle and armed groups already contain many of the characteristics that militaries would retain until the present day. In the accounts of the Battle of Kadesh (ca. 1274 BCE) we can already observe groups of up to five thousand men operating as an aggregate fighting unit under unitary command (Ferrill 1985). The Egyptian divisions could operate both tactically – turning to face the enemy and directing the line of fire – as well as strategically – crossing large distances in order to attack the Hittites. The Pharaoh Ramses exercised control over these movements and could alter their movement and position depending on the information he received.

These already vast armies (20,000 is a consensus estimate) were organized in the standard form familiar to any soldier today: individuals belonged to units consisting of fifty warriors. These in turn were grouped in formations of 250, and these configured into even larger groups of one thousand men. We find a similar "layered" and segmented structure across armies in the ancient world; it would appear that the basic military configuration of squad-platoon-company-brigade with a rough proportion of 10–100–1,000 and so on is universal (even if decimal ratios are not) and quite old (Gabriel 2005). Along with the centrality of smaller sub-units came the significance of maintaining a core of veterans who would not only command them, but serve as examples and mentors to the recruits. The central role of what would later be called non-commissioned officers is ancient and speaks to the central organizing logic of all militaries.

The formations already possessed an impressive mixture of arms, including infantry, artillery (archers), and cavalry (chariots and, in

India, elephants), each fulfilling specific and sequenced roles. As in every era, specific weapon technologies help define tactics and vice versa. Infantry weapons would probably have been limited to spears and perhaps axes. The key weapon system would have been the chariot carrying one or more archers armed with a composite bow. The apparent uniformity of weapons and basic tactics across the Eurasian landmass for about one thousand years beginning in 1800 BCE is remarkable. The centrality of the chariot is striking, as is the simultaneous use of specific archery technology. To what extent this was due to diffusion and to what extent it reflects the expansion of the Indo-Europeans is still subject to a great deal of debate (Keegan 1993; Ferrill 1985).

The key resource constraint appears to have been enough material and labor with which to produce the necessary weapon systems (e.g. lumber, metal, and horses for chariots). Geographical context was critical: for the armies of the Mesopotamian plains, cavalry in one form or another was decisive. In more mountainous terrain, or where horses were not available (as in the Americas), infantry became critical. Because of the relatively small size of the populations and the forms of battle, a single victory or defeat could permanently alter the geopolitical balance of power and even lead to the disappearance of a major group. In all cases, armies consisted of a mass of conscripts used during wars, but otherwise usually devoted to agricultural work. They would have been led by a core of warriors permanently devoted to military service and free to thereby consume the agricultural surplus produced by new technologies and the more complex forms of economic organization.

The consensus is that the importance of the chariot indicates the centrality of some form of aristocracy to war making. It is not surprising then that most of the surviving accounts of battle focus on individuals and their heroic deeds. Yet, militaries could be meritocratic arenas where relatively humble born could climb the social ladder based on martial deeds. The biblical story of David is an obvious example of this. In the Americas, Aztec militaries included all commoners and these had the opportunity to rise to elite status through merit (Clendinnen 1985; Hassig 1992).

Despite the social and material limitations of ancient warfare, the evidence indicates that already by the mid-second millennium BCE, and certainly one thousand years later, armies were capable of considerably complex maneuvers (Gabriel 2005). Sargon II's campaigns in eighth-century BCE Assyria and the wars over five hundred years leading to the battle of Jingxing and the consolidation of the Han Empire in 205 BCE are in a different tactical and strategic universe from the encounters described in the *Iliad*.

The Phalanx, the Fleet, and the Legion

Two major shifts occurred over the next few hundred years: the replacement of the chariot by cavalry and the rise to supremacy of the infantry.[4] The first shift had much to do with the expense involved in fabricating the battlewagons, their limited mobility, and their limited use outside of specific physical terrains. As the technology, breeding, and skills of horsemanship improved, cavalry evolved from simply a device to shock infantry and to deliver missiles, to one that expanded the size of the battle and created the need for a much more sophisticated understanding of it. We will focus on the second change, as it had a much more revolutionary impact on wars and the societies that fought them.

While it appears that early armies did organize infantry in something of a square, the Greek phalanx ranks as its most sophisticated elaboration in the Ancient World (Lendon 2005). Its use in other parts of Eurasia may have been limited by the fragile hold that any sovereign had over the mass conscript armies and the use of chariots, which made any dense formation on a battle plain practically suicidal. The rough terrain of the Greek peninsula and the relative material poverty of ancient Greek poleis made chariots less of a factor. The challenge of discipline and holding a large mass of soldiers together was more of a problem. Without cohesion, massed infantry is useless, as it will be broken by threats or weaknesses. To use infantry properly, a social context had to exist or be created that supported the cohesion of the formation.

According to Victor Davis Hanson (2002), the phalanx was born out of the particular agricultural structures of ancient Greece. These created the foundation for a type of battle that would be at the very core of the "Western way of war." These conditions and accompanying cultural beliefs favored a type of war where armies would meet at agreed-upon sites and fight what would be considered "decisive" battles in order to resolve any conflicts. The social order of the ancient Greek poleis also prohibited the raising of the mass conscript armies: the fighters would be a much smaller group of free citizens, the vast majority of whom were independent farmers. The resource limits of these polities also required that each warrior be responsible for his own material.

Phalanx battles were tactically simple, but socially complex. They were also a particularly terrifying form of battle. They consisted essentially of two square blocks of armored men, each wearing perhaps 30 to 50 pounds of armor and carrying a 7–9 foot spear, racing toward each other in formation across a plain. As the squares collided, the respective front rows would shove and thrust at their opponents, while the ranks behind them would push forward and, when needed, replace those in the front who had fallen or who were too exhausted to fight any longer. The central tactical logic of the phalanx was based on the *hoplon* or round shield, held with the left arm and helping to secure flank of the hoplite and part of the neighbor to the left. Phalanxes were solid and unstoppable, but inflexible. Victory required either breaking the will of the opponent or being able to flank him through strength against the traditionally weak left side.

Such a struggle required a particular form of cohesion. The phalanx was a pure expression of collective as opposed to individual power. Broken, it was virtually useless as the armor and armament of the soldiers would not have been adequate for other forms of warfare. The form of battle also meant that individual courage (while always praiseworthy) possessed less than the usual premium; the phalanx created a sum greater than the total of the individuals involved. Each warrior depended on his neighbor to the right to protect his body (thus the position of far-right corner was usually occupied by a veteran with a good reputation). The battle worthiness of the phalanx required unanimous participation and considerably more effort in the first two or three ranks. At the same time, too much fervor would be equally disastrous as the whole point of the enterprise was to maintain formation. The phalanx did this perhaps better than any other military formation: it did an incredible job of suppressing "the flesh" of instinctual fear of battle (Ferrill 1985, 104).

How did ancient societies create this formal cohesion? As in all military organizations, there was an element of coercion. The phalanx made it impossible for non-participation to be anonymous: a hole in any rank or file would be visible to all. Moreover, those in the front ranks and middle files would have a very difficult time escaping from the battle, given that they would be surrounded. Equally important was a mixture of the motivations described in Chapter 2: the column or files would be composed of friends, providing psychological support and incentive. Given the small size of the ancient Greek polis, reputation would also be fragile and the fear and consequences of shame would be great. Finally, the warriors had a clear incentive. For the Spartans, success in battle was the very basis of a social order dependent on large numbers of slaves; one too many routs and the entire hierarchy would come down. In other cities, many of the soldiers were small farmers and it was their lands that they were protecting through participation in battle.

While there remains considerable scholarly debate on the origins and operations of the phalanx, the consensus is that the social structure of the ancient Greek polis significantly influenced the structure of the phalanx, but that the phalanx in turn supported the social structure of that very society. The phalanx also functioned in a fairly culturally homogeneous world and this provided the basis for its broad use. Note that, more than most other forms of battle, the collision of the phalanxes depended on a consensual understanding between the two warring sides. Phalanxes were most effective against other phalanxes. Calvary and archery might have certainly made them ineffective. Once the basic constraints of phalanx warfare began to be violated at the Battle of Leuctra in 371 BCE and later by the Macedonians, this particular form of warfare and the society which was built on it disappeared.

The same symbiotic relationship between form of warfare and social structure could be observed with the development of the Athenian navy. More than any other ancient Greek polis, Athens was dependent on maritime trade for its economic survival, and had already developed a sizable navy by the sixth century BCE. As the military role of the navy expanded in the wars against Persia and later Sparta, the ever-increasing number of rowers used this military dependence on their labor to extract more economic, social, and political privileges. The radical changes that defined Athens in the fifth century partly had their roots in these military transformations.

A similar military and social transformation, which accompanied the rise of the phalanx in classical Greece, occurred in China in the sixth century BCE. In the lower Yangtze region, some of the "warring states" found that their geographical and social contexts favored the creation of disciplined infantry armies and these were quite successful. The rise of these armies meant the end of the heroic and aristocratic form of warfare practiced by the traditional aristocracy on its expensive chariots. The eventual victory of Shih Huan Ti and the consolidated Han Empire was in part a product of a militarization of society. The subsequent "rationalization" of warfare and of the political order had its greatest expression in Sun-tzu's *Art of War,* written in this period (Herwig et al. 2003, 54–7).

This correlation of military functions and social structure was perhaps best expressed in ancient Rome. The ancient Roman army was in many ways the culmination of these trends (Goldsworthy 2003). It dominated the entire Mediterranean basin for close to five hundred years and it did so not because the Romans were braver or necessarily better led than their opponents, but because they were better trained. Each soldier in the Roman army knew his exact place and role and, perhaps more importantly, knew that his fellow soldiers also knew theirs and would do their duty.[5] The coherence provided by the training, devotion to duty, and confidence in a "system" was the key to the Roman success. In the words of Vegetius, "Victory was granted not by mere numbers and innate courage, but by skill and training . . . [Romans] owed the conquest of the world to . . . military training, discipline in their camps, and practice in warfare" (quoted in Parker 1995, 57).

The basic Roman formation began from very similar social structures to the Greek polis and shared many of the same attributes of the phalanx. But, as Roman society changed and as the military needs expanded, the tactical and strategic inflexibility of the phalanx became more and more of a problem. The solution was the legion: a much larger unit of about five thousand men that used the phalanx or maniple as the basis for a much more adaptive battle formation. Rather than a box, the legion in battle resembled a checkerboard: three lines of ten maniples, each with alternating squares allowing the lines to move forwards and backwards, thus presenting any opponent with a regular front of fresh troops. The Romans also continued Alexander the Great's preference for greater variety of weapons and also featured cavalry, though infantry was at the very heart of the legion.

As the Roman army became more professionalized and the kinds of social cohesions that held the phalanx together dissipated the emphasis on training, a sense of duty born within the legion itself and loyal to it above all else was created. Instead of a hoplite fighting for his land, the Roman soldier sought, in the words of Roman Emperor Severus Alexander, to be "properly clothed and well armed, [with] a stout pair of boots, a full belly, and something in his money belt" (quoted in Hanson 2005, 49). The professionalization of soldiering came at the cost of divorcing the military from the society which wielded it, but did allow for a much greater tactical sophistication, given the greater dedicated training and the skill level one could assume of the typical soldier.

The reliance on mass infantry and the shift of the Roman aristocracy toward domestic politics meant that, more than any other previous military institution, the ancient Roman army was a child of the state as an institution rather than the direct arm of a class. In this, also, it presaged the modern army that would arise in the eighteenth and nineteenth centuries. It also foreshadowed the kind of destructive power of later militaries: Roman armies were not interested in the limited (if decisive) phalanx skirmishes, but in conquest. This required a military ferocity unprecedented in that part of the world, but which also helped create as large a geographic zone of domestic peace and social order as the world had known.

The Return of the Horse

In the West and East, the disappearance of imperial armies led to a fragmentation of military authority and a return to the value of individual prowess in battle where "strength, skill, and courage meant more than the organization and training" (Archer Jones 1987, 94). Combined with the diffusion of the stirrup, this produced the heyday of aristocratic war in the West. Along its frontiers and toward the East, the same general collapse of imperial powers helped foster the return of the nomad to military centrality following the millennia-long domination by military based on sedentary culture represented by the infantry.

Both the aristocratic and nomadic forms of war were based on the supremacy of the horse. The dominance of the cavalry was not new. Despite its well-deserved reputation, the Roman army did have weaknesses, and one of these was in conflict against cavalry-dominated militaries. The Mesopotamian frontier remained a fragile one from the defeat of Crassus by the Parthians in 53 BCE and their successors the Sassanids. This was not necessarily the result of some generic imperial problem with cavalry, as the Chinese Qin and Han dynasties were very successful in defeating their horse-riding opponents during this same period. But once imperial authority disappeared, the supremacy of cavalry re-asserted itself. This provides an interesting clue to the relationship between political authority and military prowess: the mass and disciplined infantry is very much a product of centralizing political states, and imperial political power and reach, in turn, seem to be a function of their ability to construct such formations; infantry and state are thus in many ways co-occurring.

Feudalism and knightly war are yet another example of how military organization and social structure reflected and produced one another. The collapse of imperial power in Western Europe meant that after the sixth century no political authority existed capable of taxing the population enough to pay for an army, nor having the organizational and institutional capacity to train and utilize such a force. The need to protect territory and resources and to preserve social order remained. The feudal system replaced the centralized army with "sub-contracted" services to an aristocracy willing to exchange military service for land (Arrighi 2010). The combination of a return to heroic warfare and the hierarchical construction of society produced a return to the culture of individual honor reminiscent of Homeric ideals.

As with any military system, knightly warfare not only reflected its underlying social foundation, but also required mutual acceptance of a set of military rules. Much as was the case with the phalanx, the onslaught of armored knights wielding lances was particularly effective against enemies who either fought in the same way or facilitated this type of warfare in one way or another. When opponents refused to stand and receive the shock (as was the case with the Muslim armies in the later Crusades) or when the wall of infantry stood fast (as in the first half of the battle of Hastings) or when archers were used to disrupt the charge (as in Crecy or Agincourt), the weakness of the knightly charge was quite evident. This is a pattern that we will observe repeatedly in warfare: military success in a particular form of battle can be completely irrelevant if the rules of combat change.

The political and military system of the nomads and their use of the horse were quite different from that of European aristocrats (Keegan 1993). Throughout most of Eurasia, there does seem to be a general turn to the military supremacy of the nomad from 500 to roughly 1300 CE. The first pattern to be observed is that in almost all of the cases, the initial rise to supremacy followed the weakening or disappearance of a political authority able to defeat the different nomad groups. Whether we speak of Huns in the fifth century, Arabs in the seventh, Vikings in the eighth, or Mongols in the thirteenth and fourteenth centuries, each faced a military that was a fragile obstacle to their expansion.

Second, the nomads were the most successful military actors to not originate in or attempt to establish a unitary territorial state. Rather than the war being part of a political project, for many, war was an end in itself. In some cases this was because of plunder, in others because of the need to propagate an idea, but overall, the nomads had a very different military agenda than their competitors.

The form in which they fought was also quite different. In many cases, the distinction between the armed force and the society (or at least the male society) was non-existent. This, and their reliance on the horse (or on ships in the case of the Vikings) meant a very different form of battle with tactics more resembling that of hunters cornering prey than the geometric exactitude of the Roman legion. This is not to say that nomad war was as chaotic as their charges may have appeared to their enemies. Certainly the Mongol battle order and the underlying hierarchical structure were far removed from the individually oriented battle of European knights or of the Sioux. But the fluidity of movement made it a very different social organization.

Despite their apparent power, however, both of these forms of warfare were also products of their historical context. When the context changed, their strategic and tactical rationale no longer served any purpose. While the horse and the individual warrior could dominate the battlefield for centuries, they could not resist the twin developments of increasing centralized political authority and the technological development of weapons based on gunpowder. The first development was able to create a human mass against which military charges would break; the second provided a weapon that soldiers could not escape or evade. Note that the former development, centralized political authority, is social in nature, while the latter is technical. The Asian "gunpowder empires" (McNeill 1989) relied on cavalry, but new organizations of infantry made their previously irresistible charges increasingly futile.

Military Revolution: Gunpowder

The interaction between military technology, tactics, and social structures is perhaps most visible in the case of gunpowder. As an invention in and of itself, gunpowder was already centuries old when it began to dominate the battlefield in the seventeenth century. Various chemical combinations of explosive powders were known in China before 1000 CE, and firearms were already available in most parts of Eurasia by 1300. By 1368, Ming soldiers possessed advanced firearms whose use had "far reaching implications" (Kiernan 2007, 105). Most of the earlier innovation in the use of gunpowder in Europe, however, was with artillery, and already by 1500 cannons were an important part of war for several militaries.

Variations in the use of even such limited munitions often had dramatic strategic consequences. In Europe, artillery meant the end of localized and autonomous aristocratic powers based in impregnable castles. On a larger scale, the fall of Constantinople in 1453 was partly the result of the use of gunpowder, and the Battle of Lepanto, which determined control over the Mediterranean in 1571, was arguably won by the Christian superiority in firepower. Javanese empires from the 1300s until the arrival of Europeans used their impressive arsenals to establish control over much of Southeast Asia.

But the true "gunpowder revolution" (if there was one)[6] required innovations beyond artillery. The rise and fall of the Spanish *tercio* may provide a good illustration of the change (Herwig et al. 2003). At the core of the *tercio* was the "hedgehog" formation of pikes in a square that might have looked familiar to a hoplite or a legionnaire. The *tercios* were an important transitional tactic because they culminated a centuries-long shift back from the more heroic aspects of nomadic and aristocratic battle to the discipline and professionalism of their Roman forebears.

Yet, while it dominated the battlefield for the last part of the sixteenth century, this type of massed formation was disastrous when faced by well-utilized artillery as in the Battle of Rocroi in 1631.

It was in the organizational more than the technological or purely tactical aspects of battle where we see the broadest impact of gunpowder. The kinds of tactics made necessary by the potential and limitations of gunpowder did bring about dramatic changes in the practice of war. The combination of improvements in the design and manufacture of firearms and new formations led to the creation of the characteristic element of warfare for the next two centuries: the volley or what we might call a "wall of lead" that replaced the previous obstacle of swords and spears.

The success of firearms in the European military tactical market was crucial for later developments (Martines 2013). Many in Europe would have envied the successful contemporaneous Japanese efforts to prohibit firearms altogether. For many, gunpowder represented an evil new way of killing. From Ariosto to Cervantes to Shakespeare, we find literary references to gunpowder and guns as works of the devil that took away the romance and value of war.[7] Most importantly, they signaled the end of the privileged position of the aristocratic warrior astride his horse, or in the Japanese case, merely armed with his katana. But, in the European cases, the success to be enjoyed by armies with the new weapons and the security they brought to the increasingly dominant sovereign houses made opposition futile.

From a sociological perspective, the most important aspect of the gunpowder revolution was the creation of a new form of organizational discipline required by the new form of war. The gunpowder revolution produced radical changes in the way men were trained and what was expected of them in battle. This arose from three interrelated changes: tactical, cultural, and demographic. In a repeat of phalanx military culture, the emphasis increasingly was on the control and manipulation of the collective with declining emphasis on the power of individual initiative and bravery.

First, given the inaccuracy of sixteenth-through-eighteenth-century firearms and the time needed to reload, success in battle came down to the ability to coordinate large groups of men so as to assure a continual wall of fire facing any offensive charge (McNeill 1989). In order for them to perform the basic procedures of firing their weapons, and to carry out the increasingly complex maneuvers required, armies created exercises to train soldiers to fire in organized volleys. The competition to increase the delivery of lead at ever-faster rates often determined who would win not just a battle but also a campaign.

The faster delivery of firepower and the larger percentage of men facing fire (as the firing line lengthened and thinned, fewer would find themselves removed from danger) required the development of what John Lynn has called the "culture of forbearance" (Lynn 2003), in which soldiers were expected stoically to accept extreme punishment and death. Consider that for roughly two centuries, most battles consisted of formations of men marching toward each other and, as they approached, letting loose and withstanding withering volleys of fire power. The combination of apparent geometric order with the increasing power of firearms brought the need for courage to a new level. What was expected of the soldier was simply the ability to accept his probable death or dismemberment as he calmly marched toward the enemy and loaded and shot his musket in time.

This expectation for courage under fire required discipline. In many ways, it required precisely the characteristics that had defined the phalanx two millennia before. Unlike the phalanx, however, these armies were not made up of land-owning neighbors but often of what one observer described as "slime of the nation and of all that is useless to society" (count of St. Germain, French secretary of war, quoted in Lynn 2005, 180), or in many cases well into the eighteenth century, mercenaries. The general assumption was that the common soldier could be trained, but never trusted. Since the officer corps remained aristocratic (with meritocratic – and lower status – niches such as artillery), the key to running an effective army and navy was to have the men fear and respect their commanders more than the dangers to which they were exposed. Tactics and strategy were partly designed to keep men disciplined and obedient. During training, the lash was a popular tool, but in battle the visibility of the line and the impossibility of hiding non-performance were equally critical.

A complicating factor was the increasing size of armies. In

the Hundred Years War of the fourteenth and fifteenth centuries, armies of ten thousand had been the norm. Two hundred years later, seventeenth-century Swedish king Gustavus Adolphus invaded Germany with over 130,000 men, and a few decades later, French king Louis XIV would operate with armies of several hundred thousand. This required ever-greater organizational sophistication as the logistical maintenance of such huge hordes became crucial for success (Lynn 1993; Van Creveld 2004). One of the keys to successful support was standardization of more and more aspects of military life. This included weapons, encouraging not only national industries capable of delivering large numbers of arms, but also discouraging variance in style or technology or even dress as uniforms increasingly became the norm.

In an interesting contradiction that would remain constant through the twentieth century, the standardization, bureaucratization, and general imposition of order on what had been an often-chaotic enterprise was accompanied by greater passive destruction. Not only was the killing power of an army increasing, but also as its size grew, the consequences of an army merely passing through any region became ever more dire. This destructive potential then required ever more discipline to manage it and direct it to the proper object of military policy.

These shifts signaled the end of whatever romance of war existed. Changes in war and its practice became part of what Norbert Elias calls the "civilizing process" whereby the chaos and the violence were moved from the public face of conflict ([1939] 2000). Certainly we see this in artistic representations of war where the action tended to move away from the heroism and great deeds of individual soldiers and where perspective moved farther and farther away so that what was left were depictions of large apparently anonymous bodies of men across gigantic canvases. It also created a new form of "military refinement," which sought to remove itself from emotions and reflect ever more the perfection of manners.

Perhaps no episode best exemplified this than Voltaire's anecdote of French and English armies meeting at the battle of Fontenoy in

1745 when the rival commanders each beseeched the other to shoot first (Voltaire 1757; but see Buchan 2011). Simultaneously, with the Enlightenment spirit of science came efforts to create a new form of military rationality which would leave nothing to chance and where battles could be fought on paper with precision and prediction. Such niceties, of course, hid the tactical imperative to hold fire until close enough to do damage, and the fact that, refinement aside, thousands died in the subsequent battle.

The Birth of Total War: Napoleon's Revolution and the American Civil War

The next revolution in the manner in which wars were fought had less to do with the specifically military aspects and more with the social bases of political authority behind them. The political revolutions of the late eighteenth century challenged not only the domestic political orders of the relevant states, but the very international system under which they operated.

The checkerboard armies of eighteenth-century Europe represented the disciplining of political violence to the will of increasingly centralized states. They accompanied the territorial expansion of a small number of strategic centers and their ability to claim the monopoly over the legitimate application of violence within their territory. But they were also the tools of monarchs and were openly used to foster their interests. Accompanying Enlightenment efforts to create a science of war came increasing rationalization of its use. Armies were meant to protect and expand interests and a lost battle need mean nothing more than a lost province. Because they were the institutional epitome of the state, because they were so expensive, and because the conflicts were really more about inter-family feuds than about primordial differences, much of the strategic emphasis was on the avoidance of battle either through maneuver or through the protection of borders by natural obstacles or fortifications. The apparent order of the battlefield reflected the instrumental rationality of the politics behind it (Weigley 1991).

The American and French Revolutions transformed the relationship between politics and war. The new forms of war were uncertain and inchoate and the struggle was increasingly existential (Strachan 1983, 91–3). Carl von Clausewitz, the great Prussian general and military strategist, recognized that wars could no longer be limited or choreographed, but required an absolute commitment and with this, new forms and levels of violence ([1832] 1984). Although still debated, many see the birth of total war (Aron 1954) in the French Revolution (Bell 2007a; Esdaile 2008),[8] carried on through the American Civil War (McPherson 1988), and finding its apotheosis in World War II (Weinberg 2005; Hastings 2011). Clausewitz would call the kinds of war "absolute" which demanded the utmost not simply from a class of officers, or a group of soldiers, but of the people from which the military was drawn itself. This relationship between war, politics, and the people would develop into total war.

The embodiment of this new spirit of war was Napoleon but the changes were also inherent the outcomes of previous developments. Tactical conventions, for example, were already being challenged by the theoretical advancements of French military tactician Comte de Guibert's *ordre mixte*, technological developments in the quality of all weapons, but particularly artillery, and the increasing success of skirmishing (Rothenberg 1980). But the most significant transformation was that armies stopped being seen as the playthings of rulers and became emblems and tools of the nation.

The transformation of the French army in part was caused by its internal dissolution as large parts of its officer corps found it impossible to operate in the post-1789 order. More important, however, was the threat the Revolution represented to the European monarchies and their responses after 1791. Faced with external threats and without an adequate military response, the Paris government created a new form of armed force: its officers would no longer be aristocrats appointed by status, but commoners advanced by their skill. The common soldiers would no longer be St. Germain's despised dregs of society, but the very representatives of the people. In any case, the line between the soldiers in the battlefield and the civilians behind them would be blurred, as each part of the nation would be called upon to do their part so that the Revolution and France (the two made synonymous) could survive.

The purpose of battle was also transformed. No longer was it sufficient to win a rare encounter that would be settled with a territorial transfer. The struggle had to be carried to the enemy and the threats must permanently be assuaged by the destruction of opposing armies. To this political shift we need add that the French army relied less on the multiyear imposition of discipline through drill (impractical given the time needed and impossible given the political and ideological context), but on a new form of morale and fighting spirit. Lacking the organizational capacity to maintain an army through complex logistics, Napoleon used these new circumstances to force decisive battles. But these battles would now encompass hundreds of square miles and campaigns would range across the entire continent. The level of violence and the number of dead increased as well.

We can appreciate some of these transformations by considering three campaigns: Austerlitz, Spain, and Russia (Bell 2007). The first in 1805 required the redeployment of massive armies over hundreds of miles and in combination with the campaigns between 1805 and 1807 produced hundreds of thousands of casualties. Austerlitz is perhaps most notable for the fact that Napoleon sought a decisive battle even after his defeat of the Austrians in Ulm two months previously. Gone were the days where one battle and a retreat would finish a war. Napoleon sought to decimate the allied Austrian and Russian armies in order to solidify his control over central Europe. The peninsular campaign begun in 1808 was notable again for the bloodshed involved – at least half a million dead in total. More importantly, the French occupation produced a popular and nationalistic revolt which, while eventually defeated, produced a political and military ulcer from which Napoleon never recovered.

The brutality of tactics on both sides of this struggle also marked a critical turning point away from the "gentlemen's wars" of the previous century. The sheer size of the campaign of 1812 merits attention. At the battle of Borodino of September, over a quarter-million men were arrayed on both sides, and total casualties may have reached 100,000. In this campaign, the annihilation of the enemy as championed by Napoleon was applied to his forces (as made most graphically clear by the famous chart by Minard, glorified by Tufte (2007)).

If Napoleon's military method met its match after 1812, the legacy of the new form of war continued. In part, this was because of two of the most famous intellectuals produced from that war – the Swiss Baron Jomini and Prussian Carl von Clausewitz – who sought to analyze the new era of war and whose readers sought to emulate (or defend themselves from) the great successes of the French armies. More importantly, once the power of national military forces and total war became clear, it was difficult if not impossible to return to the status quo ante. Prussia under Frederick the Great, for example, had served as arguably the epitome of eighteenth-century European warfare. Yet the defeat in Jena in 1806 led to a complete rethinking of the relationship between state, military, and population and began a process that would culminate in the creation of the most powerful army by the end of the century (Paret 2009).

The next stage in the development of total war occurred in the United States. The American Civil War was a critical moment in the path to total war for six interrelated reasons. First, it involved an existential threat to the protagonists. For the North, defeat would have meant a radical transformation of the Union and for the Confederacy it meant the destruction of a way of life. In part because of this, the later years of the war were categorized by an ideological intensity and an accompanying savagery still rare in military conflicts of the time. Non-professional armies largely fought the war. Both sides depended on their civilian populations not just for the lowest privates, but even the highest levels of leadership. This was not a war between soldiers, but between peoples. The size and scope of the war also distinguish it from its predecessors. The four years of war included battles in at least three major campaigns separated by hundreds of miles as well as a continual blockade of thousands of miles of coast and included over three million men. It remains the bloodiest war in US history, as over

620,000 died with perhaps another half million wounded (total casualties were over 5 percent of the male population) (Clodfelter 2008; DeBruyne and Leland 2015; Chambers 1999). The level of killing may have been unprecedented, as some units lost over 80 percent of their men in single battles. Civilians were not immune and, particularly in 1864 and 1865, the Confederate population was subjected to the harshest possible punishment and deprivation while the economy of the South was destroyed. Finally, the war was arguably the first in which industrial resources were critical for victory. The strategy of the North was at least in part one of attrition in which it could use the massive imbalance of practically every good to its advantage.

What was perhaps most remarkable about the American Civil War was that its conclusion did not lead to a major transformation of how military conflicts were viewed and organized. To a large extent, European militaries ignored the lessons of the war (Keegan 2009, 358–9), and even Americans did not reconsider the viability of war in the new industrial age. The next century would reveal their folly.

A Century of War

In many ways, war and the twentieth century defined each other. These one hundred years were marked by a bloodletting unprecedented in its reach and barbarity. While the precise number of victims remains a scholarly debate, the overall picture is indisputable. If we simply count the deaths from inter-state wars, we have a count of roughly eighty million. To this number we may add the estimated forty to fifty million victims of colonial, civil, and revolutionary wars – that is, where only one side represented a formally institutionalized state. Finally, if we include as wars efforts by states to "reform" their populations along ethnic, religious, or socio-economic criteria, we may add another eighty million dead (Clodfelter 2008). The figures are historically unprecedented. This is not to deny previous incidents of mass violence (the death counts for the Mongol invasions, the European conquest of the

Americas, and the various religious wars of sixteenth and seventeenth-century Europe were equally impressive), but it is critical to appreciate the manner in which political violence was transformed during the century. These changes are the climax of the processes that we have been analyzing in this chapter: the aggregation of ever greater collectives, the increasing complexity of organization and the centrality of technological development, the resulting level of lethality, and the subsequent transformation of the relevant societies.

This was the first time in history when wars occurred across the globe simultaneously. Where previously one region had undergone an intense period of conflict while the rest of the world remained relatively peaceful, the twentieth century saw a universality of organized violence.[9] Some regions largely avoided inter-state violence, but suffered from revolutions and civil wars.[10] In practically every region, each decade of the century witnessed a major war. Some wars occurred across the world. In 1915, for example, anyone trying to follow the course of the war would have needed detailed maps of Flanders, Polish Galicia, Eastern Anatolia, Tanzania, the North Atlantic, and the Southwest Pacific. Consider the strategic map of 1942: with the exception of Latin America and sub-Saharan Africa, the Axis and the Allies confronted each other in every major region from the North Atlantic to the South Pacific, from China to Egypt to the skies above London and Berlin. In the case of the Cold War, the entire world was held hostage to the potential outcome of nuclear Armageddon.

In part because of this geographical scope, the numbers involved were also unprecedented. During World War I, an estimated sixty-five million (overwhelmingly men) were mobilized globally. That some of these millions ended up fighting for their colonial masters against foes with whom they had no historical contact, much less conflict, and thousands of miles away from their homes added to the global nature of the war. For World War II, the distinction between civilian and military participants became increasingly meaningless, but the total global involvement was at least one hundred million. For many countries, over half of the relevant male population was in uniform at some point during the war, making these truly generational phenomena. Single battles could include more men on both sides than had previously fought in entire wars. For example, two million soldiers were involved in the battle of Stalingrad and three million soldiers were involved in the battle of Berlin. The unprecedented numbers changed the notion of battle: Stalingrad took several months while the so-called Battle for the Atlantic took three years.

The materiel involved increased accordingly. In 1915, there existed parallel systems of trenches and earthworks along thirteen hundred miles of front (Keegan 1999, 175). Along the four hundred miles of these in the West, intricate systems of communication supply and reserve trenches made for an intricate spider web that stretched for miles on both sides of the front. The millions of men stationed in these had to be fed, clothed, and armed on a regular basis, requiring supply systems over thousands of miles and involving millions of workers and farmers (Winter 2014).

Thirty years later, in World War II,[11] the opposing sides had over one thousand divisions in Europe alone, representing over ten million men, each requiring a vast communication and infrastructural network (Kennedy 1987; Overy 1997; O'Brien 2015). These were protected by roughly fifty thousand aircraft flying thousands of missions per day and over 300,000 tanks, one-half million of which were built during the war, as were five million vehicles. As the arsenal of the allies, the US economy almost doubled and its industrial production increased by over 100 percent (Calvocoressi, Wint, and Pritchard 1999). By 1943, the US was producing a tank every five minutes, a plane every half-hour, and an aircraft carrier per week (Davies 2006).

We can best appreciate the logistical demands by looking at individual battles. On the morning of June 22, 1941, for example, the Germans began their invasion of the Soviet Union with 3.5 million men, 3,300 tanks, 3,000 planes, and 600,000 horses (Bellamy 2007, 173–5; Beevor 1998, 13). A year later in Midway, seven aircraft carriers, over forty other ships, and over five hundred aircraft, whose technology had not existed a few decades before, met in a contest over hundreds of square miles (Symonds 2011).

The Normandy landings of 1944 were first preceded by an

airborne assault of three divisions, carried and defended by twelve hundred planes and followed by over seven thousand ships, including six battleships, ferrying 130,000 men supported by over ten thousand aircraft (Wieviorka 2008). Each of the American invaders was carrying an average of seventy-five pounds of equipment, which included extra ammunition, explosives, a variety of tools, several thousands of calories worth of food, cigarettes and enough Benzedrine to keep them awake. The fact that most of this equipment had to be transported across the Atlantic makes the logistical challenge even more astounding (Beevor 2009, 80; Murray and Millett 2000, 420–1). Finally, the March 10, 1945 bombing of Tokyo included 334 B-29s. Arguably the most sophisticated industrial product of the war, these machines allowed for the destruction of the enemy's homeland from bases thousands of miles away.

The role of command had been transformed along with the logistical sophistication with the development of an ever-greater divide between strategic operations and tactical leadership. Consider that at Borodino (at least as described by Tolstoy ([1869] 2007)), Napoleon was but a few command levels removed from the common foot soldier. Even in the American Civil War, the hierarchical structure was relatively simple. By World War I, the process of sending orders down the line, receiving reports, and adjusting commands accordingly was chaotic at best and resulted in attacks that should have been canceled and assaults not taken.

Perhaps the best indication of the increasing complexity of all military operations was the development of a general staff, first in nineteenth-century Germany and then throughout all militaries. These officers were to be experts in railroad timetables, killing ratios, and the movement of thousands of men across massive maps. By World War II, the distance between Eisenhower and the lowest GI was interspersed with front, army, and corps commands before reaching levels that might have made tactical sense to a general a century before. The link between supreme leadership and the soldier in battle had become increasingly tenuous.

This distance was partly a function of the sheer size of the operations involved. Even "soldiers' generals" like Zhukov and Bradley could not cognitively follow movements below divisional level, and even that might be a strain – consider that in 1945, Bradley commanded four field armies, each comprising two-to-three corps, each of which had three-to-five divisions of 10 to 20,000 men each. The most infamous example of operational and strategic complexity is no doubt the German Schlieffen Plan of 1914. It was meant to bring about a decisive battle with the French army so that Germany could then switch attention to its eastern front. The "Plan" was really a set of memoranda based on an apparently precise and exact movement of hundreds of thousands of men and accompanying supplies. Technology and planning would eliminate the chaos of the battlefield. It did no such thing, but it did succeed in making the organization of war itself a major factor in the outbreak of hostilities.

Explaining the Progress of War

What made this new form of killing possible? As in previous transformations described above, the industrial-level killing of the twentieth century was based on technological, organizational, and social and political developments.

Each of the previous "revolutions" was associated with the advent of a type of technology: the working of metal into durable weapons, the taming of the horse, or the invention of gunpowder. The nineteenth century also saw critical developments: by 1900, all of the leading armies were equipped with breech-loading rifles, permitting much more accurate and faster fire and allowing for greater tactical flexibility. Developments in artillery meant that commanders had to think of threats coming from miles away and the invention of the machine gun made massed frontal assaults suicidal. In World War II, the development of air forces literally created a new dimension for combat and made the distinction between soldier and civilian irrelevant. Without the industrial revolution, the sizes of armies and their geographical reach would have been impossible. The twentieth-century wars are ones that mirror the technological and economic advancement of modernity.

But each of these physical developments had to be shaped into a military device. The phalanx and the flanking cavalry charge are not inherent in either bronze or in horses. They involve the utilization of aspects of the technology and the organization of men in such forms as to maximize the violence of impact. All the equipment available to the US army in World War II would have been useless without the managerial wherewithal to assure that some reasonable percentage of ammunition, for example, was delivered at the right place and at the right time. The production flow chart and the carbon copy may have been as critical in assuring victory as the B-29.

These efforts to tame the new technology also required a context of political authority that made the harvesting, packaging, and delivery of resources possible. It would appear, for example, that the mass use of infantry requires a fairly consolidated state and that in its absence, the supremacy of the individual warrior can be reestablished. The discipline of the eighteenth-century volley required a state able to conscript enough men and to coerce them into military formations and into action. The logistical chain attached to the armies of the great twentieth-century wars would be unthinkable without a massive bureaucracy taxing a population and organizing thousands, if not millions, of commercial transactions. Without the political legitimacy of nationalism, no armed force could rely on the support of their society for such long periods and with such immense sacrifice.

Finally, these wars occurred in specific international contexts that helped shape their strategies and methods. The phalanx was a reflection and a creation of the geopolitics of the ancient Greek polis, and the limited warfare of the seventeenth and eighteenth centuries could not survive the Napoleonic revolution. What characterizes total war form the mid-nineteenth century on is the continual breaking of a series of norms and expectations where the only limits to absolute war were technical and organizational.

We have seen in this chapter how wars of armies developed from and shaped broader political and social structures. The increasing scale of warfare demanded ever greater planning and organization, requiring new military formations and effecting social structures. Greater numbers of armed forces also called for developing technology, and the military revolutions involving the horse and gunpowder were transformative to military conflict. With the development of total war, the war that spreads from the battlefield to the home front through political and economic channels, the role of war in society would take on unforeseen directions. In the next chapter, we will focus on the consequences of such total wars, focusing particularly on conquest and genocide.

4

War of Societies

Largely due to the focus on Western Europe in our analysis of war, the advent of total wars in the twentieth century may appear as the culmination of a process of aggregation: from battles of warriors to wars of armies, and culminating in the national industrial competition of the two world wars. In this way, the indiscriminate killing and erasure of borders between military and civilians that occurred during World War II is portrayed as an historical anomaly, the product of the new technologies of killing.

In fact, it is the limited wars of the roughly five hundred years of the military revolution in Europe that are really the exception. For much of history and across the globe the distinctions drawn between combatants and populations made little sense. The point of war *ad romanum* was often the displacement of a population or its eradication (Burleigh 2011, viii). At best, the fate of the members of a defeated society was an inconsequential aspect of military strategy and war aims. Wars were always between societies, and survival was often uncertain.

There is an essential paradox in the development of war over the past century. On the one hand, the reach of military destruction expanded and cities thousands of miles from any front line could be obliterated. The productive capacity of home societies and the legitimacy of the struggle on the home front became critical strategic considerations. On the other, and especially after World War II, normative sanctions and guidelines arose which made the divisions between legitimate and illegitimate targets more explicit.

It is only in the last few decades that the notion of the spoils of conquest has been challenged and it has become broadly accepted that victors do not necessarily make the rules. Part of the challenges of warfare in the twenty-first century, and particularly for superpowers, is the apparent contradiction between our technologically driven destructive capacity and the normative constraints placed upon its exercise and use. As American President Lyndon B. Johnson famously declared, "the only power I have is nuclear, and I can't use that" (Shogan 1991, 5). But for most of human history, there were few political limits on the exercise of destructive power, and if we are to understand the relationship between war and society, we need to look beyond the formally defined battlefield.

Living in a time and in societies where war can feel quite distant, it is important to realize that we live in very much of an historical anomaly and we need to understand better the nature of this much more brutal kind of struggle. We may call such struggles "wars of societies." They can be characterized by one or more qualities. The most obvious is a dependence on civilian society (the "home front") for military success and a subsequent implicit permission to target civilians. This usually involves a continued flow of logistical and personnel flows as struggles extend beyond a single battle or campaign.

A much more ominous characteristic of wars of societies, and one that has been historically more significant, involves clear intention to displace, destroy, or fundamentally alter the society of an existing people of a particular territory. These are wars where it is not sufficient to defeat an enemy on the battlefield, but where the aims of war include the devastation of the losing side. In some cases the destruction of a society is merely the consequence of a takeover of territory. In other times, the eradication is the very purpose of the war, and in yet others the lines between intention and consequence may not be clear. The first kind, the take over of territory with the latent outcome of displacement, elimination, or fundamental takeover of a society, we are calling conquest and it has been the most typical form of warfare for much of human history. The second form, the intentional eradication of an entire people, we may refer to as genocide, which, while rarer, also has

a considerable history. The third we may call Armageddon and its
ultimate expression may be found in the late twentieth century.

Conquest

The concept of conquest involves two related phenomena: acquisition and domination. Thought about in this light, conquest is the
fundamental expression of war. Much of military history can be
described as attempts to appropriate some resource through the
use of violence. The founding myths of many cultures involve
the conquest of some primal birthplace or the displacement of
some prior occupant found unworthy by gods or by fate. The law
of conquest, or "might making right," is as old as coercion and
the imposition of authority. Because of its ubiquity, it is often easy
to ignore the role of conquest in shaping human history; victors
tend to forget and losers disappear. Yet our political, economic,
and social worlds are very much products of conquest. It is arguably the central narrative behind the historical and contemporary
distribution of language, ethnicities, and global stratification.

The link between conquest and territory is fundamental.
Generally, we cannot speak of conquest unless there is some
concept of societal ownership or claim over the resources and
products of a region. This does not necessarily imply formal states
or even advanced agriculture. Pastoralists have been especially
adept conquerors as they moved to more desirable lands. While
the line between conquest, diffusion, adaptation, and imitation
may be difficult to establish historically, the current distribution
of cultures across the world cannot be understood without reference to conquest. Certainly the dominant position of monotheistic
religions would be impossible without it.

Waves of conquest and the often associated construction of
empire have helped shape our world from the campaigns of
Sargon of Akkad in third millennium Mesopotamia, through the
creation of the Hellenistic and Roman empires and the consolidation of Qin China, the Islamic expansion beginning in the seventh
century, and the Mongol explosion of the thirteenth century.

Closer to our time, the history of Europe over the past two hundred years could be summarized as leading and resulting from attempts at continental conquest. Yet, no war or series of wars has had a greater societal impact than the victory of the "West" beginning in the fifteenth century.

Consider that after the 1400s, no society has been able to challenge the supremacy of military power based in Northwest Europe and its satellites. The supremacy of the West is based on a five-hundred-year process of military conquest, and the contemporary world cannot be understood without reference to that military prowess. There is perennial debate regarding the reasons for Western domination, but it is undeniable that a part of the world was able to achieve a monopoly over the means of violence for close to half a millennium. The apparent comparative military advantage of the West can serve as useful lens with which to examine the interaction of war and society. Moreover, it is impossible to understand the challenges of warfare in the twenty-first century without understanding how these developed and how they have been progressively constrained.

Why did the West win? We can identify four different categories of advantages that have been cited in the relevant literature (Moor and Wesseling 1989; Diamond 1999; Raudzens 2003; Headrick 2010). The first argued advantage[1] is that Europeans enjoyed a significant lead in military technology and used it in extremely effective ways. The second advantage, argued most famously by anthropologist Jared Diamond, is that Western conquerors brought with them disease to the New World to which local populations had no immunity. Third, the West appears to have enjoyed an organizational and managerial sophistication in bringing a large and effective killing force to bear. Their political organization appeared to have been superior in delivering violence. Finally, in case after case, we find that the Europeans by no means defeated their indigenous opponents alone, but only when they made strategic local alliances.

While the first argument privileges gunpowder, the third emphasizes the organizational foundation of military revolution, both tied to capitalizing on technological and strategic developments in war making. Why did the West have this advantage? There is considerable support for the idea that the competitive market of war in Western Europe produced organizations well-designed and developed for conflict (P. T. Hoffman 2012).[2] The West had the combined good luck of competing prior to the conquest and thereby honing its military skills and then found mutual enemies in the conquered lands who could be used one against the other.

None of these in and of themselves explains the Western conquest, and each played different roles depending on time and place. One general lesson we can observe is that repeatedly the West could win when it was able to establish to strategic and tactical agenda. For example, when antagonists met in open battle, Europeans won, but when indigenous groups used their local knowledge and flexibility in smaller campaigns, they were much more successful. For our purposes, we will focus on three conquests and see how these factors played out in each one: the Americas in the sixteenth century, Asia from the fifteenth through the eighteenth centuries, and Africa in the nineteenth century.

The Americas

The basic narrative of the Spanish conquest of the Americas is too well known to require much elaboration here. Following the destruction of the indigenous population of the Caribbean, the Spaniards then took only twenty years to conquer a territory vastly larger and more populated than the Iberian Peninsula. How was it done and what does this tell us about war?

We can easily dismiss accounts which emphasize some special heroic attributes to the Spaniards and paint the indigenous people as passively accepting their fate or being incapable of avoiding it. Neither the Aztecs nor the Incas gave up easily. Their societies, their entire political, social, and economic worlds, were essentially destroyed by a force that was much better able to apply violence to its enemies, and it did so with tremendous effectiveness.

The epidemiological luck of the Spaniards should not be underestimated. The elimination of the peoples of Mesoamerica and the Andes was almost total. A rough consensus would place losses through the sixteenth century at 70 to 90 percent (Diamond 1999). This wave of mass death made the long-term subjugation of these lands and people infinitely easier.

Despite the considerable loss of life due to disease, there are arguments against this being the primary factor of success for the Spanish. The Aztecs did begin to feel the effects of European illnesses almost immediately after Cortes entered Tenochtitlan at the end of 1519. By the time Pizarro met Atahualpa in 1532, the Inca Empire had already suffered the first waves of epidemics. Yet, in neither case did these waves so decimate the native military forces as to make the Spaniards' job easier. That is, the Spaniards fought against enemies that might have been doomed by disease, but at that time the native people of what would be called Latin America still had considerable life in them.

The main effect of the epidemics was in the political and social disruption they caused (Clendinnen 1985; Hanson 2002). In the case of the Aztecs, the death of Montezuma's immediate successor made it difficult for the polity to organize itself. The foreign maladies also shattered the legitimacy of the Aztec worldview and, like any other catastrophe, disrupted basic social structures. In the case of the Inca, smallpox had already killed one ruler and arguably precipitated a civil war when Pizarro arrived. What disease did was massively to disrupt the conquered societies, but the Spaniards still had to enact their military superiority.

This was partly based on technology. The most obvious technological advantage was that the Spaniards had the transportation capacity, enabling them to invade the Americas instead of the reverse (Headrick 2010). While carrying out a long-distance engagement across a vast ocean is a considerable challenge, this enabled the Spaniards to enjoy several benefits, including using the shock of the new, as well as exploiting local allies. It is also indicative of the advanced state of technology that the Spaniards enjoyed over the Aztecs and Incans.

We may also count the horses and dogs available to the Spaniards as a military advantage. The efficiency in battle gleaned from these animals may not have made a huge tactical difference, but the disorientation they caused was considerable, especially in early encounters. Native Americans had no previous understanding of horses, and dogs in battle were unknown. The bewilderment they caused upon their use may have given the Spanish early advantages more so than anything they did on the battlefield.

Spanish armor may not have been much of an advantage (they soon switched to more local protection), but helmets were critical in protecting them from the barrage of small missiles used by the indigenous armies. There is some debate regarding the effect of gunpowder, as the Spaniards simply did not have that many such weapons, but again the sheer shock value and the advantage this gave in early battles or in the early stages of any encounter should not be discounted. Finally, Spanish steel could best the wood and soft obsidian weapons of the Aztecs and Incans, and in close-quarter combat this advantage was considerable.

Here we can argue that "soft" technology – organization, discipline, and doctrine – were much more important than any material difference. First, we should not ignore the makeup of the Spanish forces and the social process that had produced them. The legacy of the Reconquista, the prior socialization, and the idiosyncratic leadership qualities of people like Cortes and Pizarro made a critical difference in the success of Spanish conquest of the Americas. These factors did so not by creating any type of "superman," but by producing a collective commitment to a common enterprise (Elliott 1984, 156).

This is not to discount the considerable forces and organization of the Mexica or the Incas. Much like most other complex societies, they also fought in formation and had clear battle orders. But all indications are that, at least in the case of the Mexica, they focused more on what we might call "Homeric" styles of warfare – emphasis on symbolic engagements and warriorhood over the collective – and much of their social order was based on individual performance (Hanson 2002). The Spaniards, on the other hand, were trained much more to fight as units and their incentive system strongly discouraged individual acts of futile bravery. There was also a significant difference in the goals of battle. For the Mexica, for example, the point of battle was capture. For the Spaniards, it was killing.

War of Societies

As Swedish author Sven Lindqvist (2001) has argued, the colonial wars were the precursors to the total wars of the last two centuries. Spaniards and other colonial conquerors practiced a form of intense and ferocious warfare with few bounds, what the Dutch East Indian army called *indische taktiek* (Moor and Wesseling 1989, 5). Whether taking place between individuals or between larger groups, the advantage would have surely gone to that one who sought to kill in the fastest and most efficient way possible. The Incas were also constrained by their culture of war: the capture of the Inca severely disrupted their entire political organization while the Spaniards fought with no constraints (Guilmartin 1991).

However, even if we attribute all the technological advantages to the Spanish that have been suggested, it remains impossible for a few hundred Spaniards to have defeated tens of thousands of well-trained, courageous, and increasingly desperate Incan and Mexica warriors. The diseases and the technological differences perhaps would eventually doom the indigenous empires, but the manner in which the role of indigenous allies has been left out of traditional accounts speaks perhaps to a political desire to espouse European supremacy rather than acknowledge the important role of local alliances.

Neither the Mexica nor the Incas had established anything like absolute rule in their respective region. Each was resented and there seems to have been little inclination on the part of allies or subjugates to treat the Spaniards as any different from their indigenous overlords (and thus requiring unity against a common enemy). The Spaniards enjoyed the logistical and military support of the Tlaxaltecs and others in Mexico, and of various competing factions in Peru. This is where the timing and control of the transport technology was particularly critical. The Spaniards were the product of a political organization with a finely tuned model of violence evolved from constant competition against a wide variety of enemies. They were able to exploit the local divisions for their benefits. Perhaps if a fleet of Mexica warriors carrying a particularly virulent version of syphilis had landed near Calais after Henry V's death in 1422 and had united with the English to conquer France, history might have been quite different.

An interesting take on the combination of technology, organization, and geopolitics has been suggested by American anthropologist Ross Hassig (1992). In this instance, the Spaniard did possess a particularly well-suited fighting style and technology. But this was really only useful for breaking the initial battle line (a sort of conquistador *blitzkrieg*). Such a breakthrough would eventually have been suicidal, were it not followed by a significant force able to exploit it. This is what the Tlaxaltecs and other allies did, and Hassig argues that, in their eyes, they were using the Spaniards as much as vice versa. In this telling, historical agency remains with the Mesoamericans, but they could not comprehend the epidemiological or colonial fate that this strategic decision entailed.

Finally, the considerable political organization which the Mexica and the Inca did possess also ended up benefitting the Spaniards. In both cases, conquering one city or dominating one group was enough to deliver much of the remaining imperial territories. In this way, the Spaniards did not conquer the Americas, but actually succeeded two very well developed polities that had done much of the work for them. When they met opponents who were not as centralized and who refused to battle on the Spaniards' terms (as in the American West), the outcome was quite different. This is a lesson that no post-imperial insurgent could forget.

Asia

The European military advantage becomes clearer when we move halfway around the world to the Portuguese, Dutch, and English dominations in East and South Asia. Here, the epidemiological luck played no role. The Europeans did not decimate the native population through infection, nor did these locations present an ecological barrier to the conquerors.

Technology however is a different story. It is critical to distinguish here between military technology and science. On the latter, various locales, but especially Sung and Yuan China, vastly outdistanced their Western counterparts. The most obvious case is with the use of gunpowder, which was developed in China but never converted for use in mass killing. What the Europeans did – and many of their eventual opponents did not – was to use what science they did have for the purposes of mass destruction of others. This is not to valorize one culture over another, but to recognize that the Europeans applied their science in a particular way.

The first technological gap had again to do with the monopoly over transport, or more specifically, violence purveying transport (Headrick 2010; Lenman 1989). Obviously, several groups on all three sides of the Indian Ocean had seafaring technology of one sort or another. But the Portuguese innovation was to place early forms of naval cannons on their ships. These effectively gave them control over any disputed passage and allowed them to increasingly monopolize the spice trade, which, of course, further enabled them to produce more powerful ships than their competitors. They were only defeated by those using the same technology in the same way, namely the Dutch and British. The indigenous kingdoms of the Indian Ocean littoral could maintain their independence (or at least be swallowed by the Ottomans, the Safavids, or the Mughals) and they maintained control over land. But the sea had become European territory.

Explaining the later expansion of European power into that land (Britain in the eighteenth century) then requires we go to our other two mechanisms: organization and local political conditions. The numbers involved in the British conquest of India and in such iconic battles as Plassey in 1757 rival the ratios of the Spanish in the Americas. As in that case, the British enjoyed some initial supremacy in technology and this again played an important role not so much in killing as in disrupting the battle order of their opponents.

The real key to the success of the armies of the British East India Company was organizational (K. Roy 2005; T. Roy 2012). The indigenous troops were skilled as individuals, but not subject to the discipline and control that is so central for aggregation of military might. This would lead to lines being more easily disrupted, collective charges being undermined, and, too often, non-participation or even early retreat by many. The military revolutions discussed in Chapter 3 were, at this time, unique to

Europe and they provided the British with the critical advantage in mass battle. Another critical element was that while the British were able to co-opt indigenous groups and cultures to produce the militarily effective *sepoys*, their Indian counterparts had great difficulty in ensuring the loyalty of their European mercenaries (Kolff 1989; Lynn 2003).

However, as in the Americas, it was the geopolitics of the subcontinent that made the critical difference (Barua 1994; Ray 1998). The British (and others) walked into the political vacuum produced by the collapse of the Mughul Empire. While this prevented them from replacing one hegemon with another, it meant that the polities of the sub-continent found it impossible to unite against a common enemy. The subsequent disunion in the Maratha Confederacy further inhibited an Indian response (Duffy 1998). Worse, the British were able to create temporary alliances against whoever happened to be strongest at any particular time. The British also benefitted from the fact that in many cases the indigenous rulers did not enjoy a great deal of legitimacy with their troops. Combined with the absence of the post-seventeenth-century style military discipline, this again disadvantaged them in any open battle. Finally, the British alliance and then control over Bengal allowed them access to arguably the wealthiest part of India and these resources were more often spent on military investment than was the case with indigenous armies (Lenman 1989; Bryant 2004; Prakash 2008).

Africa

We may separate the European campaign in Africa into two very broad periods, each providing its own lessons. The first begins with the sixteenth century and ends halfway through the nineteenth; the second includes the infamous "scramble" that is arguably more familiar.

In the first phase we see a similar pattern to other conquests, but with interesting twists. First, in this instance, Europeans did not bring disease, but were stymied by it (Thornton 1999; Headrick 2010). The geographical and epidemiological challenges of Africa restricted the European incursions to limited sovereignty over some coastal areas anchored on fortifications. Attempts to penetrate deeper were consistently frustrated by high disease mortality, and also by the inability of the Europeans to utilize their technological and organizational strengths. The technology gap was often bridged through trade and the conditions in the region prohibited the kind of massing of even medium-size forces effectively.

However, as in our other two examples, the Europeans did not need to "conquer" Africa when in many senses others would do it for them. Here, what is critical is that warfare and conquest in the sub-Saharan setting was rarely about resources defined by territory, but rather control over human beings. This reflected the relatively low population density of the region.

For several centuries, the Europeans expressed no interest in penetrating past their bases as long as the supply of the key resource – human slaves – was assured by other means. It is in terms of this slave trade, and not in control over land, that this first phase of the European expansion involved a "conquest." The numbers will always be the subject of contention, but estimates place the numbers of Africans enslaved at over twelve million, with perhaps an equal number of Africans dead who never made it to the New World (*BBC News* 2001; Eltis and Halbert, n.d.). Such figures of enslavement and death created a demographic shock of global historic proportions, affecting the global economic, political, and social context to this day.

What weapons were used to inflict servitude on these people? Even more than in the case of the Americas and South Asia, European military agency was limited. The Europeans provided an economic and political incentive structure that catalyzed the trade and may have played a role in providing the indigenous slaving militaries with a significant technological advantage (Thornton 1999).

The second phase is much more familiar and arguably begins with the French conquest of Algeria beginning in 1830 and effectively ends with the start of World War I. Once again, disease was not a factor, except that medical advancements made penetration of the African interior progressively more feasible. As in the other cases discussed above, the colonial population not only paid for their own conquest through their own labor but also participated in the conquest, as colonial militaries used only a minority of European soldiers (Moor and Wesseling 1989). Technology did play a much more important role than in the other cases as the development of rifles and machine guns and the dearth of possible sources for Africans made battles often little more than exercises in mass slaughter. Despite some prominent examples (Isandhlwana in 1879 and Adowa in 1896), encounters between indigenous and European militaries were unmitigated disasters for Africans. Even the most militarily sophisticated entities such as the Zulu and Ashanti could not withstand a situation that French poet Hilaire Belloc famously summarized as, "Whatever happens, we have got/The Maxim gun, and they have not" (Belloc 1898).

But the technological advantage has again to be placed in the appropriate organizational and geopolitical context. First, machine guns, artillery, and breech loading repeating guns were only useful in the type of battle for which they were designed (Killingray 1989; Headrick 2010). So in Omdurman in 1898, the ratio of casualties was as lopsided as in any other colonial struggle, but only because the battle was fought on European terms. When indigenous militaries refused pitched battle and forced Europeans to fight on their terms, as was the case of Abd el Kaber before 1844, the Europeans were stymied.

Whenever frustrated by an enemy refusing to open battle, the European powers would, to paraphrase Mao, "drain the sea to catch the fish" and depopulate whole areas. Throughout the history of colonial conquests one hears references to the need for "war to assume an aspect which may shock the humanitarian" (Callwell [1896] 1996, 40). Perhaps the extreme case was the German pursuit and killing of the Ovaherero in Southwest Africa. The acts and declarations of the colonial authority leave no doubt that the purpose of the campaign was to exterminate a people (Steinmetz 2007, 190–202).

Whether intentionally or not, all these European conquests involved the slaughter of millions. Whatever other characteristics made the European conquest possible, one shared by all of these was the dehumanization of the enemy. Only once the enemy had been made less than human and uncivilized could the violence be unleashed.

Genocide[3]

There is an extensive judicial and theoretical debate about the definition of genocide and an even more contentious one about when and where it should be applied. For the purposes of this book, we are not interested in defining a term within some empirical closure, but rather in using the general concept as way of understanding the link between wars and societies. What do cases of genocide teach us about the sociology of war? With that purpose in mind, we will define genocide as the organized use of violence in order to eradicate a population defined by a given categorical characteristic. It is important to distinguish between conflicts that have had secondary genocidal consequences (e.g. the conquest of the Americas) and ones where the very point of the violence is to kill all members of a community. Historical intention is not easily established and is the subject of considerable discussion, but we can draw the boundary broadly enough that sensible readers can distinguish between mass killings that were incidental to the conflicts and ones where they served as the very point of it. These latter cases are pure "wars of societies" in that they represent an explicit existential threat to a large cohesive group.

There are sadly many candidates for inclusion as genocides, including the battle of Carthage in the second century BCE, the Mongolian conquest of Asia, some medieval Islamic conquests, the Crusades, the European conquest of North and South America, the European settlement of Australia, Germany in Southwest Africa, England's treatment of Ireland, the Armenian massacre during World War I, the history of Soviet collectivization, the partition of India, and Rwanda. Scholars have tried to be both inclusive and analytical in their attempts to clarify and explain the process (Staub 1989, 2011; Kiernan 2007; Moses 2008; Adam Jones 2011). We wish to focus on a single unambiguous case in order to draw broader lessons about the relationship between violent conflict and social structures.

Wherever one may stand on intentionality vs. function, or whether all were guilty, or just a few perpetrators, or millions of ordinary men, there is no doubt that the Shoah was genocidal (Browning 1992; Y. Bauer 1991). The attempt to eliminate the Jewish people was not a by-product of conquest (although it was related to it), and it was not the unfortunate consequence of violence directed at state institutions. It was about the eradication of a group of people whose specific categorization the Nazis were extremely careful in delineating. Both perpetrators and victims could agree that this was very much a "war against the Jews"[4] (Snyder 2010, 188). In Hitler's words: "Now [the Jewish population] is suffering a gradual process of annihilation that it had intended for us and that it would have unleashed against us without hesitation if it had the power to do so" (Mazower 2008, 374).

The Shoah[5]

Some may object to classifying the Holocaust as a war, as this is to grant political legitimacy to mass murder. There is the even deeper concern that by classifying it as war we may be taking the first step into normalizing what all authorities agree is inexplicable. To treat Auschwitz as merely another data point in the violent history of humanity is to obscure the particular evil that occurred there. Others might argue that since only humans go to war, the Holocaust does not classify, as it involved a descent into inhumanity. Even the perpetrators knew that this was a different kind of violence; thus their care never to speak its name and efforts to disguise it (Friedländer 1989, 2007).

If its intensity and extent was extreme, the Holocaust shares with most wars a common theme: the notion of the enemy. It is the rare war where each side does not see the other as evil, dangerous, or both. Genocides and certainly the Holocaust require enough social hatred as to make actions not just possible, but permissible. There is no doubt that anti-Semitism had a long and deep history throughout Europe and in Germany (Goldhagen 1996). The Jewish people were long considered an "other." Turning this into a campaign of extermination required more, however.

Our principal primary cause is a leadership willing to use every instrument available to perpetrate the horror. The killing machine was begun and fed by Hitler's pathological obsession with the Jews and his apparently real terror of what they represented. As with most such crimes, the motivation was not simple hatred, but a great deal of fear (Evans 2009, 269). The private correspondence, diary entries, and subsequent testimony of most of the relevant individuals are full of references to vast Jewish conspiracies and practical omnipotence. The spark of this murderous hatred was required to set the dry timber of anti-Semitism on fire and was fanned by an extremely effective machine of propaganda. The role of the Jews as the "other" is important to keep in mind not only for the role this played in the Holocaust, but also because it is an extreme example of the "us–them" dynamic common to wars described in Chapter 1. More pessimistically, the creation of the Jew as enemy no doubt contributed to the sense of greater national cohesion noted by most observers of Germany in the 1930s. The unity of one was purchased by the exclusion and subsequent extermination of the other.

But even taking into account the cumulative effect of a decade of incitement, the strength of the devotion to Fuhrerprinzip, and the barbarization that might come from war, we need to differentiate between the different anti-Semitic sentiments and policies that led from initial discrimination to extermination. The violence against Jews began with the thuggery of the Brown Shirts in 1933, evolved into the pogrom of Krystalnacht in 1938, followed by the systemic killing of the Einsatzgruppen in 1939 to 1941, and then, and only then, into the "industrialized, assembly-line mass murder" of 1942 through 1944 (Evans 2009, 315) for which it is most infamous (Longerich 2010). Thus, the existence of pre-war hatred is not sufficient to explain the evolution of the barbarity. We need to look at how the dynamics of war itself fed into the genocidal outcome. That evolution may be the most important sociological lesson the Shoah has to offer.

There is a massive literature regarding who ordered extermination as a "final solution" (Kershaw 2008). What is clear is that
even the leading Nazis did not begin their anti-Semitic campaigns
in the 1920s with the slaughter of millions in mind. There was no
question that the Nazi leadership sought a Germany (and later, a
Europe) that was free of Jews (*Judenfrei*), but the specific means
of achieving this goal were ambiguous and developed across time.
For the first five years of the regime, the emphasis appears to have
been on forced migration through systematic intimidation and
persecution, but relatively limited physical violence. There were
Jews in concentration camps from early in 1933, but they were
not the exclusive focus of persecution. The autumn of 1938 marks
a clear turning point.

Why the increased intensity of the movement at this point? One
possibility is that the fiscal pressures on the state required the
appropriation of whatever Jewish capital and resources remained
in Germany. Another is that the Nazi leadership became too frustrated with the reluctance of other countries to solve their Jewish
"problem" by allowing greater immigration. There are others who
argue the change in policies were attempts to garner Hitler's favor
(Longerich 2010). The result was the complete "social death" of
the German and Austrian Jewish population as they were pushed
out of the few public spaces and institutions allowed them.

There are already hints at the horror to come. In his speech to
the Reichstag on January 30, 1939, Hitler made explicit the threat
of the "annihilation of the Jewish race in Europe." Nevertheless,
even after the war begins and the Einsatzgruppen are unleashed
on Poland, there does not appear to be a systemic campaign of
extermination. Ominously, the Jewish population was forcibly
concentrated in ghettos, but it appears that this was a first step in
their forceful removal toward the East in order to provide "living
space" (*lebensraum*) for German migrants into the Polish coun-
tryside. The Nazi expectation that the "Jewish problem" could
be solved through forced movement, however, was ultimately
frustrated.

The invasion of the Soviet Union in June 1941 marked the
beginning of the third phase of the Shoah (Mazower 2008, 369).

For the next year, a part of the German war machine was devoted to the systematic killing of Jews as the Soviet invaders moved East. Within this stage we may also observe other sub-stages: killings of Jews appeared to be the first part of a general campaign to eradicate Bolshevik elements and influence in the region. Soon, however, the Jewish population qua Jews was targeted. By late 1941, Jewish identity would override any other consideration, including age or gender. This holocaust by bullets resulted in the deaths of more than one million Jews.

While the Jews suffered during all twelve years of the Third Reich, 1942 stands apart in its levels of destruction. At the beginning of that year, 75 percent of the Jews who would be killed were alive, but by the beginning of 1943, only 25 percent were still living (Browning 1992; Bergen 2009). That year marked not just a change in the degree of murder but also in its method.

In 1942, the "Operation Reinhardt" camps at Sobidor, Treblinka, and Majdanek, as well as those in Chelmno and Auschwitz became operational. Between 1942 and 1944, an estimated three million Jews were killed in those camps. The numbers defy comprehension, but the concentration and industrial efficiency of the process is arguably the worst legacy of the Holocaust. The Jews of occupied Europe were first concentrated in ghettos and other camps and then transported to sites where their bodies could be "processed." The vast majority would be dead within a few hours of de-training (Friedländer 2007).

Consider that these sites were created and functioned for the purpose of human extermination. While some had double uses as slave labor camps, this was always secondary. People were not killed because they had something someone else wanted – although personal wealth and property were certainly gleaned whenever possible. Nor were they unfortunate collateral damage, the result of a greater strategic agenda. Since great efforts were made to keep it secret, their murders were not functional or instrumental in that they could be used to intimidate or terrorize. The killing was its own objective and the reason was a perceived identity – what has been called "racial warfare" (Snyder 2010, 196). While we have many accounts of daily brutality on an individual level from camp guards, most testimonies confirm our image of bureaucratic indifference – an application of the *Thoeretik des Volkermords* (theory of genocide) (Browning 1992, 61).

How could this happen? For the very same reasons as why it happened. The Holocaust was very much directed toward a perceived rational end. The methods used through most of 1941, however, were not effective enough. Despite the massive killing in places such as Babi Yar, the elimination of so many millions could not be carried out by killing squads. Over and above logistical concerns with body disposal, there were also significant human costs to the personnel involved (Hilberg 1993, 21; Rhodes 2002, 10; Evans 2009, 226). The documentary record shows a clear awareness that it was unfeasible for even those most dedicated or numb to the task to spend hours, days, and weeks killing innocents, and that finding enough of these to finish the task would be impossible (Höhne 1969; Rhodes 2002). The difficulty (as Himmler put in his speech to the SS leadership in Poznan on October 3, 1943) was to remain decent (*anständig*) in the face of such an obligation.[6] Over and again we find references to the need for hardness and for sacrifice so as to accomplish the great goal. This required a "totally unprecedented invention of synchronized killing" (Browning 1992, 83, 125).

Each camp had its peculiarities, but all shared the following critical characteristics (Hilberg 1993): First, contact with the victims was minimized to the initial arrival. Very soon afterwards, the victims would be funneled into a path, finishing in their deaths. The removal of bodies was done by Sonderkommando – prisoners forced to work in various parts of the camp. Second, because of this use of prison labor, the actual number of non-prisoner personnel involved could be kept to a minimum[7] making the process of recruitment easier. Finally, the process was depersonalized as much as possible while the personnel were encouraged to think of their work as normal, even if unpleasant. To this would be added the "honor" of taking part in a heroic victory.

What the Holocaust teaches us is how a tool of violence can be adapted in apparently rational ways. The true horror of the Holocaust was that it did not depend on orders from evil men (though these were given), but how easily the means of war could be applied to an end that any rational person would reject out of hand (Burleigh 2011, 401–10).

Strategic Bombing

Few outside of the rarefied community of military historians have heard of the twentieth-century Italian general Giulio Douhet, yet in many ways he may be the most symbolically important figure in modern warfare. His book, *The Command of the Air* ([1921] 1983), serves as the intellectual origin of the concept of strategic bombing. Douhet predicted that the wars of the future would be decided by air-power alone. Massive fleets of bombers would destroy an enemy's cities before the more traditional forces of army and navy could even be mobilized. The destruction would be total: he advocated the targeting of both the productive capacity of the enemy and the terrorizing of the population. The futility of defense was central to Douhet's thesis. British politician Stanley Baldwin, in a famous Parliamentary debate in 1932, stated, "there is no power on earth that can protect [the man on the street] from bombing . . . The bomber will always get through" (widely quoted, but see, for example, Kiras 2006, 42). While many of the particulars of Douhet's thesis were wrong, the central premise of unimaginable destruction defined warfare in the twentieth century. Baldwin well understood these implications: "The only defence is in offence, which means you have to kill more women and children more quickly than the enemy if you want to save yourselves."[8]

With the advent of strategic bombing – meaning mass civilian bombing – the means of war have become cause for their own use. We have seen the mass killing of conquest as a byproduct of the process of appropriation, and the killings of genocide being their own purpose, and now turn to the destruction caused by strategic bombing as both consequence and objective. The killings that are a result of bombing are not because the enemy is despised, nor because she stands in the way of some resource, but because military logic declares it the only possible strategy (F. M. Kaplan 1991; Sherry 1987).

The early use of strategic bombing carried many of the characteristics that would dominate its use for a century. First, it was most often used against those whose essential human kinship was in doubt. While used sparingly in World War I, Italians, French, Spanish, and British used terror bombing against colonial subjects, as did the Japanese in China (Lindqvist 2001). Second, the motivation was not purely to destroy infrastructure or even armed forces, but to destroy the will of a society to wage war. Third, the development of the strategy was closely tied to the organizational ambitions of the new military arm: the air force. Finally, it was conceived as an improvement on the efficiency of killing: it spared one's own armies and delivered a great deal of destruction for a relatively small amount of money. Of all the paradoxes presented by war, that of strategic bombing may be the greatest: an impeccably rational and instrumental logic produced incredible devastation on the world.

The apocalyptic fears of the interwar years (Patterson 2007) were realized in the 1940s. While the London Blitz may be the most memorialized and best-known example of civilian bombing in World War II, the brunt of strategic bombing was carried out by the US and Britain against Japan and Germany (Sherry 1987; Sebald 2003; Taylor 2004; Friedrich 2006; Grayling 2006; Hastings 2008; Van Creveld 2011).

Initially used to target industry and transport, bombing campaigns were frustrated by inaccuracy and danger. It was difficult, if not impossible, actually to hit an intended target, and extremely dangerous to do so during the daylight hours, when it was most feasible. In a perfect example of strategy or ends following technique or means, the logic of bombing evolved to include not only military and industrial targets but later the very societies in which these resources existed.

In Europe, the purpose of "promiscuous bombing" was simply the destruction of Germany's cities (Burleigh 2011, 484). The British Royal Air Force (RAF) and US Air Force (USAF) dropped nearly three million tons of bombs in Europe, resulting in an estimated half a million deaths and the destruction of most of urban Germany. The most infamous raids occurred in Hamburg in 1943 and Dresden in 1945 when more than half of each city was destroyed and roughly 100,000 civilians were killed.

The campaign against Japan was arguably worse. First, the damage was concentrated in the last year, and particularly the last six months of the war. The targeting of civilians in a campaign of terror was even more explicit than in Germany, and the technological advances made the firebombing ever more efficient and destructive. In March 1945, a firestorm destroyed sixteen square miles of Tokyo and by mid-summer practically every large city in Japan was ruined. The campaign culminated with the atomic bombings of Hiroshima and Nagasaki in August of 1945. By that date, little was left in Japan worth bombing except to, as British Prime Minister Winston Churchill said, "make the rubble bounce" (widely cited; see, for example, Van Creveld 2008, 175).

Was it worth it? That is, within the logic of war, was strategic bombing an effective means of achieving the political ends? Author Warren Kozak, biographer of US General Curis LeMay, argues, "Fighting the war meant killing as many Germans as quickly as possible and not waiting for them to come up with better ideas for killing first" (2009, 127). From this perspective, extermination of civilians not only made strategic sense but in a bizarre utilitarian calculus saved lives by shortening the war.

While there are debates over the relative contribution of bombing, the consensus is and has been quite clear: strategic bombing of Japan and Germany was not critical in winning the war (Sherry 1987; Pape 1993, 1996; Overy 1997). Obviously, it had significant effects on war-time production and, perhaps most importantly, required that rare resources be used in defense, but Douhet and his followers were wrong: airpower was not enough for victory, nor was it clear that the crossing of the line into indiscriminate slaughter of civilians resulted in destroying their will. Instead, for fifty years following the end of the war, the world was held hostage to a form of warfare that took the notion of inevitable and futile destruction to its logical conclusion.

Nuclear Armageddon

The strategic and ethical line between Hamburg, Dresden, Tokyo, and Hiroshima and Nagasaki is blurry at best. It seems that, while fully aware of the potential destructive power of the weapon, the first nuclear bomb was largely seen as simply an extension of the scale of strategic bombing. We have references to those who, on August 10, 1945, thought that the world would never be the same, but also considerable evidence that it took some time for the difference of nuclear power to be widely understood (Sherwin 1975; F. M. Kaplan 1991; Gordin 2007). It is now widely accepted that in terms of human suffering the two atomic bombs were on a par with some of the worst incidents of strategic bombing in the 1943–5 period.[9]

What was different was the transformation of the logistical support needed to annihilate a city. Producing an atomic bomb required considerable economic, scientific, and industrial infrastructure. But to deliver the deathblow merely required one bomber. In the case of Japan, there was not even any need for escorts other than for recording the event. The ratio of resources per casualty had been transformed even more dramatically than during the gunpowder revolution.

The question would then become how to use this new weapon. Certainly at first the mystery and novelty of the weapon sufficiently served to give the United States an inestimable advantage. While few knew how many bombs there actually were, the promise of even more destruction may have played a role in the timing of the Japanese surrender. It certainly served an important deterrent role for any Soviet consideration of utilizing their massive advantage in armor and manpower in the European theater. The existence of and monopoly over the bomb provided the US with a strategic safety switch, allowing the rapid disarmament critical for the post-war economy.

After 1949 and the Soviet success in producing their own bomb, this strategic advantage was somewhat altered. Even with limited numbers of weapons, each side could threaten the destruction of whole armies and significant parts of Europe. Because of the limitations on delivery, however, its potential for total annihilation remained uncertain. Certainly in the mind of some, like Douglas McArthur, the bomb could be analytically treated as an immensely powerful battlefield weapon. Yet, the aura of its power must account for at least part of the absolute restraint in use during that pivotal first few years when the level of destruction remained limited.

Two developments transformed nuclear weapons into a very different sort of war instrument. The first was the exponential increase in destructive power brought about by the mutual and almost simultaneous development of the hydrogen bomb by both the United States and the Soviet Union in the early 1950s (Gordin 2009). To give a sense of the scale involved, Little Boy, the bomb used in Hiroshima, had roughly four times the destructive power of the 48-hour bombing of Dresden. By the mid-1950s, the US was testing devices with 1,000 times the yield of the first atom bombs. Moreover, the physical size of these weapons was reduced, vastly increasing the yield/weight ratio. This made it possible to deliver enough bombs via bomber as to threaten the viability of an opponent's society.

The second, and arguably most important, development was the evolution of missile delivery systems, beginning in 1957. The scale and speed of these meant that the warning time of an attack would be reduced to hours if not minutes, and the possibility of preventing enormous damage rendered null. By the 1960s, the US and the USSR could hold each other hostage. Winning a nuclear war was impossible by any conventional meaning of the term, and mutually assured destruction (MAD) would be achieved at the first use of a bomb (Rhodes 1995, 2007; N. Sheehan 2009).

The response to this quandary had several stages, at least in the US – we assume a similar parallel story in the USSR. The key distinction between strategies has to do with tactical vs. strategic use. The first involves using nuclear weapons in a battle setting as a form of ultra-artillery. Contemplation of such use fluctuated during the Cold War between periods of relatively causal consideration to absolute rejection of any first use at all.[10] The use more associated with nuclear weapons is strategic, following the logic of World War II bombing to its ultimate conclusion: to defeat an enemy one must defeat, and if necessary, annihilate the enemy's society.

With the development of two great powers capable of such destruction, the dilemma of how to handle nuclear warfare and mutual destruction arose. Great efforts were made to escape this dilemma. Game theorist and strategist Herman Kahn spent years trying to convince many of the "winnability" of nuclear war. Improvements in civil defense measures and anti-missile defense also promised that some sort of protection could be impermeable enough to make post-nuclear war survival possible. Unfortunately, for each advancement in protection, technology and strategy soon made it superfluous.

One might imagine that such a situation would produce an uneasy equilibrium at a relatively low level of mutually assured destruction, and this was the case until the early 1960s. But the pursuit of strategic dominance required that each side produce enough weapons, first to assure that enemy targets would be destroyed no matter what, and second, that one's own side always had enough left over to produce total destruction of the other. Fueled by intra-service competition, institutional inertia, domestic political coalitions, and an ever-increasing desperation to resolve the dilemma by sheer numbers, the number of bombs and the complexity of delivery grew for decades. By the mid 1980s an equilibrium had been reached, but only after the construction of a system with the capacity to produce 60,000 Hiroshimas leading not only to the destruction of the opponents, but the obliteration of the human race (Freedman 1981; Craig 2003; Rhodes 2007; D. E. Hoffman 2009; Reed and Stillman 2009; J. Miller 2010).

How does sociology explain the development of such a massive scale of weaponry intended for social destruction? We can focus on four key processes: the "other-ization" of each side, the apparent surgical precision of the strategies, the sheer industrial capability and wealth of the two societies, and, strangest of all, the mutual agreement and understanding required to maintain the system.

War of Societies

On the first, the United States witnessed several waves of "Red scares" throughout the twentieth century that produced images of "communists" often not dissimilar to more racialized constructions against the Japanese in World War II (Dower 1986). It is remarkable to read critiques of the even mild approaches of détente with a few decades of distance. Any apparent gap in one side's destructive capacity, even if that was multiple times what was required, was considered not only a sign of inherent weakness, but a dangerous signal to the other of a lack of resolve. Attempts to tone down the discourse of dehumanization made the inherent logic of the strategy more absurd. Representatives of both powers would regularly proclaim their friendship with the other side's people and appreciation for their culture, but still insist that the inescapable logic of the opposing political economic system sadly made the possibility of annihilation possible if not likely.

Experiments have proven that the more immediate and messy the violence, the more human beings are reluctant to use it. Nuclear strategy was the ultimate expression of this logic. A pair of air force officers in a silo somewhere in the Great Plains or the captain of a Polaris-armed submarine would be unlikely physically and psychologically to withstand the stress of killing millions of individuals. Yet, by a press of a button they would accomplish in a few minutes what they could not do over hours or days. All authors note the technocratic distance which characterized nuclear planning. For decades, extremely intelligent and well-educated men (and it was almost exclusively a male group) would speak of biblical levels of destruction with dispassion and precision. One could argue that the much more explicitly horrific consequences of biological warfare, for example, always made it much more of a taboo than the perhaps more destructive nuclear alternative. Strategic bombing developed a particular discourse where statistics and operations research served to remove much of the horror of what was being contemplated (Bracken 1983; F. M. Kaplan 1991; Galison 1994). The various doomsday devices designed by both the US and the USSR were strategies of sanitizing and attenuating the human costs of the process of retaliation, making it that much easier to enact (Rosenbaum 2011).

Nuclear weapons were also a product of their relative cost. This was certainly a major factor for the United States, for whom global projection of power might have been impossible or at least unsustainable without a nuclear umbrella. Nuclear strategy was a product of the technological advantage enjoyed by the two superpowers. While in some ways crude atomic weapons would be an ideal weapon for poorer nations, maintaining an arsenal, and more importantly, a delivery system, required sophisticated organizations and a considerable amount of money. Joining the nuclear club became something of a rite of passage as it indicated – sometimes falsely – a high level of institutional and socio-economic development. In that, atomic bombs were an easy expression of the American standard of living (Sherry 1987, 177).

Perhaps the most astonishing aspect of nuclear strategy was that it was premeditated on mutual agreements about the appropriate use of such weapons (Keeney 2011). More so than in perhaps any other form of warfare, nuclear arms required that the adversaries be in constant communication, mutually assuring each other of intentions and safeguards. By early in the 1950s, the tactical use of nuclear weapons outside of accidental or catastrophic circumstances was inherently prohibited. For example, we have found no reference of a serious contemplation of use during the height of the Vietnam War. Exceptions to this rule include the stationing of tactical nuclear weapons in Cuba prior to the Missile crisis of 1962 and the arming of the Israeli arsenal in the darkest moments of the 1973 Yom Kippur War. But despite the limited number of scares, all of the nuclear powers agreed that lines would not be crossed.

We have claimed that the arc of the development of war in human history has been one of an ever-increasing scale and complexity. We have also argued that the technological developments that have accompanied this massification of war have also been the engines that have pushed further expansion. With the refinement of lethality and greater efficiency of the instruments of war, these weapons became hammers in search of a nail. And with the increased capacity to destroy large numbers of people, the inevitable conclusion of conquest and weapons development would be societal breakdowns and genocide. World War II was the absolute zenith of the complexity and destructive capacity of total wars.

While World War II was the apotheosis of total war, complexity, scale, and destruction, it was also a source of creation. In the next chapter we turn from the death and annihilation of total wars of societies to the creative powers of human conflict.

5

How Wars Build[1]

In 1969, American soul musician Edwin Starr famously asked what war was good for and responded with "Absolutely nothing!" While this song was partly a product of the opposition to the Vietnam War in particular, it expresses a commonly held view in much of the modern world. War is seen as destructive, cruel, brutal, and useless. Such a view makes perfect sense, given the legacy of wars and their consequences. Nevertheless, wars throughout history have been the sources of fantastic social, technological, and political development. In this chapter, we argue that, while it is certainly destructive, war's social consequences are often greater than we realize and, whether we like it or not, we are very much the children of battle.

We have seen that war is a particularly good reflection of the kind of society that practices it. Forms of war reflect the social organization, political authority, and material resources of the involved societies. Wars in turn shape their societies – they provide a picture of what will happen to those societies afterwards. Precisely because wars are such extreme events they may serve as catalysts for dramatic social transformation. The demands of war create opportunities for innovation and adaptation. These demands also require the creation and maintenance of institutions that effect far more than a soldier's efficiency at the moment of battle. In this chapter we will focus on war's contribution to macro- and micro-level social outcomes. First, we examine three critical components of modern society: the nation state and nationalism, democracy and citizenship, and group rights. We then examine the effects of military service on the individuals who participate in war-making.

Wars and Big Outcomes

The idea that wars make states and in turn states make war (Tilly 1975, 1985, 1992) has come to be a truism.[2] As charted by the great American sociologist Charles Tilly, pre-state political formations in Europe increasingly engaged in warfare, requiring capital and manpower. An outcome of war-making was the development of a number of institutions to extract capital from the land and people and coerce men into war. These institutions were critical to the development of the nation-state as we understand it today. Further, these newly developing states were pressured into providing returns to the people for these fiscal and human capital extractions in the form of market protections and regulation and, eventually, political representation and rights.

These macro-processes hinged upon the relationship between the state and the people with military service as a critical mediator between the two. The development of conscripted militaries and standing armies was critical to not only state institutional development but also sentiments of national identity. Much like in Western Europe, military service in other parts of the world has proven to be the origin of a number of institutions that, when viewed with a broad lens, have contributed to the expansion of state powers and therefore the expectations of the citizenry as to the obligations of the state to its people.

States and Nationalism

States are the institutionalized rules by which a society governs itself. They are the foundation for social and economic life. Without states there no markets, no courts, no elections, and no public services. Hobbes was right in noting the critical importance of leviathans as a way of preventing the struggle of all versus all. At the very foundation of states is the monopoly over the means of violence. In order to enforce rights and obligations, states must have the means by which to enforce their edicts and rules. This requires that they be the strongest military institutions in a given territory. Moreover, for states to function as anything more than armed gangs or "protection rackets," they must enjoy some form of legitimacy or the support of the population for their claim to absolute rule (Tilly 1975; Tilly 1985).

Wars help build the institutional basis of modern states by requiring a degree of organization and efficiency which only new political structures could provide; they are the great stimulus for state building. States, in a sense, are by-products of rulers' efforts to acquire the means of war; war is inherently an organizing phenomenon from which the state derives its administrative machinery. So, for example, the advance of bureaucratic forms may be partly explained by increasing demands for administrative efficiency generated by the needs of growing armed forces and the escalating costs of waging war.

The rise of the modern European state may be traced to the military revolution of the sixteenth and seventeenth centuries. During this period, three critical political and organizational developments changed the nature of military struggle and its relationship to state-making: control over the means of violence shifted from private to public control; the size of armies increased dramatically; their composition became less varied and more based on a specific national identity.

War made the territorial consolidation of a state more feasible and more imperative. Only those states that could wield great armies and guarantee control over their own territories could play the great game. Only those states able to impose that central control could survive the military revolution. Countries unable to do so disappeared. The decline in the number of European states after the fifteenth century (from fifteen hundred to twenty-five by 1900) is an obvious indicator of the centralization of power wrought by military conflict. In this sense, we may think of war as a form of competition between a variety of organizations. Following the logic of competitive markets, the threat of wars places a great premium of the efficient delivery of violence. This in turn may produce institutional by-products that promote further state development.

The key to the relationship between war and state-making in Western Europe is what British political scientist Samuel Finer called the "extraction–coercion" cycle (1975). We begin with the obvious fact that wars require capital: By the sixteenth century, war became so expensive as to require the economic mobilization of an entire country. Professional armies clearly outperformed any rivals, but these required ample and continuous amounts of money.

The need for strong armies causally linked military and political development. On the one hand, states penetrated their societies in increasingly complex forms in order to obtain resources. The organizational innovations that occurred during war-time did not disappear with peace, but often left an infrastructural residue that Ardant (1975) calls the "physiology" of the state. On the other hand, the new form of the post-Westphalian[3] state was particularly well suited to the organizational task of managing this penetration and channeling the resources thus obtained into "productive" violence directed at some external enemy. Thus, wars both created and expressed political power.

Taxation has been used as a measure of effective political authority and institutional development. Taxes are, in the words of Oliver Wendell Holmes, the price we pay for civilization. They are taken to both represent and augment the strength of the state as measured by the capacity to enforce centralized rule on a territory and its population. The logic behind this assertion is rather simple: assuming that most people will not freely part with their resources in exchange for a set of public goods with no guarantee of delivery and great possibilities for free-riding, the ability to extract such resources reflects the state's strength. Taxes are even seen as the very expressions of citizenship: "[they are] the economic expression of the individual's cohesion with the nation ... [taxes] represent the nation's entire civic sense on the economic plane" (Stein [1885] 1964, 28).

In short, the history of taxation is the history of the state. How a state taxes may help define how it fights (and vice versa).

Functional states will try to get as much resources as they need to survive and prosper. Today we can understand various political regime types through the ways in which they collect taxes. At one end of a scale, regimes that view the role of the state as very limited, only for selected public goods such as military provision, will have small governments and limited taxation of the people. Regimes that view the role of the state as a broad guarantor of social safety and inequality reduction will tax its people rather highly in order to fund a wide variety of social services for the people within its territory. And at the other extreme of the scale, regimes interested in short-term profits for a very limited number of people (often dictatorships and kleptocracies) may tax the people extremely highly, but offer limited or no social services in return. Taxes are therefore the concrete expression of the ideological orientation of the state.

Yet, no revenue comes free. The costs of taxation can be measured economically and politically. In order to extract resources, the state must pay for them in a variety of ways. Collecting taxes often requires a significant expenditure of that same revenue and so states have often to increase the efficiency of their fiscal capture in order to assure the most return for their taxing investment.

Political costs are more difficult to measure. These are based on estimates of a population's preference order of services, the quality expected, perceived availability of alternatives, willingness to pay a premium to the state for delivery, and views of the "fairness" of the bargain in general. For each relevant social sector involved, these estimates must be multiplied by the respective actor's political capacity to protest or enforce a bargain. We must then take into account conflicts between and among these actors.

In short, taxing is hard – and what helps taxing, helps the state. Wars generate greater needs for resources while also providing temporary declines in the state's social constraints. Wars also provide an organizational focus around which the state's organizational capacity may improve. Finally, armies raised for war might also serve as a means with which to collect resources.

The evidence for the positive link between war and the rise of taxes in early modern Europe is exhaustive. In the four cases

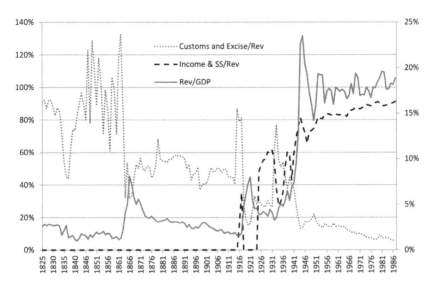

Figure 5.1 USA Revenues and Source
Compiled with data from Mitchell, B. R. (1998)

analyzed by Ames and Rapp (1977), tax systems were the product of negotiations between royal houses and their respective societies during times of war or preparation thereof. According to them, the birth of tax systems in Western Europe is tied to the military transition beginning with the Hundred Years War (170).

The pattern is also obvious in the United States. Figure 5.1 can be read as a parallel history of American wars and American government revenues. This shows the percent of revenue from customs duties and overall government expenditure. Revenue from customs and estates are often the easiest and least politically and organizationally demanding of any taxes. There are limits, however, to how much anyone can extract via these instruments. At a certain point the demands of war so escalate that the state must penetrate further into a society, develop its bureaucratic reach, and extract directly from the population via individual income taxes. As the graph indicates, as the United States relied less on customs as a sources of revenue during the 1930s, it increased its reliance on individual income taxes. Also note that expenditures as a percentage of GDP have also increased over time, which is one measure of the size of the state.

War makes a significant contribution to national wealth.[4] The economy of the US is partly shaped by the result of the Civil War, which provided the economy of the North with an immense boost and allowed the Federal government to increase its control over economic policy and integrate a national market as never before (Bensel 1991). Similarly, the recovery of the US from the Great Depression may owe more to World War II than to the New Deal: the productive capacity of the US economy was unleashed by the war effort. The war also produced an international system centered on the US and the dollar. For the losers, the very destruction of war may be beneficial as it eliminates outdated technologies, reallocates state spending on non-military investments, and allows the creation of new industries (D. R. Lee and Vedder 1996; Hartley 1997).

Wars can also develop group cohesion within the state. Describing the aftermath of an Athenian naval battle toward the end of the Peloponnesian War, military historian Barry Strauss (2004) nicely evokes the spirit often associated with war:

> For a brief moment they were all Athenians. On an afternoon in September 406 B.C., the city of Athens achieved a unity that usually eluded it. It was imperfect unity, with no women and only a small percentage of Athenian men present – less than one percent. Yet those men represented a cross-section of Athens' male population. They ranged from the richest to the poorest, from cavalier to knave, from representatives of families so old that they seemed to have sprung from the Attic soil itself to immigrants from obscure villages somewhere in Thrace or Sicily. As a group they comprised citizens, metics (resident aliens), foreign mercenaries, and slaves. They spanned the ranks of the Athenian military, from horsemen to hoplites (infantrymen), from deck-soldiers to rowers, from the home guard to scouts. On this afternoon, men who normally would have scorned each other became brothers. They extended their hands to each other, literally, because they had to hold on for dear life. (Strauss 2004, 40)

The above passage exemplifies that oft-cited claim that wars create nationalism, a sort of civil religion that celebrates the nation and its people. The idea is that through the organization of the military, the shared experience of battle, and the antagonism of a common enemy, wars create cohesion within a state. Others, however, argue that nationalism actually precedes and causes wars, through its emphasis on difference and competition. There are also claims that war has a completely different relationship with nationalism. For example, Winter (2010) argues that wars can actually lead to anti-nationalist or certainly anti-bellicist movements.[5] Yet, we would argue that there is fairly clear evidence for war making a strong contribution to not a state centered nationalism, but a less institutionally coherent united, if imagined, community (B. Anderson 2006).

This is the sense of unity that Rustow (1970) claimed was an essential part of the foundation for democratic rule and may be an essential product of war. It is a unity born out shared sacrifice, a sense of danger, and the euphoric celebration of community. This sense of oneness can then translate into a recognition of the less fortunate in the society as worthy of assistance, it can serve to expand suffrage, and it may also provide the basis for the recognition of minimal civil rights that all in the community can share.

This sense of inclusiveness, however, is defined by exclusion. We are the same because *they* are different from *us*. It is this sense of exclusive community, even more than the institutional basis of territoriality, which might make notions of transnational citizenship so difficult to achieve. War is an important part of the construction of this community, but in the absence of collective enemies that serve to underscore what we share, how to create a democratic unity on a non-national basis?

There is perhaps no better example of this "Janus-face" of war, on the one hand welcoming its citizens, and on the other seeking to crush those against its walls, than the Athenians in Thucydides. On the one hand, Pericles can claim:

> It is true that we are called a democracy, for the administration is in the hands of the many and not of the few. But while there exists equal justice to all and alike in their private disputes, the claim of excellence

is also recognized; and when a citizen is in any way distinguished, he is preferred to the public service, not as a matter of privilege, but as the reward of merit. Neither is poverty an obstacle, but a man may benefit his country whatever the obscurity of his condition. There is no exclusiveness in our public life, and in our private business we are not suspicious of one another, nor angry with our neighbor if he does what he likes; we do not put on sour looks at him which, though harmless, are not pleasant. (Book 2.34–46)

Yet, some pages later, the Athenians can speak to Melians with nothing but threats and disdain prior to their destruction of the city:

For ourselves, we shall not trouble you with specious pretences . . . since you know as well as we do that right, as the world goes, is only in question between equals in power, while the strong do what they can and the weak suffer what they must. (Book 5.85–113)

Nationalism is an ideology based on the premise that the individual's loyalty and devotion to the nation-state surpasses other individual or group interests. Obligations to the state and to the community outweigh more individual or personal allegiances. To go into battle is to risk emotional and material crises for all of one's kin. Such a sacrifice cannot be effectively accomplished through pure coercion, but requires an overlaying system of beliefs that justify such a risk. It implies the identification of the state or nation with the people – or at least the desirability of determining the extent of the state according to ethnographic principles. Nationalism is sociologically paradoxical in that it stresses the particular and parochial, the differences, and the national individualities spearing one group from another, but simultaneously emphasizes how the commonalities within the group outweigh any differences. In the words of the British philosopher and anthropologist Ernest Gellner ([1983] 2006):

Durkheim taught that in religious worship society adores its own camouflaged image. In a nationalist age, societies worship themselves brazenly and openly, spurning the camouflage. At Nuremberg, Nazi

Germany did not worship itself by pretending to worship God or even Wotan; it overtly worshiped itself. (quoted in Malešević 2015, 95)

Obviously the creation of this sense of community is not new. But nationalism is a new phenomenon to the extent that political allegiance was not previously so exclusively defined by the combination of ethnic identity and geographical proximity. The rise of national feeling to major political importance was encouraged by a number of complex developments: the creation of large, centralized states ruled by absolute monarchs who destroyed the old feudal allegiances; the secularization of life and of education, which fostered the vernacular languages and weakened the ties of church and sect; and the growth of commerce, which demanded larger territorial units to allow scope for the dynamic spirit of the rising middle classes and their capitalistic enterprise. This large, unified territorial state, with its political and economic centralization, became imbued in the eighteenth century with a new spirit – an emotional fervor similar to that of religious movements in earlier periods. War was central to all these developments.

Military references are a popular part of nationalist rhetoric. War served to construct icons with which to teach nationalism. For some periods in some states, such references are central to the task of identity formation. To choose one example, consider any random assortment of flags and national symbols (Cerulo 1995; Marvin and Ingle 1999). Now analyze either the explicit images or the historical basis for the more abstract representations. The very choice of symbols has now become expected: think of the apparent absurdity of Ben Franklyn's suggestion of the turkey for the national bird. Similarly, national anthems are notorious for their saber-rattling prose. To choose two from the earliest national revolutions, consider the bloodthirstiness of *La Marseillaise* or the battle references in the American national anthem.

Perhaps the best example of the centrality of war to the iconography of national identity is the ubiquitous reference to and from war in the public landscape of most major cities. This visual background serves as the foundation for many taken for granted identities. In the words of British historian Raphael Samuel (1989):

Continuous national history, whether we study it or not, is something we are all brought upon. It is perpetuated in street names. It is
commemorated in public statuary. (10)

Monuments objectify the ideals for which the nation is supposed
to stand. Memorials make the past not only bearable, but also
usable; they re-write history as a glorious beginning. "Monuments
transform historical figures into symbols and myths: they transform the political into the religious" (Mosse 1975, 50). They
indicate the hierarchy of official memory. Monuments and the
like also help create an illusion of unity. As has been said about
patriotic literature, "they develop a narrative formula for resolv-
ing continuing conflicts" (Sommer 1991, 12).

Service, Citizenship, and Democracy

Since the mid-nineteenth century and through the immediate
post-World War II period, the European and North American
armed forces served as social institutions whose tasks included
not only national defense, but also the forging of young men into
productive and responsible members of the community. Through
mobilization, exposure to nationalist doctrine, and the cohesion
encouraged by shared danger, armies made citizens and nations.
For individuals, the transformation can be both dramatic and
positive. The initiation into and training by the armed forces may
improve the physical health of the recruit and teach him basic
skills as well as discipline and self-respect. For the society as a
whole, the collective experience could introduce previously isolated individuals to the variety of ethnic groups with whom they
share a territory and build camaraderie among all while exposing
them to nationalist themes and a sense of patriotic duty. As we will
see in the next chapter, the changes in these policies may imply a
significant social transformation (J. J. Sheehan 2008).

Conscription, understood as forced participation in a military, is
by no means new or unique to modern Western Europe. What dis-
tinguishes the European pattern after the mid-nineteenth century
is theoretically universal conscription including all social sectors,

legitimated by a common membership in a nation-state.[6] This universal conscription of national members, it has been argued, is the foundation of the citizen-soldier paradigm, and it has played an important role in the self-definition of Western civilization. What better contrast with the despotism of the East with its slave armies than the phalanx of Greek hoplites?

Yet this tradition was breached more often than honored for much of the past two thousand years. At least since the end of the Roman Republic, fighting in the army was seen as the job for professionals, and not a very well respected job at that. During the Middle Ages, the gulf grew between those who fought for honor and the large mass who merely obeyed orders and whose status was in no way enhanced by military activity. In fact, much of so-called universal service has not been universal in history. For example, as historian Beth Bailey has astutely pointed out, the Selective Service System of the United States is just that – selective. To be liable for conscription was a good index of one's inability to avoid it.

Beginning in the sixteenth century, armies began to require a greater imposition of the state on their societies. In 1544 Sweden became the first country to organize a permanent army based on military obligation. After the late seventeenth century, European states came to expect that their subjects had an obligation to serve in some vague form (M. S. Anderson 1998). The Prussian state climbed from insignificance to minor power status in the eighteenth century because of a modified version of compulsory service. But resistance to conscription was practically uniform. To be in the army still meant that one was part of the rural poor, without money or corporate sponsors able to remove the yoke of conscription. It was widely perceived that "the army must inevitably consist of the scum of the people, and of all those for whom society has no use" (M. S. Anderson 1998, 163). Generals may have been exalted, but one has to look far to find an ode to the common soldier of Marlborough or Frederick. Before they were "nations in arms," such forces were more likely to be considered armed hordes. Brutal discipline, not nationalist devotion, kept the troops literally in line.

The French Revolution and Napoleonic Wars provided a strong enough threat to require the radical rebalancing of military forces. The French General Assembly, when debating the policies through which it would reform the army of the *ancien regime*, was quite aware of the costs and benefits associated with universal conscription; with giving the army to the people and vice versa. The notions of soldier and citizen were seen as diametrically opposed. The Revolution and its radicalization after 1791 bridged these two identities. The *levée en masse* of 1793 was inspired in part by external threat, but also by the need to mobilize the population for the Revolution. It represented a radical rupture with the past in that it called the "people" to defend their newly acquired status of citizen. The important break was neither technical nor strategic, but rather had more to do with the relationship between state and society. The state stopped legitimately being the possession of the few and came to represent the aspirations of the many. As such, it had the right and obligation to call on them to defend their property.

We should not exaggerate the extent to which this re-definition mirrored an authentic and enthusiastic popular response. Few human beings long to put themselves in mortal danger, no matter the cause. But an important change did take place. War stopped being a game of kings and became the business of the people. The various stages of conscription in Napoleonic France raised an army of one million men. France's enemies had to respond in kind.

The fear of a French invasion transformed the British military and the state (Paret 1992). If the army was to grow enough to counter the threat, administrative systems had to be established to count, select, coerce, arm, and transport men. Perhaps more importantly, the Napoleonic scare transformed the English, Welsh, Irish, and Scots men who served by giving them a new sense of common identity with their fellow (British) soldiers, by showing them the larger island which existed past the boundaries of their shires, by granting them a new status within that society, and by inculcating them with a new sense of loyalty to it. War and the response to it made them into Britons in ways that had been unimaginable before the 1790s (Colley 1992).

Conscription encouraged a different attitude toward the state – one based on collective identity and shared citizenship. War and military experience also helped break down provincial allegiances and networks and replace these with ones more centered on a national community. This point is certainly relevant for the French, where the military played an important role in standardizing language and symbolic repertoires (E. Weber 1976).

After 1870, military powers or those who aspired to that role could no longer ignore the new means of doing war. This was not just the case in Europe (Ralston 1996). Despite the harshness of the army, conscription did help create a greater sense of national identity among the Egyptian fellahin. The army played a critical role in the development of Japanese nationalism following the Meiji Revolution. The Israeli experience has been more along these lines; the army represents the institution in which most young Israelis crystallize their national identity. Mass conscription resulted in a series of parallel and complementing processes that would arguably define the relationship between people and their state. Conscription and citizenship were two sides of the same coin.

Along with compulsory education and the right to vote, conscription was seen as one of the pillars of the democratic state. On the one hand, the state came to demand more from the population than passive obedience. On the other, the population came to see themselves in the state and to demand more from it in part as recompense for their ultimate sacrifice. One could see this as a form of political exchange:

> Considered in purely mechanistic terms, the state needed unobstructed access to the citizen; in turn to gain his willingness to work and fight for the state, the individual had to be offered political power, or – if that was impossible – new psychological inducements and social opportunities to enable him to reach his full potential. (Paret 1992, 46)

In exchange for the obligation to participate in war, citizens were rewarded with greater rights and more welfare services. The vote and national military service were corollaries. Historian William

McNeill (1967) concludes that military service is the "ball and chain attached to political privilege" (64). In the words of Max Weber ([1927] 2003), "Military discipline meant the triumph of democracy because the community wished and was compelled to secure the cooperation of the non-aristocratic masses and hence put arms, and along with arms political power, into their hands" (325).

War and Rights

The foundational right in a democracy is that which recognizes the basic autonomy and inviolability of the individual. Civil rights are those that protect that status by assuring constraints on the actions any state can take regarding the life or property of a citizen. Further, as citizenship develops, people begin to demand more from their state, including social and economic guarantees. How does war affect this?

The foundation of civil rights through military service rests on citizenship (described above) and the exchange of rights for service between the state and soldiers (see Turner and Hamilton 1994). This can be played out in many ways, but essentially involves citizens (even if the term is used anachronistically) demanding some rights in exchange for their participation in war. This participation need not necessarily involve violence. Arguably the most important instances of such an exchange have involved groups of citizens agreeing to provide financing in order to pay for the tools of war. Similar exchanges have been a mainstay of the history of the rise of the constitutional state in Britain and the institution of a militia in various parts of the world. Perhaps the best contemporary argument for the link between war and the welfare state is by political scientist Theda Skocpol (1992). Such contracts between states and populace are not solely historical artifacts. Today in the United States, for example, there exist programs offering "expedited citizenship" through military service (M. M. Lee and Wasem 2003).

Sometimes, the relationship between citizenship and military service is less of a bargain between soldier and state and more the product of the need of the state to defend its reputation. The argument has been made that the competition for global legitimacy during the Cold War forced the Federal Government to support a broader civil rights agenda than might have been the case otherwise (Dudziak 2000). While war has often been associated with the elevation of civil rights for previously persecuted minorities, however, the institution of military service may actually also serve as a bulwark of ingrained power. In these instances, military service legitimizes a hierarchical ordering of society. The resistance of the samurai to the Meiji reforms, for example, was in part based on their awareness that these would elevate previously discountable peasants into potential soldiers (Turnbull 2006). Similarly, one might trace many of the gender- or sex-based barriers to full citizenship to the historical male monopoly on military service.

As Krebs (2010) notes, war can have very different effects on the concentration of power inside a regime and the manner in which that power is exercised. On the one hand, wars provide "emergencies" during which legal rights are perceived as possibly unnecessary and even dangerous luxuries. The suppression of basic civil rights has often accompanied wars: freedom of speech is limited, the obligations of government are lessened, and individuals are required to give up some of their "negative freedom" to the collective needs of the endangered whole.

The appeal of such calls for limits is considerable. In the wake of 9/11 and considerably after, it was a brave and often rare American public figure that warned about the dangers of giving federal and executive authorities too much power. The notion that torture might save lives (no matter how empirically falsifiable) had many adherents. Obviously, the effect of this sometimes dissipates in the post-war period. In fact, as Krebs (2010) notes, the excesses of war often can turn into the lessons that help us better protect our rights. Nevertheless, a variety of regimes justify the limitation on individual freedoms by either claiming that the enemy remains undefeated, or by pulling ever-new terrors from the global political environment.

There is also a relationship between voting and war. The key historical step here, as Avant (2010) notes, is the creation of mass armies, where the nobility no longer battles with mere support from the rabble, but where the nation as a whole is called to arms. Here there is the mechanism of conscription which, following the logic of the discussion on civil rights, triggers the exchange mechanism as exemplified in a Swedish folk saying: "One soldier, one rifle, one vote" (Ben-Eliezer 1995). In this process, each individual willing to risk his life is paid off by the state with a promise of suffrage.

Conversely, wars can elicit states of emergency where elections need to be postponed, as New York Mayor Giuliani sought to propose in the aftermath of 9/11. Wars also potentially limit suffrage by forcing the creation of grand coalitions that not only obscure political difference, but also retain power through an agreed deferment of elections, as was the case with the British War Cabinet of World War II.

The relationship between electoral democracy and the military has been the subject of the most study, and Mansfield and Snyder (2010) provide a richly rigorous foundation for discussion. When we include the entire globe of democracies there appears to be a weak relationship between suffrage and conflict, or between war and democracy. Given the extent to which the relationship between the polling booth and the barracks is widely held to be, these are unexpected results.

The relationship between war and the political import of election results is therefore harder to unwind than one might suppose. First, there is the tricky historical question of causal order. Which really comes first, the soldier or the citizen? Do mass armies produce mass citizenship, or polities of existing citizens produce mass armies? Even accounting for the Western European history of military formation given above, we do not have enough historical detail on these questions. We know, for example, of Machiavelli's approval of "citizen armies" as opposed to the mercenary variety, but how much evidence do we have of debates inside Italian city states regarding this relationship?

The second difficulty is that suffrage does not mean democracy. Even if war plays a significant role in expanding voting rights, there is no reason to believe that these votes will have any meaning. The Spanish expression "elección búlgara" (Bulgarian election) refers to those elaborately staged rituals of popular participation where the regime receives overwhelming support.[7] Bermeo (2010) comes closest to proposing specific conditions through which military conflict can promote democratic government. Her findings seem to indicate that military defeat is often a good predictor of some democratic reform. Yet, at the core of this effect is not necessarily a military component. It is the public failure of a regime to accomplish some goal that so delegitimizes authoritarian rule as to provide an opportunity for democracy. Such delegitimation could come form an economic crisis or a simple failure to perform adequately. Rather than war making democracy, we might better speak of a failure of war-making in doing so.

Third, there is that other supposed child of war, state development (Centeno 2002). For democratic state power and control to be established in any meaningful way, the state has to have enough capacity not just to run an election but also to make its results mean something in policy terms. Wars have been cited as producing both states and democracies, but the order of their creation might be critical. It may be that for a functioning democracy, one needs to two wars: one to create a state, the next to make it democratic. Efforts to do the latter without the former may lead to failure and a return to simpler authoritarian rule.

It is also important to recognize the many instances of wartime mobilization that did not lead to democracy. Combinations of effective propaganda and coercion can produce a significant popular support for military victory with no democratic institutional legacies. The totalitarian regimes of World War II certainly mobilized their masses with the same fervor, and arguably effectiveness, as the democracies. Note, moreover, that the negotiation between state and populaces need not imply institutionalized social rights, much less welfare states. Populations may bargain for schools and hospitals, but also settle for bread and circuses.

Yet another way that war may lead to greater social rights is through the instrumental use of welfare policies to produce citizens more prepared for war-time service. Individual education is an example of this, and it is discussed further in the section on individual outcomes and military service. In the United States, state universities were established as a means of broadly educating the citizen soldier. Today we have come to expect national and local governments to provide accessible, quality education for free to all citizens. Thus policies originally aimed at the soldier become extended to broader social rights for all.

Finally, there is a close connection between the level of military participation and the degree of egalitarianism in the society as a whole. The armed forces may offer the best opportunities for employment and promotion for disadvantaged members of a society. Certainly in the US no other major employment sector has seen the rate of success of African Americans in positions of power as in the military.

Reasons for this are relatively simple. One the one hand, the military operates on a highly bureaucratized meritocratic system of assessment. This system limits the extent to which manifest or latent forms of racism can impede an individual's ability to move up the ranks in service. Further, the US army, particularly after the Korean War, began actively recruiting from minority groups and women, offering service as a path to travel, learning, and post-service employment (Bailey 2009).

Militaries and the Individual

Now we turn to examining the role of military service at the individual level. Participating in a standing military, we argue, has contributed to the development of citizenship claims, state responses to those claims, and to the material and social well-being of those who serve. As such, the military has been a critical vehicle for macro-level phenomena like citizenship and social development. But military service is also responsible for micro-level, individual improvements. In this section we will touch upon the effect of military service on education, health, and economic mobility.

Historic longitudinal studies of health, educational, and economic outcomes are rare. As such, much of the data presented below has been cobbled together from a wide variety of sources, mostly emphasizing the US experience. The effects of personal service to the nation for war-making are far from uniform: different sectors of society have experienced different outcomes, and era of service, length of service, and combat exposure all have an effect. That said, there is evidence of greater health (even accounting for war-time casualties), greater education, and more money for at least some individuals, and particularly for those individuals serving before Vietnam and those coming from lower socio-economic classes, for minorities, and for women (Modell and Haggerty 1991; Settersten 2006; MacLean and Elder Jr. 2007).

Health[8]

There is precious little written in history of the care taken by polities to improve the health of their soldiers. Yet we know that a good soldier is strong and obedient, and capable of carrying out orders. This has meant that militaries have clothed, fed, and housed their soldiers and generally provided for their care, to ensure their battle-readiness. We also know that wars and the need to care for wounded soldiers was a driving factor in the development of emergency health care and health services more generally. For example, the development of the International Red Cross was a direct reaction to war-time casualties and the need for organized response to emergencies. Similarly, both the French and USSR acknowledged war-time need as the driving force for improving and modernizing its health services ("Military Health Services in the USSR" 1945; Lefort 2014). This process of improved health service as a response to war needs is no doubt mirrored the world over in history. A doctor writing to the *Lancet* in 1914 even remarked, "It has, indeed, become an axiom that whatever may be said for or against war, its anticipation and preparation by universal military service will regenerate the health of the nation" (Warden 1914).

The difficulties in studying the effect of military service on individual health are numerous. First, there is no standard long-term system dedicated to tracking the health of people prior to service, during service, and following service. Second, militaries the world over screen potential soldiers for health and readiness to fight. Because of this, it is difficult to know whether servicemen are in better shape because of military service, or if it is simply that militaries accept only fit soldiers. Third, militaries provide regular physical training, health care, and health education to their soldiers. In some countries, including the United States, this may be more specialized and individualized health treatment than is available to the general population, particularly for the poorer classes. Finally, there is the question of short-term versus medium-term versus long-term health outcomes. When comparing military servicemen to their non-serving age mates, we may not see health differences for many years after service. This is all to say that there are numerous barriers to comprehensively answering the question, both today and historically, of what the effect of military service is on individual health outcomes. What data we do have, however, points to a generally positive effect when compared to non-serving age mates.

Given the extreme fighting conditions, threat of bodily harm, and risk of death, one might expect military service to have a negative effect on health. In fact, it seems that military service has a negligible negative and even a positive effect on health. One recent study of over twelve thousand men finds that male veterans have significantly more health conditions but fewer daily living limitations and better self-reported health than non-veterans up to the mean age of sixty-six (Wilmoth, London, and Parker 2010). After the age of sixty-six, they found that as veterans aged they continued to have more health conditions, greater daily living limitations, and worse self-rated health. Another major study shows no statistically significant health disparities with respect to self-reports of poor health, chronic conditions, or psychological distress for veterans under the age of forty-five (Kramarow and Pastor 2012). Similar to the previous study, however, Kramarow and Pastor found that as veterans age they report poorer health, more chronic conditions, and greater psychological distress than civilians.

Why there appears to be improved health of veterans over non-veterans until middle age and then declining health is not fully explained. One obvious conclusion is simply that the effects of military service may not appear until later in life. That is, there are relatively few acute health conditions that are the result of service, and most effects take longer to occur. Another explanation is the fact that over 90 percent of veterans have access to health care, which may also lead to greater identification and treatment of physical and mental conditions. This means that they are in better health during and in the near-term post-service years as a result of their greater access to care, but that long-term health conditions remain unaffected due to the state of health service in general.

A major risk, of course, in the course of military service is death. Modern warfare, however, has seen a steady decline in fatalities since World War II. Indeed, data show that for some groups the risk of poor health outcomes and death is *greater* for civilians than those in the military (Segal and Segal 2004). Specifically, the rate of homicide for African Americans is lower for those in the military than for civilians. Segal and Segal also demonstrate that historically the rate of suicide is considerably lower for servicemen and women than their civilian counterparts. Disturbingly, however, recent data indicate that suicide by service members is increasing, even surpassing civilian suicides for comparable groups (Williams 2012; Lazar 2014).

With the decline of combat fatalities has been the incredible increase of wounded survival. The wounded–killed ratio has dramatically widened in the past half century. In World War II, there were 1.7 wounded servicemen for every fatality for a ratio of 1.7:1 (DeBruyne and Leland 2015). In Vietnam, that ratio grew to 2.6 wounded for every fatality. In Afghanistan and Iraq today, the ratios are 7.4:1 and 7.2:1 respectively ("Casualty Status" 2015), nearly four times the rate of wounded survivors of World War II. This has led to a situation in which there is an increasingly larger population of physically traumatized veterans who must be cared for and re-integrated into society.

In addition to the attention to the soldier's physical health, there has been greater awareness of the soldier's psychological health. Considerable recent research has been devoted to the effects of service generally, and combat specifically, on mental health outcomes since the Vietnam war to the present (Modell and Haggerty 1991). Perhaps unsurprisingly, studies indicate that depression and PTSD are more prevalent among men and women who have combat experience when compared to servicemen and women who do not (T. C. Smith et al. 2011). This has been a robust finding across service members from all wars. With respect to service members deployed versus those who are not deployed, recent studies have shown that both deployed men and deployed women report greater adverse mental health than their civilian counterparts, while non-deployed women (but not men) also reported greater adverse mental health than their civilian counterparts (Hoglund and Schwartz 2014). There is some evidence that resilience is protective for service members who face combat, but there are many questions remaining about how to foster and maintain such a protective trait in service (Sinclair and Britt 2013). While mental health access is increasing greatly among active service members and veterans, comprehensive mental health care is still unattained and remains a goal (Weiss and Albright 2014).

Education

Historically, the educational benefits that came with military service were unmatched by those that could be obtained in the civil sector. Prior to the Vietnam era, military service was not an alternative but a pathway to education. Over a century and a half ago in the United States, military service was tied to nationalized education. The Morrill Land Grant Act of 1862 was developed specifically with citizen-soldiers in mind. It granted US states donated federal land and money upon which to found universities, specifically "without excluding other scientific and classical studies and including military tactic, to teach such branches of learning as are related to agriculture and the mechanic arts." Note that military tactic is specifically listed as a subject. Further, land-grant colleges are required to maintain reserve officer training corps (ROTC) and programs in agriculture and engineering. Sixty-nine colleges were funded through this program, including major state flagship universities such as the University of Wisconsin as well as private universities like Cornell and the Massachusetts Institute of Technology. This act was passed as a means to ensure a broad base of technically and militarily educated citizens upon which to draw during war-time.

Later, World War II veterans were the recipients of the GI Bill, passed in 1948, which gave generous financial assistance to veterans who chose to attend college. Studies show that US World War II veterans had more education than comparable nonveterans (J. Teachman 2005). This finding was even more robust for black veterans of World War II, who had even greater educational advantages over their black civilian counterparts. That military service could be a path to greater education was actively promoted by the army. In a promotional film produced by the Army Pictorial Service in 1951 (*The Big Picture: The Citizen Soldier.* 1951), a captain of the army and film narrator states:

> Your army is aware of its responsibility to turn out first class citizens as well as first class fighting men. That's why it provides news information and education for all its personnel. In fact, it's possible for a soldier to leave the army today, far better educated and informed than he was when he came in.

Indeed, for the average citizen, military service up until Vietnam provided greater education and opportunity than otherwise was available to most young men.

The educational advantages of service declined, however, during the Vietnam era. When comparing those who served in Vietnam to those who did not, there are statistically significant differences in educational attainment. In fact, according to Teachman (2005; 2007), Vietnam veterans showed up to a two-year deficit in education at discharge compared to their non-servicing compatriots. Race was not a statistically significant factor when accounting for the deficit, however, indicating that minority groups still have better educational outcomes if they enter into military service.

Today, enlistees do have better education than their civilian counterparts, but this is in part a function of the high-school diploma requirement for enlistment (Clever and Segal 2013). This is to say, 100 percent of enlistees are required to have a high-school diploma – a statistic that non-enlistees do not come close to reaching, particularly for minority and lower-class groups. Officers are actually less educated than their civilian employed equivalents according to the same report. This is because those who are better educated have more to gain financially and socially by entering the civilian workforce than the military. This finding is echoed internationally as well. In Germany and Holland military service is associated with less educational attainment (T. K. Bauer et al. 2012; Hubers and Webbink 2015). This is all to say that for some groups, particularly minorities and lower-income groups, military service remains a pathway to greater education (Wang, Jr. and Spence 2012).

In an exciting development, schools on military bases are testing across the board better than their civilian counterparts (Winerip 2011). They are also dramatically reducing the Black–White education gap that has proved so enduring in US society outside of the military. This begs the question as to what the military is doing right, and how it can be replicated in civilian society. No doubt the availability of high quality schooling and after school care combined with steady income for families has gone a long way to improving child education outcomes. It remains to be seen whether these gains can be replicated outside of the military service setting, or whether they will have long-term socio-economic effects.

Income

The difficulties in studying the effect of military service on economic and class outcomes prior to World War II are difficult to overstate. There is simply very little systematic record-keeping or data with which to draw conclusions. While we know that, for example, the Morrill Land Grant Act was passed in part to educate the citizen soldier, it is difficult to measure any sustained effects of service on income. Nevertheless, a few studies point to an improvement on both as result of participation in the armed forces. For example, Lee (2012) demonstrated increased geographic mobility and greater propensity to enter into white-collar professions and farming among unskilled veterans of the

Civil War's Union Army when compared to their nonveteran counterparts.

Research has shown that immediately following the World War II era, military service was associated with increased income after discharge. This is in large part due numerous government programs designed to reintegrate servicemen into the economy, such as the GI Bill and house and car buying programs, and due to the robust post-war economy (Fernandez-Kelly 2015).

Unfortunately, these gains in income and socio-economic status were lost after the Vietnam era. Studies show that veterans make less than their non-serving age mates over their lifetime (J. D. Teachman and Call 1996; J. Teachman 2005; Clever and Segal 2013). We also know, however, that the effects of military service on income are different among whites and non-whites. Teachman (2005) demonstrated that white Vietnam era veterans experienced lower incomes than non-veterans of the era, while black veterans experienced no income changes relative to other black non-veterans. In fact, active duty black serviceman saw increases in their incomes.

For the most part, men and women who are actively serving in the military make more than their comparable age mate counterparts (Hosek and Wadsworth 2013). This is in large part because most people entering military service are 18 to 24 years old. The standard income for an 18-year-old military enlistee with a high-school diploma is considerably more than his or her counterpart is making in the unskilled labor market. However data also show that incomes decline dramatically compared to their age mates once people leave the military. This is because though the 18–24 year-old serving four years in the military is making more money than his age mate, who is in the unskilled labor market or unemployed but attending school, the college graduate will command more in pay upon graduating after four years than his or her age mate after four years of military service. Thus the economic gains of military service for the most mobile people in the labor market in the modern era are temporary. This is a finding that is also found in other countries, including Germany and Holland (T. K. Bauer et al. 2012; Hubers and Webbink 2015).

Another factor in household economy is the income, if any, of the spouse (Hosek and Wadsworth 2013). Since the vast majority of people serving in the military are male, the spouse is typically a woman. Research shows that spousal income suffers a two-percent drop every time the household moves, which is not an uncommon event in the life course of a service man. Further, there is a 20 to 29 percent wage gap between spousal income and their civilian counterparts; significant enough to affect dramatically overall household income. It is believed that such a large penalty for being the spouse of a service person is due to the frequent location changes and the attendant inability to build a long-term career with a particular company or industry. Finally, undesired unemployment is higher among military spouses than in the general population.

There has been concern that an all-volunteer military draws too heavily on the lowest economic classes, or, conversely, that the upper classes do not serve (Berryman 1988; Roth-Douquet and Schaeffer 2006; Watkins and Sherk 2008). Research indicates that in fact the lowest classes are not disproportionately represented in the military, but that the top is vastly under-represented (Berryman 1988; Bailey 2009). At least in the contemporary US, the military has become the province of the middle-third of the income distribution. There has also been concern that of those who do serve, minority groups disproportionately face fatal combat service. This was the case during the early Vietnam years, but specific policies have reduced Black combat fatalities to representative levels (Segal and Segal 2004).

In understanding the macro-sociological implications of these micro-sociological outcomes, we return to the medical doctor writing a letter to the *Lancet* in 1914 (Warden 1914). He noted that:

Now, it is surely evident that any one group of the same age and sex forms but a small part of the whole population and of the complicated problem of national health . . . It is surely obvious that the real problem of national health is far other and depends upon urbanization and its consequences . . . It involves measures of dealing with tuberculosis, contagious diseases, unhealthy industrial conditions, infantile mortality. It is a question of house, of food, of drainage, of water-supply, not of the military training of healthy young men.

Indeed, the author notes and remains correct – less than 1 percent of the population serves in the military at any given time. We do well to keep this in mind when considering any effects of service on individual outcomes. While it is clear that service can have a very positive effect on health, education, and income for particular groups in the modern era, military service as a social mobility policy will never reach significant portions of the populace.

What we see, then, is that wars and the military are not only great machineries of destruction, chaos, and suffering. In fact, there is great evidence that the long-term outcomes of war include centralized political authority and institutions of state-building that promote economic and social development (Morris 2014). But in addition to these big outcomes, individuals, too, can benefit from war making. While the ultimate price may be paid in loss of life, far more often the outcome for soldiers is better health, education, and income. This chapter has shown how nation states, nationalism, citizenship, and rights have all developed specifically from the practice of war. Further, military service has had a clear positive effect on the lives of many young men, and now women, in the world.

We now turn to what may be the future of war in the world. It is rather bold for anyone to make predictions on the scale of massive human conflict and development, but, particularly when compared to the practice of war just fifty years ago, we are already seeing clear changes in the practice of war. The next chapter outlines a few of the changes, looking particularly at the decline of Western powers, the rise of insurgencies, and the changing face of military service.

6

War and Society in the Twenty-First Century

The number of books and essays on war in the twenty-first century is quite large. There are, for example, those who speak of a "new" form of war (Kaldor 1999; Hirst 2001; Kolko 2002; Coker 2004; Shaw 2005), of new geographies (Barnett and Low 2004; Kilcullen 2013), and of new technologies (B. F. Harris 2009; Singer 2009).[1] The number of parings with the word "war" grows ever longer: water, civilizational, ecological, ethnic, and narco among them. Continuing with the general theme of this book, we will not explore any of these bellic alternatives in detail, but rather focus on changes that dramatically affect the relationship between war and society.

We believe that the state of war in the twenty-first century presents yet another paradox in our study of the link between social structures and organized violence. On the one hand, we are living through something that could be called a "world war" in that practically every region is affected by at least violent threats if not a great deal of killing and destruction. On the other, the majority of humanity does not live in a state of war as we saw in the cases of Chapters 3 and 4. We cannot hope to provide a global synthesis or prediction in the few pages available, but we can use this paradox as a way of illustrating the changes in the relationships between war and society in the near future.

An Unseen Global War?[2]

We may begin with a world tour of organized violence. Beginning with North America, we note a continued state of alert in the United States and a continued commitment to defend itself from terrorism; certainly a significant contrast with the post-Cold War hopes of a "peace dividend." In Mexico, the number of dead associated with its "war on drugs" over the past decade is in the multiple tens of thousands. While no formal state of war exists, the presence of semi-organized violence is pervasive throughout the society. The degree of organization of that violence and in Central America is an empirically debatable question, but the level of bellic level ferocity is not. Certainly any reasonable person would describe the situation in parts of Mexico, Guatemala, El Salvador, and Honduras as at the very least resembling a Hobbesian anarchy. In the Southern continent, the casualties of the Colombian civil war have declined, but there remain threats to state control over its territory. In the rest of the region, such threats tend to be concentrated in parts of major urban centers. While the level of organization is again subject to debate, there is no question that violence is pervasive in selected zones (Imbusch, Misse, and Carrion 2011).

Crossing the Atlantic, we see that the traditional fulcrum of Western European wars from Flanders through to the mouth of the Danube remains relatively peaceful. Approaching the traditional "bloodlands"of Europe (Snyder 2010), the conflict over the Eastern Ukraine very much looks like a classic war. The ambivalent participation of Russian military makes this a perfect example of one of the "new" kinds of war: violent, but with unclear roles.

Africa is awash on conflict. From the Atlantic shores of the Sahara through Suez, claims of territorial monopoly over the means of violence are contested daily. The chaos of the region north of the Gulf of Guinea has declined and the respective states have at least some nominal resemblance of control over their territory. The situation in Northern Nigeria remains volatile with a variety of threats to the state. In all of these countries, some form of political violence is endemic, but as with the case of Central America, the degree of organization is problematic. While the Angolan civil war is over, Mozambique's appears always about to break out again. In general, however, and with the exception of high levels of daily crime, Southern Africa is arguably the most peaceful part of the continent. The bloodiest part of the region remains the Great Lakes (Prunier 1995), where a two-decade war and associated dislocation has produced close to ten million casualties. The very ambiguity of the death toll serves an indication of the extent to which the "organization" of this violence has been on a relatively micro scale. Moving north, we have two cases where again, while the violence is endemic, the degree to which we can attribute it to recognized institutional actors remains unclear. An imaginary rectangle stretching from the western borders of South Sudan to the Indian Ocean holds as much human misery resulting from direct and indirect violence as anywhere in the world.

Moving toward South Asia, we find the site of perhaps the best candidate for the standard form of warfare we have studied in this book. India and Pakistan have been in some form of conflict for more than sixty years, at times culminating in classic military maneuvers and tactics (Hiro 2014). The fact that both now possess nuclear weapons gives any South Asian war a global scope as the climactic consequences of even a limited nuclear exchange would be significant. Southeast Asia and east toward the Pacific is relatively militarily quiet, but with continued threats to the relevant states in isolated regions. Moving north, the East and South China seas are the site of "grand strategy" disputes between the Communist People's Republic of China (PRC) and its neighbors (Christensen 2015). The increasing resources devoted to naval forces by the PRC, and the clear American commitment to regional autonomy makes this the most likely site for some form of Great Power conflict. In the cases of both the PRC and Eastern Russia, as well as parts of the former Soviet Central Asian states, there do not appear to be any significant inter-national disputes, but the possibility of internal disruptions and threats to centralized power remain. The Korean peninsula remains a permanent "hot-zone" and the discrepancy between the North Korea's military threat and its productive capacity represent a new kind of puzzle for war.

Finally, we come to the region most associated with military conflict in the twenty-first century: the Middle East widely defined. The complexity of conflicts here belies even a summary, but these include at least inter-national conflicts (Saudi Arabia vs. Iran, Israel vs. all neighbors), religious or ideological conflicts (Salafi vs. Shia vs Sunni; secular vs. religious; democratic vs. authoritarian), conflicts over resources (oil and gas, water), as well as the cultural bellicosity and group dynamics detailed in Chapter 1. The level of violence ranges from the possibility of a nuclear exchange to fights between isolated partisans armed with AK-47s. The level of organization of the violence ranges from global alliances (with the US's strategic partnership with both Israel and Saudi Arabia), to national (Israel vs. all others), to the numerous, sub-national entities (Assad Alawaite group, Hezbollah, ISIS, etc.) (Karsh 2015, among his many works on the region).

Obviously each of these conflicts is producing massive numbers of casualties. For those killed, wounded, raped, or exiled by war, it appears as traumatizing as ever. Yet the global statistics show that the percentage of humanity killed by war is certainly lower than any point since the 1940s, and some point to a "decline of war" (Gleditsch 2013). While there seems to be some quantitative proof of the "waning of war" (Lacina and Gleditsch 2013), there are several problems with such statistics.

First, the twenty-first-century wars and their fatalities tend to occur far from media centers and the killed-in-action census is not nearly as precise as that available, for example, for US losses in Vietnam. Unlike in the thirty years of war in the twentieth century (1914–45), much of the destruction is taking place away from major urban centers and is particularly concentrated on some of the poorer parts of each region and the world in general. Mexico's sixty thousand homicides would draw much more attention in Mexico City than that same number spread out over Guerrero, Michoacán, Coahuila, and other Mexican states. The millions of victims in the African Great Lakes region are dying anonymously and largely unnoticed. To put it most crudely, unlike the first half of the twentieth century, in the first decade of the twenty-first century few of the victims are of European heritage. Moreover, the technological advantage of the US and allied countries, combined with the professionalization of the military, means that civilians in large parts of the rich world can live in a world where war is nothing but an element of a video game, or perhaps a news item. After the first Gulf War and the development of new precision weapons, our coverage of war has been transformed where the line between it and an action movie seems increasingly blurred. Certainly the US has experienced its longest period of continuous warfare in the twenty-first century while leaving a bare ripple in the civilian cultural consciousness.

Second, because of the nature of the weapons used and the quality of medical care, survival with lasting mental and physical scars is much more likely now. The value of measuring war by deaths may be declining at a time when the consequences are not necessarily fatalities, but life-changing events such as rapes, decapitating wounds, or exile. Wars do not just kill, but can destroy societies without a significant number of bodies. Certainly in the case of Iraq and Syria the destructive tsunami of war is much greater than that measured by the already considerable number of dead.

Relatedly, the share of civilian deaths in these conflicts has increased even in the absence of the kind of strategic bombing used in World War II. In Iraq after the 2003 invasion, over 70 percent of those who died of direct war violence were civilians (Crawford 2013). These "collateral" casualties are hard to count. This has largely to do with the fact that the wars of the twenty-first century are not between countries but largely within them. The Westphalian model of war may no longer be relevant and we need to understand war on a different level of aggregation than we do below.

We are faced, therefore with interesting dilemmas for students of war. In many ways war remains very much a part of history in practically every part of the world. On the other, the social ramifications of war appear to be increasingly diluted in the West and the rich East. What does this mean for the relationship between war and society?

Return of the Warrior[3]

The story narrated in this book so far would appear to be a fairly linear progression in the social and organizational complexity of war. Beginning about ten thousand years ago, we find groups of humans uniting in order to fight other humans (Ferguson 2003). Some six hundred years ago such efforts on the European peninsula consolidated into what we might recognize as nation states, making possible ever more complex forms of delivering violence. In some periods and in some areas, this progression went backwards and more individualized and chaotic forms of violence came back to the fore. The overall global pattern, however, appears straightforward. Wars both required and produced institutionalized structures designed to aggregate resources and point them in the right lethal direction. Whichever society could do a better job of organizing violence came out on top. The explosions over Hiroshima and Nagasaki in 1945 would appear to represent yet another stage in this evolution of war.

Yet, with the hindsight of some decades, that same year might better represent a zenith in the societal complexity of war at which point a more basic form re-asserted itself. The continued capacity of several nations' abilities to destroy significant parts of the planet remained. In fact, the collapse of Communism led not a few to believe that American military power could feasibly establish the first truly global empire (Nye 1990; Muravchik 1991; Ikenberry, Mastanduno, and Wohlforth 2011; but note Layne 1993; Layne and Thayer 2007). The attack on the World Trade Center in New York City elicited calls for the greatest of American military and political responses (Boot 2001). The resultant victories over Iraq in 1991 and 2003 made ever more apparent the sheer virtuosity of the American way of war (Weigley 1977). The United States could deliver unprecedented amounts of industrial levels of violence across the world with relatively little effort. It seemed the American legions were invincible.

And to a certain extent they were. No regular armed force could ever hope to match the American military might, but that very same omnipotent capacity might have become increasingly politically irrelevant at the same time that it announced itself in August of 1945. If the past ten thousand years has been the progression from the wars of warriors to those of societies, the last few years may mark a new trend with a return to the warrior.

The rest of this chapter will explore this shift along two lines. First, it analyzes the decline of massed military engagement and the increasing relevance of irregular warfare in defining the outcomes of conflicts. Then, it will discuss how a concurrent change in demographics of the American military calls into question the role of armed forces in society today, and may represent a departure from the long history described throughout this book.

The End of Empires

While much of the discussion on war since 1945 has focused on confrontations between superpowers and the global consequences thereof, nuclear standoffs were arguably not the most important military development of the end of the last half of the twentieth century. If we think broadly and globally, the most significant trend since World War II has been the increasing divorce of military might from social resources.[4] While much of the war for the previous five hundred years was a reflection of relative organizational effectiveness and access to physical resources, the past few decades have witnessed a reversal to the apparently endless aggregation of empires. The accretion of power culminated with the bi-polar balance of power between the United States and the Soviet Union during the Cold War, but already there were indications that a post-imperial line had been crossed.

Consider that in 1945 the European empires and their direct descendants controlled the vast majority of the world's landmass and population. The maps of the European empires still dominated globes. The United States was supreme in its political, military, and economic power, and there was a reasonable belief that it would continue as a global imperial force along side the other traditional political powers. A few decades later, the world of empires looked remarkably different. Even the Soviet empire had fallen and the ability of global powers to dictate everywhere and anywhere in the world was severely limited. At the same time, the destructive military capacity of these same powers, and particularly the United States, had grown exponentially. How can we explain the decline of imperial powers that coincided with the growth of military force (Burbank and Cooper 2010; Mann 2012)?

We may begin by summarizing the standard reasons offered for the ability of the West to dominate the globe for roughly five centuries. First and most often noted was the technological monopoly on the delivery of violence possessed by the imperial powers (Adas 1989). This did not just involve the capacity to inflict violence locally, but to project it globally. With the exception of the Japanese empire, no non-European power could project its military might across oceans. This meant that colonial and imperial wars could be fought on the territory of the other, with any associated benefits that could incur. The monopoly over transcontinental transport may have been the most critical component of Western imperial power. This monopoly allowed the West to use local allies to support their own land grabs. While some have remarked on the cultural superiority of the Western powers (Hanson 2002; but see Morris 2014), we might better focus on the specific military and organizational practices that had been honed by the perpetual warfare in Europe for several centuries. The West was "better" at conquest in part because it had been practicing for a very long time (Tilly 1992). Another component is that the societies behind the empires were willing to bear the cost of empire, and the empire was able to extract those payments (Kennedy 1987; Tilly 1992). Conquest was seen as both necessary and inevitable and the populations were usually willing to pay the blood and resource price for imperial grandeur. Finally and most importantly, the process of Western conquest depended on the other side being willing to fight on Western terms. When these conditions disappeared after 1945, the military logic of Western supremacy disappeared.

The key element for understanding the end of empires after World War II may be by considering a very different kind of warfare than the ones discussed in previous chapters (Boot 2006).

We argue that the end of empires came as a result of the political and moral costs of war escalating because of the advent of nuclear technology and the subsequent increased use of small war tactics by non-imperial forces.

The standard definition of guerrilla war or insurgency[5] is that it is an irregular conflict carried on by small groups acting independently (Laqueur 1976). This is essentially a direct reversal of the more direct and unidirectional forms of battle that dominated after 1500. While regular armies concentrate their violence and seek decisive battle, guerrilla forces disperse and seek the slow destruction of the enemy. In most cases, a guerrilla force cannot hope to destroy a regular armed force, but it can debilitate it to the point that it can no longer function. This has been called the war of the flea (Taber 1965), as it relies not so much on sheer resources or size, but on small continual bites to drive the adversary mad.

In this way insurgency and its close relative, terrorism (M. Carr 2007; Burleigh 2009) are the perfect confirmation of the Clausewitzian maxim of war as politics by other means. Insurgency returns our attention to the politics behind conflicts and the kind of social and cultural supports regular wars require. Rather than seeking to defeat the enemy on the battlefield, it seeks to drain the home societies' willingness to pay the price of war. In this way, it is similar to the purposes of strategic bombing: not focused on the actual destruction, but on the withering away of a fighting spirit.[6]

Insurgencies are not meant to eradicate an enemy, but to make the opponent decide that the struggle is not worthwhile. In many ways they bring forward the psychological and cultural foundations that make conflict possible. The rise of industrial war and the increase in the sheer destructive capacity of militaries has diverted our attention from a basic principle of war: it is not necessarily about the elimination of an enemy force, but about destroying the effectiveness and coherence of that force. Phalanxes did not win by necessarily killing more or better, but by shattering the cohesion of the enemy and its faith in a possible victory. Perhaps the best example of this is the success of the German Blitzkrieg against the arguably superior French army in 1940 (May 2000; Nord 2015).

The Germans did not destroy the French army, the French state simply fell apart. The logic of the guerrilla takes these lessons to their conclusion. Against the Clausewitzian logic of decisive battles, fighting to physically and politically exhaust the enemy rather than destroy can yield victory.

The potential power of guerrilla war has always been clear (Boot 2013). Groups organized enough to inflict constant (if relatively small) damage on regular troops have always been feared. The most obvious example of the power of irregular forces – and the origin of the term guerilla – was Napoleon's experience in Spain after his invasion of 1808 (Laqueur 1976). Similarly the victorious Union army's greatest fear was that the Confederate population would not accept Lee's surrender and require a military operation much more intensive that involved in reconstruction (Winik 2001). The German army was triumphant at Sedan, but required another year to pacify an armed French populace. Imperial powers from Spain to Britain to the United States found that defeating an enemy not interested in a decisive battle but in incremental resistance required much greater resources than defeating an equally organized and formal opponent.

Critical to the success of an insurgency is the perceived legitimacy of the struggle. Organizational competence and physical resources are important to win wars, but guerrilla warfare demonstrates the power of the will of the people to persevere. An enemy unwilling or unable to accept defeat requires a level of destructive violence that its opponents may not be able to deliver or – equally important – justify. Mao Tse-tung's notion of a protracted war argues that a nation trades space and materiel for time during which the enemy can exhaust itself (Mao 1961). The key effort is not to defeat the enemy militarily but to force the enemy to lose its political and social support – the "hearts and minds"[7] of the home front – so as to make conquest practically impossible. Consider the dilemma for the form of war as perfected by the West: unless empires are willing to engage in genocidal struggles, the military conflict is potentially endless.

The roster of imperial defeats after 1945 is practically a continuous proof of the power of such irregular warfare.[8] While the colonial powers relied on the same weapons they had used in World War II including heavy artillery and air forces, the insurgents depended on the AK-47, the RPG-7 and the SAM-7 (Chivers 2010). None of these weapons could guarantee victory, but they could blunt the military advantages of the higher technology weapons. The key to the success of practically each of these struggles was a lesson learned by the Irish Republican Army in its war with Britain: "matching operations to its means, it could ensure its survival for long enough to achieve psychological victory out of a military stalemate" (Foster 1989, 501–2).

Pride of place in the post-independence era obviously belongs to India. While violence was certainly a part of the process, it played a very small role in Britain's final decision to leave. The Amritsar massacre of 1919 and the political fallout and the success of Gandhi's campaign had already made it clear to the British that it would be impossible to prolong its rule by military means (Sayer 1991). Given the size and complexities of the challenge before them, the British left the subcontinent to two successor states and departed in a hurried, but dignified exit. A similar dilemma faced the British in Palestine during the civil war of 1947–8 (R. Miller 2010).

The centuries long Dutch Empire in the East Indies had a much more violent end (Adams 1996). Dutch authority had disappeared after the Japanese conquest and while the Europeans were initially successful in reestablishing control after 1945, it was limited to the major towns and roads. It is possible that the significant Dutch military presence could have prevailed in maintaining control over the major exporting zones in Sumatra and Java, but the Indonesian national Revolution made it clear to the United States and other imperial powers that any successful decolonization would be extremely violent and expensive. The Indonesian war evidenced the post-World War II political climate and marked a turning point in the global legitimacy of war (Ricklefs 2001). It had become politically impossible for the Dutch to use their still considerable military advantage following the Nazi occupation of Europe and the attendant rejection of that occupation.

A similar process occurred in 1956 when the British and French attempted to retain control over the Suez Canal (Neff 1981;

Pocock 1986). Despite the overwhelming military victory of the Europeans and their Israeli allies, no war could continue without US support and this was expressly denied. Combined with significant domestic opposition in the UK, this made the politics of military victory impossible. Despite the fact that there was absolutely no question that the invasion could and would be successful, Egypt retained control over the canal.

A very different situation occurred in parallel in Hungary (Borhi 2004). As in the case of Suez, the Soviet Union and her "allies" had invaded Hungary in order to assure continued control over the territory. As in the case of Suez, there was no question of realistic military resistance. The Soviet Union, on the other hand, could resist international pressure and whatever domestic protest might have existed was obviously moot. If not clear before, the twin crises of 1956 made it clear that in dealing with empires, military might had long given way to political expediency.

France suffered the most significant colonialist defeats in the decades following the end of World War II. In Vietnam, the victory of the Viet Minh was by no means guaranteed as late as 1950. Subsequent scholarship has clearly proven that the anti-French forces were starving and exhausted and very much at their breaking point by 1954 (Karnow 1983). The outcome of the battle in the Dien Bien Phu valley decided the war, not the significant resources lost by the French (Lacey and Murray 2013). The Viet Minh would probably not been able to launch another similar operation and, moreover, a massive bombing campaign would have guaranteed their defeat. The fall of French Indochina was not a military one, but something out of a piece of theater: having made their bet on Dien Bien Phu and facing significant domestic resistance, the French government could not politically sustain their effort. The fact that France was then able to mount a full military operation in Algeria following the Vietnamese defeat clearly indicates that the French colonial military apparatus was not destroyed in Vietnam.

In the case of Algeria, the overshadowing of the military by politics was even clearer (Horne 1978; Stora 2001). No one disputes that the French had been able to destroy much of the insurgency in the major cities and had even created safe-zones in large parts of the country. What the military could not do, however, was to convince enough of the French population that *Algérie française* was worth the moral, physical, and fiscal sacrifices required.

Perhaps the extreme example of how insurgencies do not need to win wars, but simply wait for the colonial power to recognize its inevitable defeat, may be found in the case of the fall of the Portuguese empire. Portugal represented arguably the greatest distance between the size and scope of its imperial pretentions and the ability of the domestic society to support and maintain it. The poorest country in Western Europe controlled an empire centered on the massive territories of Angola and Mozambique. The independence struggles in these had begun in the early 1960s. Yet in part because of divisions within the insurgency and because of the willingness of the Portuguese army to use whatever means were necessary to keep control, the situation in the early 1970s remained stalemated (Cann 1997). It was when the Portuguese military lost its institutional willingness to continue anti-insurgency and when elements within it led a successful coup against the regime that Portuguese Africa gained its independence.

While not formally an independence war, the Cuban Revolution of 1956–9 (Pérez-Stable 1993; García Luis 2008) can also serve as an example of what we might call the insurgent's dictum: don't try to win, just make the other guy lose. By any military standard the forces working with Fidel Castro in early 1957 were inconsequential. The "invasion" of the island by the guerilla force had ended up in disaster while the urban underground was decimated by its mis-planned and mis-executed actions in support of those in the mountains. In early 1957, Fulgencio Batista could count on a well-equipped and supplied army of nearly fifty thousand men. Against him, Fidel Castro had fewer than a few dozen badly armed men. A year later, the situation had not changed very much except that the revolutionaries' domestic and international cachet had increased dramatically. The Cuban armed forces attempted to destroy the guerillas in 1958, but lack of morale and political corruption made it impossible to do so. By later 1958, Batista still could count on a sizable military force and faced a still insignificant rebel military.

Yet by the end of the year Batista had left Cuba and Fidel Castro triumphantly entered Havana in January 1959. The revolution had not defeated the government. The legitimacy and the morale of the latter were so low that it essentially collapsed on itself.

While this process has been seen as one of decline of the West (Smith 1975), it may be better to understand it as the decline of the power of accretion. For thousands of years the capacity to aggregate and organize ever-larger groups of soldiers and support them with the appropriate materiel has been the key to victory. The outcome of global wars of the twentieth century and the development of the super-weapons of nuclear power seemed to indicate that a new imperial age had arrived. Yet underneath that apparent power lay an important political fragility: the costs of using it were geopolitically profound and fraught and the legitimacy of its use was weakly founded in the home countries. The process of aggregation required that a military enjoy enough social support to maintain itself. That made any divorce between what was militarily feasible and politically acceptable impossible. The two great post-war powers did have the capacity to destroy any civilization, but in the absence of public approval to do so – and under threat of self-destruction – their military prowess had limited political application.

Perhaps the contemporary example which best illustrates the divorce of statehood or social resources from military capacity is post 2011 Syria ("Syria: The Story of the Conflict" 2015). Over and above the devastation in that country what may be most significant from a scholarly point of view is the increasing fragmentation of power and the ability of even relatively small and under-resourced actors to reinforce the decline into chaos. Moreover, Syria seems a perfect example of proxy wars where major protagonists are not present, but merely provide enough resources to allow even the almost defeated to survive. In the case of Syria, for example, most ISIS fighters are foreigners with no link to the society. The nominal limits placed on Assad's use of chemical weapons and the ISIS execution videos also highlight how media politics and global legitimacy may be more important than straightforward military capacity.

The Limits of Firepower:
Vietnam, Afghanistan, and Iraq

For insurgents to defeat declining empires may not seem surprising. The last forty years, however, have shown that even the most destructive firepower ever assembled may be humbled.

A standard story about Vietnam is that the United States did not try to win the war. While it is true that the US did not use nuclear weapons or invade the North, to call Vietnam a "limited" war or one fought with hands tied behind the back is simply incorrect. Consider that roughly 3.5 million men and women served in Southeast Asia, with 2.5 million in Vietnam (US Department of Veterans Affairs 2010; Gelman 2013). Of these more than a million fought in combat or provided close support. At the peak of the war, the US had more than half a million troops in the country, consuming nearly half of Army and marine personnel. The US built dozens of airports and deep-water ports and millions of square footage of storage, hundreds of miles of roads bridges and pipelines, and spent more than $750 billion, or 2.3 percent of GDP at the peak of the war (Daggett 2010). Millions of tons of bombs were dropped in the region leading the deforestation of large parts of three countries. Over 59,000 Americans lost their lives, as did perhaps two million Vietnamese and Cambodians.

An often-alternative story is that Vietnam was something of an anomaly and not representative of the military might used by the US (Hanson 2002). This is also incorrect, as the war, certainly as fought for its first five years, was an exemplary model of how the US military was taught and sought to fight (N. Sheehan 1988; McMaster 1997). American policy in Vietnam reflected the perspective which Henry Kissinger described as "built on the assumption that technology plus managerial skills gave [the US] the ability to reshape the international system" (Gibson 1986, 15). This was a natural extension of the experience in World War II: given that the US was bigger and much more technologically capable and that the other side was a peasantry and industrially weak, winning was assumed. Or as one colonel quoted by Michael

Herr said, the meat eaters should be easily able defeat the rice eaters (Herr 1991, 56).

And yet, the US lost precisely because the military attempted to make war into a managerial game and a production function. The logic used was a war of attrition, reflecting the experience of the two world wars, in which the Vietnamese would be overwhelmed into defeat. What such a perspective forgot was that defeat is not just a tactical or strategic goal, but a political one as well.

A classic example of such a strategy was the so-called "search and destroy" missions where the US would use the well-announced arrival of troops so as to attract and then destroy the enemy. Unfortunately, what made some sense in Washington, Guam, Saigon or a helicopter one thousand feet above the battlefield made little on the ground. The enemy simply and quickly learned not to walk into obvious traps. Another example was the institution of "body counts" by which progress was measured statistically depending on reported numbers of those killed in action, supplies destroyed, and yes, even battalion fitness reports (Milam 2009).

The US military succeeded in everything it sought to do in Vietnam and displayed awesome power: it moved half a million soldiers in and out of a battle zone on an annual basis, it projected its air and naval superiority half-way around the world and it did win every battle. It just didn't win the war.

Practically the same story could be told of the Soviet experience in Afghanistan (Borovik 1990; Feifer 2009; Tanner 2009; Braithwaite 2011). Seeking to support a weak ally and to institutionalize formal authority, the Soviets spent more than $50 billion and fifteen thousand lives in a war in which they suffered "a thousand cuts" from a motivated insurgency (S. G. Jones 2009). The Soviets used much of the incredible military technology they possessed and certainly went further than the Americans in creating a rule of terror in the countryside. The toll on Afghans in terms of deaths, mutilations, and refugees was in the millions and accompanied the collapse of what existed of a nation-state In the end, "[it] was absolutely meaningless, like subtracting from zero" (S. G. Jones 2009, 25; see also Kalinovsky 2011). The American experience in Afghanistan after 2001 was depressingly similar (S. G. Jones 2009; Tomsen 2011; Gall 2014).

Almost four decades later, the US made a similar error in Iraq in the early 2000s (Ricks 2006, 2009; Gordon and Trainor 2006; T. H. Anderson 2011; Bolger 2014). Once again American superiority in straightforward military power was beyond debate (Murray and Scales 2003; Keegan 2004). The US and its allies were able to conquer the major objectives of the invasion in fewer than three weeks. Once again, the numbers reflect massive US power: 1,500 air sorties a day; 145,000 troops moved across thousands of miles, and defeating a significant opponent with 155 fatalities (mostly from friendly fire). President Bush was right when he famously proclaimed that the mission had been accomplished. But as in the case of Vietnam, it was the wrong mission.

If the mission had simply been to defeat and depose Saddam Hussein, 2003 would have been seen through a similar light to that of the 1991 Gulf War. Unfortunately, what the US hoped to do in Iraq was much more complicated and involved actually controlling Iraq and recreating its society (Hahn 2012). Note the critical difference: the military centric logic is to simply destroy the enemy, but the underlying political logic is to assure some form of stability.

Even after it became clear that the US was facing an insurgency in Iraq, the US military adopted the same decade-old logic – that if you killed enough insurgents, the remaining would give up. As was the case in Vietnam, allied forces won every major set battle (even if painfully, as in the case of Fallujah). Only later in the war did the policy of "clear, hold, and build" (US Army Combined Arms Center, n.d.; Ucko 2013) begin to establish a true legitimate monopoly over the means of violence. A problem still remained, similar to that faced in Vietnam – the war mission was defined in such a way (stability and an end terrorist control) that it would take years, perhaps decades, to accomplish. Similar to Vietnam, the public support for such a campaign rarely lasts so long.

The last fifty years have seen something of a "democratization" of massive violence. There no longer needs to be advanced industrialization and a Weberian bureaucracy to inflict significant damage. This is potentially a major revolution in the link between war and society as it separates societal development from capacity for significant violence. Technology allows for a small group of individuals to gather the killing power previously limited to a regiment of soldiers. The interconnectedness of modernity also provides many more targets than were available on the simple battlefields of yore. This makes the central characteristic of states – the monopoly of violence over a given territory – much more problematic. The decline in absolute numbers of dead in war might actually be a result not of the pacifying of the globe, but of the lower aggregation of deaths associated with individual acts of violence. And of course, a nuclear conflagration would make "the waning of war" a temporary statistical aberration.

An interesting result of this trend is arguably that military violence is now occurring more in the hinterlands. While terrorism makes every civilian in the wealthiest parts of the world a potential victim, the actual result is to divorce much of the world's population from the consequences of military violence.[9] This trend is made even more significant due to the "professionalization" of the military in the wealthiest of countries (accompanied paradoxically by the "militarization" of civilians in the war zones).

Who Will Serve? The Changing Demographics of the Military

In Chapter 5, we noted the importance of conscription in many aspects of modern states. Since the 1970s in most countries, armed forces have moved away from a conscription model and more toward one based on volunteer service. In the rest of this chapter we focus on the case of the US as this is a country very much associated with the notion of military service being critical to political development, and its military is the most significant in the world.[10] The argument is that yet another result of the changes in warfare described above is a shift is military composition – a shift that may have important consequences for citizenship and social and economic mobility.

The changing demographics of the military are the result of a number of forces. First, there is the historical background of the US case, one that is not altogether unique. The military was, for the bulk of its history, filled with male white citizens exclusively. This meant that women, men of color, and non-citizens historically have not been immediate participants in (and benefits of) war. In practice, the wealthy often were able to buy their way out of combat participation, such that the core fighting forces have been young, male, poor, and white for a significant period of time (Bailey 2009).

Political currents and social developments have led to the inclusion of non-traditional groups in the military, including African Americans and non-citizens, women, and now openly homosexual soldiers. Such social shifts have had an enormous effect on the demographic make-up of the military. Below we present some data that demonstrates the profound shifts occurring in military service today.

The increasing innovation in military technology also has significantly altered the nature of participation. It has allowed armed forces to develop practices never before imagined, particularly with the advent of such elements as improved armored vehicles and body armor, night vision wear, and drone technology. While women are still officially not allowed to serve in combat positions, they are increasingly closer to full combat participation in part because of these technological developments.

Historical Military Service

Since the beginning of the United States, there has been a history of a limited standing army with rapid expansion during war and immediate contraction once the war concluded. The typical standing army from 1800 through 1940 was less than one-half of a percent of the total population. The Civil War saw a mobilization of 3 percent of the population, with nearly the same amount active during World War I (Segal and Segal 2004). World War II saw the involvement of an incredible 12 percent of the country (some 56 percent of the eligible adult male population), and then

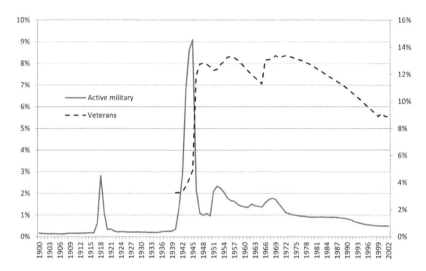

Figure 6.1 Percent of US Population Serving in US Military
Source: US Census

saw a gradual decline in the following fifty years to today's level of approximately 0.5 percent of the US population serving.

Following World War II there was not a complete draw down in armed forces as there had been in times past, and following the Korean and Vietnam Wars there remained between one and two percent of the population still participating in the armed forces. This is more than double the previous standing military strengths.

Counter to popular belief, the United States was historically an all-volunteer service. A tiny portion of the population was a part of a standing militia, and volunteers supplemented the low number of standing militia as wars developed. It was not until the Civil War made such incredible demands on the population that conscription came into effect. Table 6.1 provides the percentage of total military forces that were conscripted rather than volunteer.

As we can see, the percent of the total serving military that has been drafted has been in steady decline since World War I. Contrary to popular belief, the draftee population in Vietnam was a significant minority of military servicemen, only 16 percent

Table 6.1. Percent Conscription of Active Forces, US Military

American Civil War (1862–3)	WWI (1917)	WWII (1940)	Korean War (1950)	Vietnam (1964)
21% Confederate (210K of 1M) 2% Union (46K of 2.1M)	72% (2.8M of 3.5M)	62% (10.1M of 16M)	54% (1.5M of 2.8M)	16% (but 88% of armed infantry; 543k of 3.4M)

Source: Chambers (1999)

compared with the 72 percent of drafted servicemen in World War I. Eighty-eight percent, however, of the infantry serving in Vietnam was conscripted.

Amid the increasing professionalization of the armed forces following the Korean War and the growing domestic political resistance to military engagement, especially after more than ten years of involvement in Vietnam, Nixon declared the end of the draft in 1973. This created what is known today as the all-volunteer force (AVF). Historian Beth Bailey (2009) provides a penetrating and fascinating history of the American Army, the largest branch of the armed forces, detailing the political and military debates and aftermath surrounding the institution of the AVF.

The military as we know it today exists in the contexts of two particular trends: expansion and consolidation. The US military expanded its eligible enlistees to include African Americans and then other minorities, first in segregated units, which sometimes where integrated at larger levels of aggregation during World War II (Buchanan 1977). While women have historically served in combat support units, particularly as medics, they were excluded from combat roles by law in 1948. This law was lifted in 1994 for aviation roles, and completely in 2013, such that women can serve in nearly all positions in the US military. Finally, homosexuals have been recognized as service members since the Clinton era through a policy of Don't Ask, Don't Tell, and then officially after the Obama administration's repeal of that law.

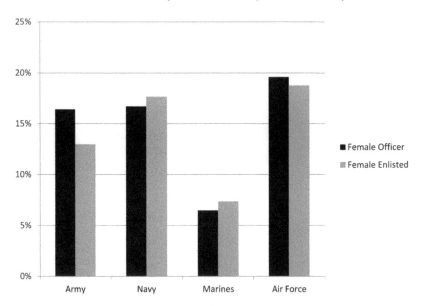

Figure 6.2 Percent Women by Branch and Rank 2012
Compiled with data from the Defense Manpower Data Center (https://www.dmdc.osd.
mil/appj/dwp/dwp_reports.jsp)

The expansion of the military to include ever-greater numbers of minorities and women is illustrated in the Figures 6.2 to 6.4. What should be noted is that the expansion of armed forces to include these groups has not occurred evenly. Across the service branches there is wide variation in the numbers of minorities and women serving. Currently Blacks are overrepresented across the military, but particularly in the Army, while Latinos are underrepresented across the board. Women are increasingly serving in the military, with just over 15 percent of the current force comprising women. Of those women, 34 percent are Black, almost three times their civilian percentage. Note the increasing number of minorities[11] at the officer level since the early 1990s. There is no official census of homosexuals serving in the military at this time, but estimates run at 2.5 percent (Segal and Segal 2004; Defense Manpower Data Center 2010).

The consolidation of the military is seen in four different areas: family history, geographic representation, political orientation,

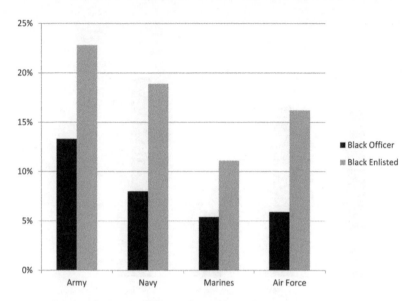

Figure 6.3 Percent African-American by Branch and Rank 2012
Compiled with data from the Defense Manpower Data Center (https://www.dmdc.osd.
mil/appj/dwp/dwp_reports.jsp)

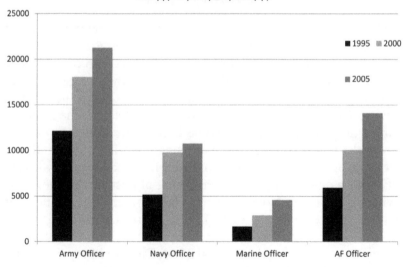

Figure 6.4 Non-White Officer by Branch
Compiled with data from the Defense Manpower Data Center (https://www.dmdc.osd.
mil/appj/dwp/dwp_reports.jsp)

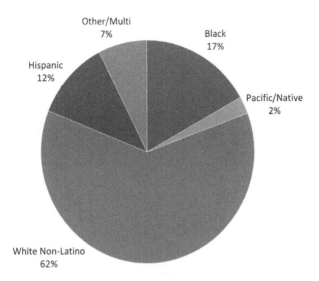

Figure 6.5 Ethnic/Race Composition 2012
Compiled with data from the Defense Manpower Data Center
(https://www.dmdc.osd.mil/appj/dwp/dwp_reports.jsp)

and socioeconomic status. Following the advent of the AVF the greatest predictor in serving in the military is having a family member who has also served. Relatedly, the greatest predictor of *not* serving is having a college-educated parent (Segal and Segal 2004) (see below). The American South and rural households contribute the largest share of men and women to the military. However, a complicating factor is the geographical location of the largest US military bases in the South. The southern contribution can be explained through the fact that the region has a greater share of eligible recruits – young males from military families. The next largest share of enlistments is from the North Central region, with the remaining military population drawn from the West and Northeast regions (Defense Manpower Data Center 2010).[12] There is some evidence that current service men and women are more politically conservative. There are greater numbers of service members who are identifying as Republican today than in previous times (Holsti 1998; Urben 2010; Pew Research Center

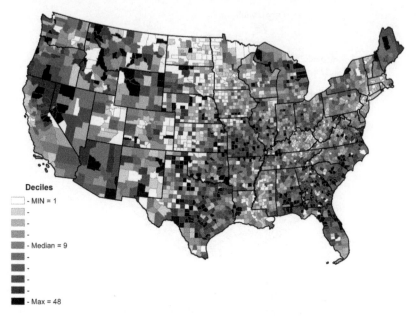

Figure 6.6 Average Annual Army Recruitment per 10,000 Residents, ages 18-45
Source: Authors' calculations from US Army Accessions Command Data (2009-2011) and US Census (2010)

2011). This is difficult to measure, however, given that previously political affiliation was not asked of enlistees. Furthermore, there is some evidence that people with service records, when asked specific questions of national policy, are no more conservative as a group than their non-serving compatriots (Joyner 2012).

The socio-economic representation in the military is a very contentious issue. Some studies indicate an over-representation of middle and upper class families across the entire military (Kane 2005). When we disaggregate the numbers by branch and type of service, however, the picture is quite different. Analyzing casualty and fatality rates over the past decade, other authors indicate that the middle third of the income distribution is over-represented while the two tails (the lowest income and especially the wealthiest) are underrepresented (Kriner and Shen 2010).

What does all of this change and consolidation mean? The

greatest topic of discussion today is over the so-called civil–military gap. Scholars have argued that a serious cultural gap is developing between the civilian and service populations, with, at worst, a sense of disdain forming between the two (Ricks 1997b; Cohen 2000; Feaver and Kohn 2000; Rahbek-Clemmensen et al. 2012). There are also claims of a decoupling of citizenship from service (Roth-Douquet and Schaeffer 2006), the very foundation of much of the creative effects of war as argued in this book. What may be more troubling, however, is the increasing "drift" seen between military and non-military families, with the former demonstrating increasing endogamy and the latter increasingly distanced from any notion of military service (Pew Research Center 2011; Eikenberry and Kennedy 2013).

Indeed, there is some evidence of change in this direction. While standing militaries were minuscule at the founding of the country, there is clear political and legal evidence that the founders of the country expected service to be a duty of citizenship when necessary (Dethloff and Shenk 2011). There is a clear decline of military participation of the elite since World War II. The current Congressional service history is only one third of what it used to be: in 1969, 70 percent of Congressmen had a service record whereas today only one quarter do (Zillman 2006). However, there is no evidence of a difference in political decision-making with respect to having a service record (Bianco 2005).

The argument for the civilian–military gap largely rests on the relationship between economic and social elites and the armed forces. With the end of the draft, the assumption has been that elites are no longer forced to participate in the military anywhere near what their previous participation was (Roth-Douquet and Schaeffer 2006). However, Bailey (2009) has convincingly demonstrated that the draft in the United States, officially called Selective Service, was, in fact, selective. Since the draft in the Civil War through the modern draft of World War II, there were always concessions for specific populations, usually the upper class. During the Civil War, men could simply buy their way out of service with either cash (in the North) or a slave (in the South) (Chambers 1999). During the second World War concessions were made for what was considered the needs of the home front: students and doctors, and for a considerable time married men with children, were exempted from service. This is all to say that elites have long found ways to limit their participation among the rabble of the military.

These developments – the decline of Western imperial control, the rise of irregular forces in conflict, and the changing face of military service – we argue are hallmarks of the future of warfare in the world. Certainly we have seen how irregular forces with negligible military power in Afghanistan and Iraq have been able to maintain long-term engagement with the United States, indisputably the greatest military power on the planet. Where this will lead us remains to be seen. We have argued that social structure has been affected by military conflicts; what we do not know yet is how these changes in war will change the nature of society in the decades to come.

Conclusion

The writers and likely readers of this book have the historical and biographical fortune of living in a world where violence, much less massive military aggression, happens in other places to other peoples or in other times. The modern world has been created, at least in part, by war, yet we now treat it as an aberration. In the United States, we publicly honor those who have served in uniform while not desiring to know much about their experiences, addressing many of their needs, or considering why their service may have been necessary. In our universities, significant numbers of students and scholars can spend their entire tenure without considering this form of human interaction or knowing very much about it except that they would like to avoid it.

This book hopes to bring war back into the classroom and into scholarly debates. We do not seek to answer all of the questions that have been asked about war, but rather we tried to clarify a set of points we consider critical.

First, we argue that war is historically, culturally, and geographically quite common. This is not an exception to human behavior that can be explained by outliers and peculiarities, but rather a fundamental part of what organized societies do. We go further and argue against the too simple notion of war being "uncivilized," but rather very much part of the dynamics and structures of the last ten thousand years of human life. It is too easy to reduce war to the destruction associated with it, and not consider how that carnage is shaped by who we are, what we believe in, and how we live together. Looking at other animals, we might go so far as to say that the organized, conscious, deliberate, collective practice of war is one of the characteristics that make us human. War can only occur because it does not solely rely on violent instincts that should be contained. Rather, war is a product of social control itself and reflects and shapes our societies. War is not about our better or lesser natures, but about what we have created by coming to live together in complex societies.

The easy condemnation of war has perhaps obscured a critical sociological mystery: given how terrible these experiences are, how have so many participated, and so many willingly? There should be no question that the supposed glory of victory cannot hope to compensate for the sufferings of battle. While coercion has played an important role in delivering soldiers to the battlefield, we have too many examples of voluntary compliance to believe that we can easily explain away participation in battle as the result of some sort of cost-benefit management. Similarly, there are too many participants to assume that any significant number suffers from some psychological or biological predisposition to violence. We argue that the answer to this question lies in the kind of organizations that practice war, the values that they teach, and the bonds that they create between individuals. In this way, participating in war, rather than an expression of beastly anger, may actually rely on the very human qualities of love, altruism, and devotion to goods greater than the individual.

War has also had an historical progression from isolated encounters of individuals to total war involving the military, economic, and political mobilization of nearly the entire world. The key revolution is the creation and development of formations of soldiers and warriors that augmented their discrete destructive capacity by creating a greater whole able to deliver even more devastating power than the equivalent number of isolates. Much of success in battle seems to rely on the whole being greater than its parts. Battle formations have some forms of emergent properties whereby the collective interaction of the single agents produces a power greater than could be achieved through simple summation.

Conclusion

The interaction of this form or organization with technological developments has shaped the progress of war. The development of gunpowder and industrialization made the managerial function of war ever more important as these reduced the marginal difference made by an individual's courage. The Second World War culminated in the ultimate technological expression of war: the nuclear bomb.

While war has at times and in places involved ritualistic encounters between representatives of different groups, it has also often involved the survival of the protagonists' societies. The history of war is often one of conquest and genocide. Arguably the greatest mass killing in the history of the world occurred thanks to the expansion of a particular form of war practiced by European powers between the fifteenth and twentieth centuries. While a relatively small percentage of the resulting deaths came from battle, there can be no denying that the European conquest brought death and destruction to more millions than died in other bloodletting, such as the Mongol invasions of the thirteenth and fourteenth centuries and the world wars of the twentieth. More than any other single military event, global conquest continues to shape our economic and political reality, and much of the wars of the twenty-first century originate in the rise and decay of empires.

The book has focused on the organizational and technological developments of war and we also discuss two cases where these advancements supported mass killing. In the first, the Nazi Holocaust may be partly understood as the culmination of bureaucratic structures combined with the dehumanization of victims. Similarly, the development of bombing technology created a scenario where societies could be wiped from existence with no more human agency than the push of a button. All of these cases would indicate that both organizational and technological models may be adapted for military uses that contradict any notion of political rationality.

In addition to its destructive outcomes, we also noted that war also has helped build our contemporary world. The evidence linking war to the contemporary political order of nominal democratic states, composed of citizens believing in some collective identity is overwhelming. We are very much an institutional product of war and questions of its disappearance must also wonder what kind of social collective device would take its place.

What then of war? We argue that the progress of war has not been toward decreasing violence, but just the opposite. Certainly through the twentieth century, the ability of wars to annihilate populations and destroy civilizations has grown exponentially. But war has also been a surprising handmaiden to civilization. Whatever the specific causal mechanism, there is little doubt that we observe significant transformations in the delivery of violence with equally dramatic changes in social structure. War and society have both become larger and more complex.

The last few decades present new paradoxes of war. On the one hand, we have not had a repeat of the massive bloodletting of the World Wars. On the other, military and political violence has increased in many parts of the world. We have emphasized the changes in the aggregation of power associated with war. On the one hand, those at the top of the bellic pyramid can now deliver such levels of destruction as to make the means unusable. On the other hand, the democratization of armament technology has also meant that groups no longer require the kind of organization and cohesion to deliver massive death. The result seems to be a world where war is omnipresent, yet unfamiliar to most. The US, for example, has been at war for almost fifteen years, yet it is hard to perceive it in the everyday lives of the vast majority of Americans. We have called this phenomenon the return of the warrior. The fighting is still taking place, but in discrete places, by small numbers of people. The major question might not be the future of war, but the future of society now lacking this fundamental mechanism in its very construction.

Notes

Introduction

1 As a short survey, this book cannot touch upon all of the facets of the sociology of war, much less summarize the entire literature on war. Other excellent surveys of the sociology of war include Malešević (2010) and Wimmer (2014). For a discussion of war and sociological theory, see Joas (2003).

I The Nature of War

1 Russell (1917; 2007) and Walzer ([1977] 2000) are classic arguments against war. Grayling (2006) provides an argument against area bombing, a common practice in war since the Second World War. Reichberg et al. (2006) provide a sound collection of readings on arguments for and against war.

2 We thank our colleagues at Princeton for their help with this. For example, Old Saxon *werran*, Old High German *werran*, and German *verwirren* all mean "to confuse, perplex," and stem from the Proto-Indo-European *wers- (1) "to confuse, mix up."

3 For arguments about the *decreasing* casualties of conflict as a proportion of the global population and decreasing levels of violence, see Morris (2014) and Pinker (2011).

4 Massey (2005) highlights the four types of social relationships that exist across all cultures and times: communal sharing, equality matching, authority ranking, and market pricing (87–9).

5 Such agreement between warring parties, the "the rules of war," become particularly evident through their absence. States fighting guerilla and terrorist forces often note the lack of adherence to standard rules of engagement, such as use of uniforms or the prohibition against civilians as explicit targets.

6   Max Weber, a German thinker at the turn of the twentieth century who is a foundational figure in sociology and economics, first argued that the definition of a state (in the international political sense) was one that had the "monopoly on the legitimate use of physical force" ([1919b] 1946, 82–3).

7   This section on gender and war draws heavily on Joshua Goldstein's *War and Gender* (2001), perhaps the best and most comprehensive book-length treatment on the topic.

8   In particular, see Wilson ([1975] 2000; [1978] 1982). For a list of sociobiological sources, see p. 52 fn 91 in J. S. Goldstein (2001).

9   Another way of looking at the same pattern might also come to the conclusion that since men are less relatively valuable for reproduction, they are also expendable.

10 Recent scholarship argues for evidence of interpersonal violence as early as the Middle Pleistocene, 430,000 years ago. See Sala et al. (2015).

11 There is another aspect of this debate, focusing on whether war developed endogenously in each locale or whether some other group imported it. See Ferguson (2008).

12 See the special issue of *Science*, Vol. 336, May 2012 for a summary of these arguments.

2 War of the Warrior

1   Given the male preponderance in war, we will consistently use male pronouns unless dealing with the specific role of women.

2   The "tooth" being the forces facing combat, and the "tail" being all of the people involved in logistics and support. Generally speaking, most people involved in war do not face direct combat situations. Thanks to the transformation of the services and the privatization of many support functions, the figure for Iraq among US personnel is probably closer to World War II levels (McGrath 2007).

3   What follows is culled from years of reading through memoirs, biographies, and journalistic account of war. For the some of the best overviews with focus on the World Wars, see Keegan (1976), Ellis (1980), Keegan and Holmes (1985), Holmes (1986), Fussell (1989b), Grossman (1995; 2008), Hynes (1997), Gray (1998), Audoin-Rouzeau and Becker (2003), Watson (2009), Kershaw (2011), Stephenson (2012), and Rose (2015). For accounts on more recent wars, see Wright (2004), Campbell (2009), Finkel (2009), and Junger (2010), and compare with Borovik (1990).

4   A cartoon from *Punch* magazine in 1917 shows a soldier writing a note and progressively asking, "wot day . . . month . . . year" it is ("Punch Cartoons on WW1, The Great War | PUNCH Magazine Cartoon Archive," n.d.).

5   Beginning with the twentieth century, militaries have become more proficient and proactive in plying soldiers (and especially pilots) with "go pills," usually

dextroamphetamine, to make sure that they can operate for the necessary 12 to 24 hours needed in some operations.

6 In three days of Gettysburg, for example, 81 percent of Union soldiers and 76 percent of Confederates escaped unhurt, and 94 percent of those who faced combat in Vietnam survived. Even on the first day of the Somme, widely understood as a particularly bloody and fatal battle, a British soldier had a four-in-five chance of surviving (Stephenson 2012).

7 Even legendary moments of contemporary individual bravery such as Dunkirk or the Battle of Britain included sailors refusing to sail or pilots turning back because of "engine trouble."

8 The term is of Malay origin and has been used to described the behavior of males (it appears to be extremely sex and gender specific) who are in a prolonged state of rage and who engage in a murderous frenzy. As a sign that characterizations of brutality are socially constructed, note that the term was picked up by British colonial authorities and used to described both the behavior of animals and of native peoples, but not of imperial soldiers. The literature on the psychological and cultural phenomenon of running amok is vast. For example, see Carr and Tan (1976), Spores (1988), and Hatta (1996).

9 For an excellent discussion of these issues in World War I, see Winter (2014, 559–638).

10 Atrocity has no precise scientific definition. We define atrocity as particularly destructive group violence that has no instrumental purpose in war. We discuss examples of atrocity below.

11 The literature on the My Lai Massacre is voluminous. We are drawing heavily on Goldstein et al. (1976) and Hersh (2000), and Oliver (2006).

12 The morphology of this ideal varies across cultures and times, but some aspects appear universal, especially masculinity and youth.

13 For an excellent contemporary portrayal of the attractions of war described below see Sebastian Junger's *War* (2010). For detailed analysis of why soldiers fight see McPherson (1997), Costa and Kahn (2008), and Reese (2011).

14 Such sentiments might also apply to larger groups of men, as seems to be the case with the devotion to individual British regiments or to the US Marine Corps. A particularly interesting form of collective cohesion is the case of the French Foreign Legion. Founded in 1831, this unit often consisted of those who had previously broken social and political taboos and who owed little obvious loyalty to France. Yet, the bravery and steadfastness of the unit are legendary no matter whom they are fighting (Porch 1991). Sledge (2007) gives an excellent firsthand account of the bonds between fighting men.

15 From the nineteenth-century English poet Percy Bysshe Shelley's poem, "Queen Mab." Full text is available at https://www.marxists.org/archive/shelley/1813/queen-mab.htm.

3 War of Armies

1 World history and legend is filled with examples. David and Goliath, Hector and Ajax, and Miyamoto Musashi and Sasaki Kojiro are three that are prominent.
2 For a fascinating examination of urban development, elite power, and economic, religious, and social institutions in Europe and the Mediterranean civilizations that touch on many of these themes but during the medieval and following centuries, see Arrighi (2010).
3 The major exception in this pattern may be the Harappan civilization of 2500–2000 BCE, which featured surplus agricultural production, cities, and commerce, but where evidence for both war making and social hierarchy appears to be absent.
4 For more on the revolutions in military practice and particularly on cavalry and infantry developments, see Morris (2014).
5 The very notion of duty was at the core of Roman identity. Perhaps no two works provide as good a contrast of the "heroic" vs. "duty bound" war ethos than the *Iliad* and the *Aeneid*.
6 There is an extensive debate in the literature regarding the degree to which gunpowder was the heart of the tactical and strategic revolution of the seventeenth century. See Parker (1995), Mcneill (1989), and Parrott (2012). For a comparison across the globe during this period see Black (1999).
7 For a discussion of how art portrays war in different periods see Paret (1997) and Rabb (2011).
8 An argument could also be made for the Thirty Years War (P. H. Wilson 2009).
9 The global struggle between France and Britain in the eighteenth century might also be considered the first "world" war.
10 The relative peace enjoyed by Latin America deserves much greater study. Even if we count intra-state violence, the lack of major conflict during the century is astounding (Centeno 2002).
11 For an exhaustive narrative history of the European war from the US perspective see the trilogy by Rick Atkinson (2002; 2007; 2013).

4 War of Societies

1 Victor Davis Hanson (2002) argues that these four elements are not, in fact, the source of Western hegemony, but instead principles of democracy, freedom, and innovation rooted in Greco-Roman culture are the explanatory factors.
2 These above three rationales could also be used to explain the Islamic gunpowder empires of the fifteenth through eighteenth centuries.
3 Critical texts in the literature of genocide include Staub (1989), Fein (1993), and Jones (2011).

4 This is not to deny the parallel suffering of other groups at the hands of the Nazis, but there is no questioning the Nazis' central obsession with the Jews.
5 From the Hebrew, meaning "the disaster," or "the catastrophe." The term *shoah* was used early on when talking about the events described here; the term Holocaust came into usage after the end of the war.
6 The speech merits reading for an appreciation of the particular combination of insanity and propriety expressed: http://www.holocaust-history.org/himmler-poznan/speech-text.shtml
7 We have been unable to locate even an estimate of the personnel working in the various camps. We do know, however, that while the concentration camps were known about, the Nazi regime tried to keep the death camps a secret.
8 Often cited, few have read the entire text of his speech, which can be found here: http://hansard.millbanksystems.com/commons/1932/nov/10/internatio nal-affairs#S5CV0270P0_19321110_HOC_284. It is an illuminating statement of the political and public attitudes during the Second World War.
9 However, compared to incredible numbers of fatalities on the Eastern front, with its thirty million-plus deaths in less than four years, the destruction in Japan in August 1945 was not exceptional.
10 The proliferation of nuclear weapons in the past thirty years and the scenarios in which they might be used has kept this discussion quite relevant.

5 How Wars Build

1 Portions of the material for this chapter have been adapted from Centeno (2010).
2 See also Morris (2014).
3 The Peace of Westphalia, signed by the major European powers in 1648, granted territorial and political sovereignty to nation states, to the exclusion of others. While today it may seem self-evident that states alone rule themselves and have specific borders, this is a relatively recent historic development. This begins the era of nation states and the global political system we currently live in.
4 And vice versa. See Brauer and Van Tuyll (2008).
5 The debates on the relationship between war and nationalism are summarized in Van Evera (1994) and Malešević (2011). The arguments and evidence can be further explored in Hall and Malešević (2013) and Wimmer (2002, 2013). On how defeat can create nationalism see Schivelbusch (2003).
6 The male monopoly and the fight over it have also been defined by war. See Gullace (2002).
7 These ceremonial approbations can often take a life of their own. Stalin supposedly had to change the 100 percent vote noted in an election of the 1940s in order to make the results more believable.

8 For an exhaustive analysis of experience in war and nutrition see Collingham (2012).

6 War and Society in the Twenty-First Century

1 Few have been able to accurately predict what shape war will take in the era of modern technology; we are wise enough to remain skeptical about military futures with respect to technological developments.

2 See the *SIPRI Yearbook* (2015) and the *State of the World Atlas* (D. Smith 2008). For detailed lists see "Global Conflict Tracker," n.d.; "Wars in the World," n.d.

3 In this section we focus largely on the warrior in insurgency. For the "rich army" version see last section in this chapter.

4 For analyses of the frustration this may cause among more traditional powers see see Turchin (2007), Lifton (2003), Bacevich (2008).

5 The literature on the topic of insurgency is vast, but contemporary accounts include Nagl (2005), Hammes (2006), Moyar (2009), and Kilcullen (2010).

6 This begs the question: just as strategic bombing failed to crush the spirits of World War II civilians, does guerilla warfare fail to destroy the home support of extended wars? Time will tell whether the outcomes of the US wars in Iraq and Afghanistan differ from Vietnam in this way.

7 This phrase as a military strategy began with the British response to the Malayan uprising in 1952, and its use has continued today. For a brief time-line of its use, see Dickinson (2009).

8 What follows is an illustrative summary of imperial decline. Rich literatures exist for each of these events and for the history of European empires more broadly, and they simply cannot be engaged here. The sources provided are representative. For a general overview of the end of empires after World War II, see T. Smith (1975) and Chamberlain (1985).

9 See, however, Kilcullen (2013), who argues that conflict and war are coming "out of the mountains" and increasingly into urban areas. He argues that the future targets of conflict and violence will increasingly be the mass urbanized areas of the world.

10 The volunteer model has become the norm in much of the world and is standard in the richest parts. The most prominent exception to this pattern is Russia. While China has nominal conscription, its military is essentially fully volunteer.

11 US Department of Defense reporting changed after 2005, when Hispanics of whatever race were no longer recorded as minorities. The total number of minorities continued to grow, however, even with different categories indicating that the trend is continuing.

12 For a statistical analysis explaining military service see Abascal and Centeno (forthcoming).

References

Abascal, Maria, and Miguel Centeno. Forthcoming. "The Geography of American Patriotism." Manuscript in preparation.

Adams, Julia. 1996. "Principals and Agents, Colonialists and Company Men: The Decay of Colonial Control in the Dutch East Indies." *American Sociological Review* 61 (1): 12–28.

Adas, Michael. 1989. *Machines as the Measure of Men: Science, Technology, and Ideologies of Western Dominance*. Ithaca: Cornell University Press.

Ames, Edward, and Richard T. Rapp. 1977. "The Birth and Death of Taxes: A Hypothesis." *Journal of Economic History* 37 (01): 161–78. doi:10.1017/S0022050700096807.

Anderson, Benedict. 2006. *Imagined Communities: Reflections on the Origin and Spread of Nationalism*. Rev. edn. New York: Verso.

Anderson, M. S. 1998. *War and Society in Europe of the Old Regime, 1618–1789*. Montreal: McGill-Queen's Press.

Anderson, Terry H. 2011. *Bush's Wars*. New York: Oxford University Press.

Archer, Christon I., John R. Ferris, Holger H. Herwig, and Timothy H. E. Travers. 2002. *World History of Warfare*. Lincoln: University of Nebraska Press.

Ardant, Gabriel. 1975. "Financial Policy and Economic Infrastructure of Modern States and Nations." In *The Formation of National States in Western Europe*, edited by Charles Tilly. Princeton, NJ: Princeton University Press.

Armstrong, Karen. 2014. *Fields of Blood: Religion and the History of Violence*. New York: Alfred A. Knopf.

Aron, Raymond. 1954. *The Century of Total War*. Garden City, NY: Doubleday.

Arrighi, Giovanni. 2010. *The Long Twentieth Century: Money, Power and the Origins of Our Times*. New and updated. London: Verso.

Atkinson, Rick. 2002. *An Army at Dawn: The War in North Africa, 1942–1943*. New York: Henry Holt & Co.

References

____. 2007. *The Day of Battle: The War in Sicily and Italy, 1943–1944*. New York: Henry Holt & Co.

____. 2013. *The Guns at Last Light: The War in Western Europe, 1944–1945*. New York: Henry Holt & Co.

Audoin-Rouzeau, Stéphane, and Annette Becker. 2003. *14–18: Understanding the Great War*. Translated by Catherine Temerson. New York: Hill and Wang.

Avant, Deborah. 2010. "War, Recruitment Systems, and Democracy." In *In War's Wake: International Conflict and the Fate of Liberal Democracy*, edited by Elizabeth Kier and Ronald R. Krebs. New York: Cambridge University Press.

Bacevich, Andrew J. 2008. *The Limits of Power: The End of American Exceptionalism*. New York: Metropolitan Books.

Bailey, Beth L. 2009. *America's Army: Making the All-Volunteer Force*. Cambridge, MA: Belknap Press of Harvard University Press.

Barnett, Clive, and Murray Low, eds. 2004. *Spaces of Democracy: Geographical Perspectives on Citizenship, Participation and Representation*. Thousand Oaks, Calif.: SAGE.

Baron-Cohen, Simon. 2011. *Zero Degrees of Empathy: A New Theory of Human Cruelty*. London; New York, NY: Allen Lane.

Barua, Pradeep. 1994. "Military Developments in India, 1750–1850." *Journal of Military History* 58 (4): 599–616. doi:10.2307/2944270.

Bauer, Thomas K., Stefan Bender, Alfredo R. Paloyo, and Christoph M. Schmidt. 2012. "Evaluating the Labor-Market Effects of Compulsory Military Service." *European Economic Review* 56 (4): 814–29. doi:10.1016/j.euroecorev.2012.02.002.

Bauer, Yehuda. 1991. "Holocaust and Genocide: Some Comparisons." In *Lessons and Legacies: The Holocaust in International Perspective*, edited by Peter Hayes and Dagmar Herzog, VII:11–22. Evanston, IL: Northwestern University Press.

BBC News. 2001. "Focus on the Slave Trade," September 3, sec. Africa. http://news.bbc.co.uk/2/hi/africa/1523100.stm.

Beevor, Antony. 1998. *Stalingrad*. New York: Viking.

____. 2009. *D-Day: The Battle for Normandy*. New York: Viking.

Bellamy, Chris. 2007. *Absolute War: Soviet Russia in the Second World War*. New York: Alfred A. Knopf.

Bell, David Avrom. 2007. *The First Total War: Napoleon's Europe and the Birth of Warfare as We Know It*. Boston, MA: Houghton Mifflin Co.

Belloc, Hilaire. 1898. "The Modern Traveller." *Internet Archive*. https://archive.org/details/moderntraveller00belluoft.

Ben-Eliezer, Uri. 1995. "A Nation-in-Arms: State, Nation, and Militarism in Israel's First Years." *Comparative Studies in Society and History* 37 (2): 264–85. doi:10.1017/S0010417500019666.

References

Bensel, Richard Franklin. 1991. *Yankee Leviathan: The Origins of Central State Authority in America, 1859–1877*. New York: Cambridge University Press.

Bergen, Doris L. 2009. *War and Genocide*. Rowman & Littlefield Publishers.

Bermeo, Nancy. 2010. "Armed Conflict and the Durability of Electoral Democracy." In *In War's Wake: International Conflict and the Fate of Liberal Democracy*, edited by Elizabeth Kier and Ronald R. Krebs. New York: Cambridge University Press.

Berryman, Sue E. 1988. *Who Serves?: The Persistent Myth of the Under Class Army*. Boulder, CO: Westview Press.

Bianco, William T. 2005. "Last Post for 'the Greatest Generation': The Policy Implications of the Decline of Military Experience in the US Congress." *Legislative Studies Quarterly* 30 (1): 85–102.

Black, Jeremy. 1998. *Why Wars Happen*. New York: New York University Press.

———. 1999. *War in the Early Modern World, 1450–1815*. London: UCL Press.

Boehm, Christopher. 2000. "Group Selection in the Upper Palaeolithic." *Journal of Consciousness Studies* 7 (1–2): 211–15.

———. 2012. *Moral Origins: The Evolution of Virtue, Altruism, and Shame*. New York: Basic Books.

Boix, Carles. 2015. *Political Order and Inequality: Their Foundations and Their Consequences for Human Welfare*. New York: Cambridge University Press.

Bolger, Daniel P. 2014. *Why We Lost: A General's Inside Account of the Iraq and Afghanistan Wars*. Boston: Houghton Mifflin Harcourt.

Boot, Max. 2001. "The Case for American Empire. The Most Realistic Response to Terrorism Is for America to Embrace Its Imperial Role." *The Weekly Standard* 7 (5): 1–5.

———. 2006. *War Made New: Technology, Warfare, and the Course of History, 1500 to Today*. New York: Gotham Books.

———. 2013. *Invisible Armies: An Epic History of Guerrilla Warfare from Ancient Times to the Present*. New York: Liveright Pub. Corp.

Borhi, László. 2004. *Hungary in the Cold War, 1945–1956 between the United States and the Soviet Union*. New York: Central European University Press.

Borovik, Artem. 1990a. *The Hidden War: A Russian Journalist's Account of the Soviet War in Afghanistan*. New York: Atlantic Monthly Press.

Bourke, Joanna. 1999. *An Intimate History of Killing: Face-to-Face Killing in Twentieth-Century Warfare*. New York: Basic Books.

Bowles, Samuel, and Herbert Gintis. 2011. *A Cooperative Species Human Reciprocity and Its Evolution*. Princeton, NJ: Princeton University Press.

Bracken, Paul J. 1983. *The Command and Control of Nuclear Forces*. New Haven: Yale University Press.

Braithwaite, Rodric. 2011. *Afgantsy: The Russians in Afghanistan, 1979–89*. New York: Oxford University Press.

References

Brauer, Jurgen, and Hubert P. Van Tuyll. 2008. *Castles, Battles, and Bombs: How Economics Explains Military History*. Chicago: University of Chicago Press.

"Breaking the Silence: Israeli Soldiers Talk about the Occupied Territories." n.d. *Breaking the Silence*. http://www.breakingthesilence.org.il/.

Browning, Christopher R. 1992. *The Path to Genocide: Essays on Launching the Final Solution*. New York: Cambridge University Press.

Bryant, G. J. 2004. "Asymmetric Warfare: The British Experience in Eighteenth-Century India." *Journal of Military History* 68 (2): 431–69. doi:10.1353/jmh.2004.0019.

Buchanan, Albert Russell. 1977. *Black Americans in World War II*. Santa Barbara, CA: Clio Books.

Buchan, Bruce. 2011. "Civilized Fictions: Warfare and Civilization in Enlightenment Thought." *Alternatives: Global, Local, Political* 36 (1): 64–71. doi:10.2307/23211187.

Bull, Hedley. (1977) 2012. *The Anarchical Society: A Study of Order in World Politics*. Basingstoke: Palgrave Macmillan.

Burbank, Jane, and Frederick Cooper. 2010. *Empires in World History: Power and the Politics of Difference*. Princeton, NJ: Princeton University Press.

Burleigh, Michael. 2009. *Blood and Rage: A Cultural History of Terrorism*. New York: Harper & Row.

_____ . 2011. *Moral Combat: A History of World War II*. New York: Harper & Row.

Callwell, C. E. (1896) 1996. *Small Wars. Their Principles and Practice*. Lincoln: University of Nebraska Press.

Calvocoressi, Peter, Guy Wint, and R. John Pritchard. 1999. *The Penguin History of the Second World War*. London: Penguin.

Campbell, Donovan. 2009. *Joker One: A Marine Platoon's Story of Courage, Sacrifice, and Brotherhood*. New York: Random House.

Cann, John P. 1997. *Counterinsurgency in Africa the Portuguese Way of War, 1961–1974*. Westport, CT: Greenwood Press.

Carr, John E., and Eng Kong Tan. 1976. "In Search of the True Amok: Amok as Viewed with the Malay Culture." *American Journal of Psychiatry* 133 (11): 1295–99. doi:10.1176/ajp.133.11.1295.

Carr, Matthew. 2007. *The Infernal Machine: A History of Terrorism*. New York: New Press.

"Casualty Status." 2015. US Department of Defense. http://www.defense.gov/news/casualty.pdf.

Centeno, Miguel Angel. 2002. *Blood and Debt: War and the Nation-State in Latin America*. Pennsylvania State University Press.

_____ . 2010. "Concluding Reflections: What Wars Do." In *In War's Wake: International Conflict and the Fate of Liberal Democracy*, edited by

References

Elizabeth Kier and Ronald R. Krebs, 253–70. New York: Cambridge University Press.

Cerulo, Karen A. 1995. *Identity Designs: The Sights and Sounds of a Nation*. New Brunswick, NJ: Rutgers University Press.

Chaliand, Gérard. 1994. *The Art of War in World History: From Antiquity to the Nuclear Age*. Berkeley: University of California Press.

Chamberlain, Muriel Evelyn. 1985. *Decolonization: The Fall of the European Empires*. New York: Basil Blackwell.

Chambers, John Whiteclay, ed. 1999. *The Oxford Companion to American Military History*. New York: Oxford University Press.

Chari, Tendai. 2010. "Representation or Misrepresentation? The New York Times's Framing of the 1994 Rwanda Genocide." *African Identities* 8 (4): 333–49. doi:10.1080/14725843.2010.513242.

Chivers, C. J. 2010. *The Gun*. New York: Simon & Schuster.

Christensen, Thomas J. 2015. *The China Challenge: Shaping the Choices of a Rising Power*. New York: W. W. Norton & Co.

Christian, David. 2004. *Maps of Time: An Introduction to Big History*. Berkeley: University of California Press.

Churchill, Winston. 1940. "Blood, Toil, Tears and Sweat." *The Churchill Center*. May 13. http://www.winstonchurchill.org/resources/speeches/1940-the-finest-hour/blood-toil-tears-and-sweat.

Clausewitz, Carl von. (1832) 1984. *On War*. Translated by Michael Howard and Peter Paret. Princeton, NJ: Princeton University Press.

Clendinnen, Inga. 1985. "The Cost of Courage in Aztec Society." *Past and Present*, no. 107 (May): 44–89. doi:10.2307/650706.

Clever, Molly, and David R. Segal. 2013. "The Demographics of Military Children and Families." *The Future of Children* 23 (2): 13–39. doi:10.2307/23595618.

Clodfelter, Micheal. 2008. *Warfare and Armed Conflicts: A Statistical Encyclopedia of Casualty and Other Figures, 1497–2007*. Jefferson, NC: Mcfarland.

Cohen, Eliot A. 2000. "Why the Gap Matters." *The National Interest*, no. 61 (October): 38–48. doi:10.2307/42897241.

Coker, Christopher. 2004. *The Future of War: The Re-Enchantment of War in the Twenty-First Century*. Malden, MA: Blackwell Publishing.

Colley, Linda. 1992. *Britons: Forging the Nation, 1707–1837*. New Haven: Yale University Press.

Collingham, Lizzie. 2012. *The Taste of War: World War II and the Battle for Food*. New York: Penguin Press.

Collins, Randall. 2008. *Violence: A Micro-Sociological Theory*. Princeton: Princeton University Press.

Costa, Dora L., and Matthew E. Kahn. 2008. *Heroes and Cowards: The Social Face of War*. Princeton: Princeton University Press.

References

Cottam, Kazimiera Janina. 1983. *Soviet Airwomen in Combat in World War II*. Manhattan, KS: Military Affairs/Aerospace Historian.

Craig, Campbell. 2003. *Glimmer of a New Leviathan: Total War in the Realism of Niebuhr, Morgenthau, and Waltz*. New York: Columbia University Press.

Crane, Stephen. 1998. *The Red Badge of Courage and Other Stories*. New York: Oxford University Press.

Crawford, Neta. 2013. *Accountability for Killing: Moral Responsibility for Collateral Damage in America's Post-9/11 Wars*. New York: Oxford University Press.

Daggett, Stephen. 2010. "Costs of Major US Wars." RS22926. Washington, DC: Congressional Research Service. http://fas.org/sgp/crs/natsec/RS22926.pdf.

Daly, Martin, and Margo Wilson. 1994. "Evolutionary Psychology of Male Violence." In *Male Violence*, 253–88. London: Routledge.

Davies, Norman. 2006. *Europe at War: 1939–1945, No Simple Victory*. London: Macmillan.

Davis, Paul K. 2013. *Masters of the Battlefield: Great Commanders From the Classical Age to the Napoleonic Era*. 1st edn. New York: Oxford University Press.

DeBruyne, Nese F., and Anne Leland. 2015. "American War and Military Operations Casualties: Lists and Statistics." RL32492. Washington, DC: Congressional Research Service.

Defense Manpower Data Center (2010) Population Representation in the Military Services: Fiscal Year 2010 Summary Report.

Dethloff, Henry C., and Gerald E. Shenk, eds. 2011. *Citizen and Soldier: A Sourcebook on Military Service and National Defense from Colonial America to the Present*. Routledge.

Diamond, Jared M. 1999. *Guns, Germs, and Steel: The Fates of Human Societies*. New York: W. W. Norton & Co.

Dickinson, Elizabeth. 2009. "A Bright Shining Slogan." *Foreign Policy*, August 22. http://foreignpolicy.com/2009/08/22/a-bright-shining-slogan/.

Douhet, Giulio. (1921) 1983. *The Command of the Air*. Washington, D.C.: Office of Air Force History.

Dower, John W. 1986. *War without Mercy: Race and Power in the Pacific War*. New York: Pantheon Books.

Dudziak, Mary L. 2000. *Cold War Civil Rights: Race and the Image of American Democracy*. Princeton, NJ: Princeton University Press.

Duffy, Michael. 1998. "World Wide War and British Expansion, 1793–1815." In *The Oxford History of the British Empire: Volume II: The Eighteenth Century*, edited by P. J. Marshall, Alaine Low, and Wm. Roger Louis. New York: Oxford University Press.

Eckhardt, William. 1990. "Civilizations, Empires, and Wars." *Journal of Peace Research* 27 (1): 9–24. doi:10.2307/423772.

References

Edgerton, Robert B. 2000. *Warrior Women: The Amazons of Dahomey and the Nature of War*. Boulder, CO: Westview Press.

Ehrenreich, Barbara. 1997. *Blood Rites: Origins and History of the Passions of War*. New York: Metropolitan Books.

Eikenberry, Karl W., and David M. Kennedy. 2013. "Americans and Their Military, Drifting Apart." *New York Times*, May 26, sec. A17. http://www.nytimes.com/2013/05/27/opinion/americans-and-their-military-drifting-apart.html?_r=0.

Elias, Norbert. (1939) 2000. *The Civilizing Process*. Blackwell Publishing.

Elliott, J. H. 1984. "The Spanish Conquest and Settlement of America." In *The Cambridge History of Latin American*, edited by Leslie Bethell, 1:147–206. New York: Cambridge University Press.

Ellis, John. 1980. *The Sharp End: The Fighting Man in World War II*. New York: Scribner.

Eltis, David, and Martin Halbert. n.d. "The Trans-Atlantic Slave Trade Database." http://www.slavevoyages.org/tast/index.faces.

Esdaile, Charles J. 2008. *Napoleon's Wars: An International History, 1803–1815*. New York: Viking.

Evans, Richard J. 2009. *The Third Reich at War*. New York: Penguin Press.

Feaver, Peter D., and Richard H. Kohn. 2000. "The Gap: Soldiers, Civilians and Their Mutual Misunderstanding." *The National Interest*, no. 61 (October): 29–37. doi:10.2307/42897240.

Feifer, Gregory. 2009. *The Great Gamble: The Soviet War in Afghanistan*. 1st edn. New York: HarperCollins.

Fein, Helen. 1993. *Genocide: A Sociological Perspective*. London; Newbury Park, Calif.: Sage Publications.

Fenichel, Otto. 1945. *The Psychoanalytic Theory of Neurosis*. New York: W. W. Norton & Co.

Ferguson, R. Brian. 2003. "The Birth of War." *Natural History* 112 (6): 28–35.

———. 2008. "War before History." In *The Ancient World at War: A Global History*, edited by Philip de Souza, 15–27. London: Thames & Hudson.

Fernandez-Kelly, Patricia. 2015. *Hero's Fight*. Princeton, NJ: Princeton University Press.

Ferrill, Arther. 1985. *The Origins of War: From the Stone Age to Alexander the Great*. New York: Thames & Hudson.

Finer, Samuel E. 1975. "State- and Nation-Building in Europe: The Role of the Military." In *The Formation of National States in Western Europe*, edited by Charles Tilly, 84–163. Princeton, NJ: Princeton University Press.

Finkel, David. 2009. *The Good Soldiers*. New York: Sarah Crichton Books/ Farrar, Straus And Giroux.

Flannery, Kent V, and Joyce Marcus. 2012. *The Creation of Inequality: How Our Prehistoric Ancestors Set the Stage for Monarchy, Slavery, and Empire*. Cambridge, Mass.; London: Harvard University Press.

References

Foster, R. F. 1989. *Modern Ireland, 1600–1972*. New York: Penguin Books.

Foucault, Michel. (1975) 1995. *Discipline and Punish: The Birth of the Prison*. Vintage Books.

Franke, Volker C. 2000. "Duty, Honor, Country: The Social Identity of West Point Cadets." *Armed Forces and Society* 26 (2): 175–202. doi:10.1177/0095327X0002600202.

Frank, Philipp. (1947) 2002. *Einstein: His Life and Times*. New York: Da Capo Press.

Freedman, Lawrence. 1981. *The Evolution of Nuclear Strategy*. New York: St. Martin's Press.

French, Shannon E. 2003. *The Code of the Warrior: Exploring Warrior Values Past and Present*. Lanham, MD: Rowman & Littlefield Publishers.

Friedländer, Saul. 1989. "The 'Final Solution': On the Unease in Historical Interpretation." *History and Memory* 1 (2): 61–76. doi:10.2307/25618581.

———. 2007. *The Years of Extermination: Nazi Germany and the Jews, 1939–1945*. New York: HarperCollins Publishers.

Friedrich, Jörg. 2006. *The Fire: The Bombing of Germany, 1940–1945*. New York: Columbia University Press.

Fry, Douglas P. 2007. *Beyond War: The Human Potential for Peace*. New York: Oxford University Press.

Fry, Douglas P., and Patrik Söderberg. 2013. "Lethal Aggression in Mobile Forager Bands and Implications for the Origins of War." *Science* 341 (6143): 270–73. doi:10.1126/science.1235675.

Fussell, Paul. 1989a. *War-Time: Understanding and Behavior in the Second World War*. New York: Oxford University Press.

———. 1989b. "The Real War, 1939–45." *The Atlantic Monthly*, August. https://www.theatlantic.com/past/docs/unbound/bookauth/battle/fussell.htm.

———. 1991. *The Norton Book of Modern War*. New York: W. W. Norton & Co.

Gabriel, Richard A. 2005. *Empires at War: A Chronological Encyclopedia*. Westport, CT: Greenwood Press.

Galison, Peter. 1994. "The Ontology of the Enemy: Norbert Wiener and the Cybernetic Vision." *Critical Inquiry* 21 (1): 228–66. doi:10.2307/1343893.

Gall, Carlotta. 2014. *The Wrong Enemy: America in Afghanistan, 2001–2014*. Boston: Houghton Mifflin Harcourt.

García Luis, Julio, ed. 2008. *Cuban Revolution Reader: A Documentary History of Fidel Castro's Revolution*. New York: Ocean Press.

Gellner, Ernest. (1983) 2006. *Nations and Nationalism*. 2nd edn. New Perspectives on the Past (Basil Blackwell Publisher). Malden, MA: Blackwell Publishing.

Gelman, Andrew. 2013. "How Many Vietnam Veterans Are Still Alive?" *New York Times*, March 25. http://www.nytimes.com/2013/03/26/science/how-many-vietnam-veterans-are-still-alive.html.

References

"General: It's 'Fun to Shoot Some People.'" 2005. *CNN.com*. February 4. http://www.cnn.com/2005/US/02/03/general.shoot/.

Gibson, James William. 1986. *The Perfect War: Technowar in Vietnam*. Boston: Atlantic Monthly Press.

Gil-White, Francisco J. 2001. "Are Ethnic Groups Biological 'Species' to the Human Brain? Essentialism in Our Cognition of Some Social Categories." *Current Anthropology* 42 (4): 515–53. doi:10.1086/321802.

Glasser, Ronald J. 2006. *Wounded: Vietnam to Iraq*. New York: G. Braziller.

Gleditsch, Nils Petter. 2013. "The Decline of War." *International Studies Review* 15 (3): 396–419. doi:10.1111/misr.12031.

"Global Conflict Tracker." n.d. *Council on Foreign Relations*. http://www.cfr.org/globalconflicttracker/.

Goffman, Erving. 1961. *Asylums: Essays on the Social Situation of Mental Patients and Other Inmates*. New York: Doubleday.

Goldberg, Matthew S. 2014. "Updated Death and Injury Rates of US Military Personnel During the Conflicts in Iraq and Afghanistan." Working Paper 2014–08. Washington, D.C.: Congressional Budget Office. https://www.fas.org/sgp/crs/natsec/RL32492.pdf.

Goldhagen, Daniel Jonah. 1996. *Hitler's Willing Executioners: Ordinary Germans and the Holocaust*. New York: Knopf: Distributed by Random House.

Goldstein, Joseph, Burke Marshall, and Jack Schwartz. 1976. *The My Lai Massacre and Its Cover-up : Beyond the Reach of Law?: The Peers Commission Report*. New York: Free Press.

Goldstein, Joshua S. 2001. *War and Gender: How Gender Shapes the War System and Vice Versa*. New York: Cambridge University Press.

Goldsworthy, Adrian Keith. 2003. *The Complete Roman Army*. New York: Thames & Hudson.

Gordin, Michael D. 2007. *Five Days in August: How World War II Became a Nuclear War*. Princeton, NJ: Princeton University Press.

Gordin, Michael D. 2009. *Red Cloud at Dawn: Truman, Stalin, and the End of the Atomic Monopoly*. Picador.

Gordon, Michael R, and Bernard E Trainor. 2006. *Cobra II: The Inside Story of the Invasion and Occupation of Iraq*. New York: Pantheon Books.

Gourevitch, Philip. 1998. *We Wish to Inform You That Tomorrow We Will Be Killed with Our Families: Stories from Rwanda*. New York: Farrar, Straus, and Giroux.

Grant, Ulysses S. (1885) 1999. *Personal Memoirs*. New York: Modern Library.

Gray, J. Glenn. 1998. *The Warriors: Reflections on Men in Battle*. Lincoln, NE: Bison Books.

Grayling, A. C. 2006. *Among the Dead Cities: The History and Moral Legacy of the WWII Bombing of Civilians in Germany and Japan*. New York: Walker & Co.

References

Grossman, Dave. 1995. *On Killing: The Psychological Cost of Learning to Kill in War and Society*. Boston: Little, Brown.

Grossman, Dave, and Loren W. Christensen. 2008. *On Combat: The Psychology and Physiology of Deadly Conflict in War and in Peace*. 3rd edn. [Illinois]: Warrior Science Pub.

Guilaine, Jean, and Jean Zammit. 2005. *The Origins of War: Violence in Prehistory*. Malden, MA: Blackwell Publishing.

Guilmartin, John Francis. 1991. "The Cutting Edge: An Analysis of the Spanish Invasion and Overthrow of the Inca Empire, 1532–1539." In *Transatlantic Encounters: Europeans and Andeans in the Sixteenth Century*, edited by Kenneth J. Andrien and Rolena Adorno, 40–69. Berkeley, CA: University of California Press.

Gullace, Nicoletta. 2002. *The Blood of Our Sons: Men, Women, and the Renegotiation of British Citizenship during the Great War*. New York: Palgrave Macmillan.

Hahn, Peter L. 2012. *Missions Accomplished?: The United States and Iraq since World War I*. New York: Oxford University Press.

Hall, John A., and Siniša Malešević, eds. 2013. *Nationalism and War*. New York: Cambridge University Press.

Hammes, Thomas X. 2006. *The Sling and the Stone: On War in the 21st Century*. Minneapolis, MN: Zenith.

Hampson, N. 1973. "The French Revolution and the Nationalisation of Honour." In *War and Society: Historical Essays in Honour and Memory of J. R. Western, 1928–1971*. London: Elek.

Hanson, Victor Davis. 2002. *Carnage and Culture: Landmark Battles in the Rise of Western Power*. New York: Anchor.

____. 2005. "The Roman Way of War." In *The Cambridge History of Warfare*, edited by Geoffrey Parker, 46–60. New York: Cambridge University Press.

Harris, Brice F. 2009. *America, Technology and Strategic Culture: A Clausewitzian Assessment*. New York: Routledge.

Harris, Lasana T., and Susan T. Fiske. 2006. "Dehumanizing the Lowest of the Low: Neuroimaging Responses to Extreme Out-Groups." *Psychological Science* 17 (10): 847–53. doi:10.2307/40064466.

____. 2011. "Dehumanized Perception: A Psychological Means to Facilitate Atrocities, Torture, and Genocide?" *Zeitschrift Für Psychologie/Journal of Psychology* 219 (3): 175–81. doi:10.1027/2151-2604/a000065.

Hartley, Keith. 1997. "The Economics of the Peace Dividend." *International Journal of Social Economics* 24 (1/2/3): 28–45.

Hassig, Ross. 1992. *War and Society in Ancient Mesoamerica*. Berkeley, CA: University of California Press.

Hastings, Max. 2008. *Retribution: The Battle for Japan, 1944–45*. New York: Alfred A. Knopf.

References

_____. 2011. *All Hell Let Loose: The World at War 1939–45.* London: HarperCollins.

Hatta, S. Mohamed. 1996. "A Malay Crosscultural Worldview and Forensic Review of Amok." *Australian and New Zealand Journal of Psychiatry* 30 (4): 505–10. doi:10.3109/00048679609065024.

Headrick, Daniel R. 2010. *Power over Peoples: Technology, Environments, and Western Imperialism, 1400 to the Present.* Princeton, NJ: Princeton University Press.

Herodotus. 1997. *The Histories of Herodotus.* Translated by George Rawlinson. New York: Knopf.

Herr, Michael. 1991. *Dispatches.* New York: Vintage Books.

Hersh, Seymour M. 2000. "The My Lai Massacre." In *Reporting Vietnam: American Journalism, 1959–1975,* 413–27. New York: Library of America.

Herwig, Holger H., Christon Archer, Timothy Travers, and John Ferris. 2003. *Cassell's World History of Warfare: The Global History of Warfare from Ancient Times to the Present Day.* London: Cassell.

Hilberg, Raul. 1993. *Perpetrators, Victims, Bystanders: The Jewish Catastrophe, 1933–1945.* New York: Harper Perennial.

Hiro, Dilip. 2014. *The Longest August: The Unflinching Rivalry between India and Pakistan.* New York: Nation Books.

Hirst, Paul Heywood. 2001. *War and Power in the 21st Century: The State, Military Conflict, and the International System.* Malden, MA: Blackwell Publishers.

Hoffman, David E. 2009. *The Dead Hand: The Untold Story of the Cold War Arms Race and Its Dangerous Legacy.* New York: Doubleday.

Hoffman, Philip T. 2012. "Why Was It Europeans Who Conquered the World?" *Journal of Economic History* 72 (03): 601–33. doi:10.1017/S0022050712000319.

Hoglund, Mark W., and Rebecca M. Schwartz. 2014. "Mental Health in Deployed and Nondeployed Veteran Men and Women in Comparison With Their Civilian Counterparts." *Military Medicine* 179 (1): 19–25.

Höhne, Heinz. 1969. *The Order of the Death's Head; the Story of Hitler's S.S.* 1st American edn. New York: Coward-McCann.

Hollander, John, ed. 1999. *War Poems / Selected and Edited by John Hollander.* Everyman's Library Pocket Poets. New York: A. A. Knopf.

Holmes, Richard. 1986. *Acts of War: The Behavior of Men in Battle.* New York: Free Press.

Holsti, Ole R. 1998. "A Widening Gap between the US Military and Civilian Society? Some Evidence, 1976–96." *International Security* 23 (3): 5–42. doi:10.2307/2539337.

Homans, George Caspar. 1950. *The Human Group.* New York: Harcourt, Brace & World.

References

Horne, Alistair. 1978. *A Savage War of Peace: Algeria, 1954–1962.* New York: Viking Press.

Hosek, James, and Shelley MacDermid Wadsworth. 2013. "Economic Conditions of Military Families." *The Future of Children* 23 (2): 41–59. doi:10.2307/23595619.

Hubers, Frank, and Dinand Webbink. 2015. "The Long-Term Effects of Military Conscription on Educational Attainment and Wages." *IZA Journal of Labor Economics* 4 (1): 1–16. doi:10.1186/s40172-015-0026-4.

Huntingford, F. A. 1989. "Animals Fight, But Do Not Make War." In *Aggression and War: Their Biological and Social Bases,* edited by Jo Groebel and Robert A. Hinde, 25–35. New York: Cambridge University Press.

Hynes, Samuel. 1997. *The Soldiers' Tale: Bearing Witness to Modern War.* New York: A. Lane.

Ikenberry, G. John, Michael Mastanduno, and William Curti Wohlforth, eds. 2011. *International Relations Theory and the Consequences of Unipolarity.* New York: Cambridge University Press.

Imbusch, Peter, Michel Misse, and Fernando Carrion. 2011. "Violence Research in Latin America and the Caribbean: A Literature Review." *International Journal of Conflict and Violence* 5 (1): 87–154.

Jacoby, Russell. 2011. *Bloodlust: On the Roots of Violence from Cain and Abel to the Present.* New York: Free Press.

James, William. (1910) 1995. "The Moral Equivalent of War." *Peace and Conflict: Journal of Peace Psychology* 1 (1): 17–26. doi:10.1207/s15327949pac0101_4.

Jarosz, Lucy. 1992. "Constructing the Dark Continent: Metaphor as Geographic Representation of Africa." *Geografiska Annaler. Series B, Human Geography* 74 (2): 105–15. doi:10.2307/490566.

Joas, Hans. 2003. *War and Modernity: Studies in the History of Violence in the 20th Century.* Malden, MA: Polity.

Jones, Adam. 2011. *Genocide: A Comprehensive Introduction.* 2nd edn. New York: Routledge.

Jones, Archer. 1987. *The Art of War in the Western World.* Urbana, IL: University of Illinois Press.

_____ . 2001. *The Art of War in Western World.* Reprint edn. Urbana: University of Illinois Press.

Jones, Seth G. 2009. *In the Graveyard of Empires: America's War in Afghanistan.* New York: W. W. Norton & Co.

Joyner, James. 2012. "Military Less Republican Than You Think." *Outside the Beltway.* February 12. http://www.outsidethebeltway.com/military-less-republican-than-you-think/.

Junger, Sebastian. 2010. *War.* New York: Twelve.

Kaldor, Mary. 1999. *New and Old Wars: Organized Violence in a Global Era.* 1st edn. Stanford, Calif.: Stanford University Press.

References

Kalinovsky, Artemy M. 2011. *A Long Goodbye: The Soviet Withdrawal from Afghanistan*. Cambridge, Mass: Harvard University Press.

Kane, Tim. 2005. "Who Bears the Burden? Demographic Characteristics of US Military Recruits Before and After 9/11." Center for Data Analysis Report 05–08. National Security and Defense. Heritage Foundation. http://www.heritage.org/research/reports/2005/11/who-bears-the-burden-demographic-characteristics-of-us-military-recruits-before-and-after-9-11.

Kaplan, Fred M. 1991. *The Wizards of Armageddon*. Stanford Nuclear Age Series. Stanford, Calif: Stanford University Press.

Kaplan, Robert D. 1993. *Balkan Ghosts: A Journey through History*. New York: St. Martin's Press.

Kappeler, Victor E., and Aaron E. Kappeler. 2004. "Speaking of Evil and Terrorism: The Political and Ideological Construction of a Moral Panic." In *Terrorism and Counter-Terrorism*, edited by Mathieu Deflem, 5: 175–97. Sociology of Crime, Law and Deviance. Emerald Group Publishing Limited.

Karnow, Stanley. 1983. *Vietnam: A History*. New York: Viking Press.

Karsh, Efraim. 2015. *Tail Wags the Dog: International Politics and the Middle East*. [Place of publication not identified]: Bloomsbury.

Keegan, John. 1976. *The Face of Battle*. New York: Viking Press.

____. 1988. *The Mask of Command*. New York, NY: Penguin Books.

____. 1993. *A History of Warfare*. New York: Alfred A. Knopf.

____. 1999. *The First World War*. New York: Alfred A. Knopf.

____. 2004. *The Iraq War*. New York: Alfred A. Knopf.

____. 2009. *The American Civil War: A Military History*. 1st edn. New York: Alfred A. Knopf.

Keegan, John, and Richard Holmes. 1985. *Soldiers : A History of Men in Battle*. London: Viking Press.

Keeley, Lawrence H. 1996. *War before Civilization*. New York: Oxford University Press.

Keeney, L. Douglas. 2011. *15 Minutes: General Curtis LeMay and the Countdown to Nuclear Annihilation*. New York: St. Martin's Press.

Kennedy, Paul M. 1987. *The Rise and Fall of the Great Powers: Economic Change and Military Conflict from 1500 to 2000*. New York, NY: Random House.

Kershaw, Ian. 2008. *Hitler, the Germans, and the Final Solution*. New Haven, CT: Yale University Press.

____. 2011. *The End: The Defiance and Destruction of Hitler's Germany, 1944–1945*. New York: Penguin Press.

Kiernan, Ben. 2007. *Blood and Soil: A World History of Genocide and Extermination from Sparta to Darfur*.

Kilcullen, David. 2010. *Counterinsurgency*. Oxford; New York: Oxford University Press.

____. 2013. *Out of the Mountains: The Coming Age of the Urban Guerrilla*.

References

Killingray, David. 1989. "Colonial Warfare in West Africa, 1870–1914." In *Imperialism and War: Essays in Colonial History in Asia and Africa*, edited by Jaap A. de Moor and H. L Wesseling, 146–67. Leiden: E. J. Brill.

Kiras, James D. 2006. *Special Operations and Strategy: From World War II to the War on Terrorism*. New York: Routledge.

Kolff, Dirk H. A. 1989. "The End of the Ancien Regime: Colonial War in India, 1798–1818." In *Imperialism and War: Essays in Colonial History in Asia and Africa*, edited by Jaap A. de Moor and H. L Wesseling, 22–49. Leiden: E. J. Brill.

Kolko, Gabriel. 2002. *Another Century of War?*. New York: The New Press.

Kozak, Warren. 2009. *LeMay: The Life and Wars of General Curtis LeMay*. New York: Regenery Publishers.

Kramarow, Ellen A., and Patricia N. Pastor. 2012. "The Health of Male Veterans and Nonveterans Aged 25–64: United States, 2007." NCHS Data Brief 101. US Department of Health and Human Services.

Krebs, Ronald R. 2010. "International Conflict and the Constitutional Balance: Executive Authority after War." In *In War's Wake: International Conflict and the Fate of Liberal Democracy*, edited by Elizabeth Kier and Ronald R. Krebs. New York: Cambridge University Press.

Kriner, Douglas L., and Francis X. Shen. 2010. *The Casualty Gap: The Causes and Consequences of American War-Time Inequalities*. New York: Oxford University Press.

Kuzmarov, Jeremy. 2009. *The Myth of the Addicted Army: Vietnam and the Modern War on Drugs*. Amherst, MA: University of Massachusetts Press.

Lacey, Jim, and Williamson Murray. 2013. *Moment of Battle: The Twenty Clashes That Changed the World*. New York: Bantam Books.

Lacina, Bethany, and Nils Petter Gleditsch. 2013. "The Waning of War Is Real. A Response to Gohdes and Price." *Journal of Conflict Resolution* 57 (6): 1109–27. doi:10.1177/0022002712459709.

Laqueur, Walter. 1976. *Guerrilla: A Historical and Critical Study*. Boston: Little, Brown.

Layne, Christopher. 1993. "The Unipolar Illusion: Why New Great Powers Will Rise." *International Security* 17 (4): 5–51.

Layne, Christopher, and Bradley A. Thayer. 2007. *American Empire : A Debate*. New York: Routledge.

Lazar, Susan G. 2014. "The Mental Health Needs of Military Service Members and Veterans." *Psychodynamic Psychiatry* 42 (3): 459–78.

LeBlanc, Steven A. 2003. *Constant Battles: The Myth of the Peaceful, Noble Savage*. New York: St. Martin's Press.

Lee, Chulhee. 2012. "Military Service and Economic Mobility: Evidence from the American Civil War." *Explorations in Economic History* 49 (3): 367–79. doi:10.1016/j.eeh.2012.03.001.

Lee, Dwight R., and Richard K. Vedder. 1996. "The Political Economy of the Peace Dividend." *Public Choice* 88 (1/2): 29–42. doi:10.2307/30027250.

References

Lee, Margaret Mikyung, and Ruth Ellen Wasem. 2003. "Expedited Citizenship Through Military Service: Policy and Issues." RL31884. Washington, DC: Congressional Research Service. http://www.fas.org/sgp/crs/natsec/RL31884.pdf.

Lefort, Hugues. 2014. "A Spectacular Revolution: Evolution of French Military Health Service." *Soins*, no. 786 (June): 36–40.

Lendon, J. E. 2005. *Soldiers and Ghosts: A History of Battle in Classical Antiquity.* New Haven, CT: Yale University Press.

Lenman. 1989. "The Transition to European Military Ascendancy in India, 1600–1800." In *Tools of War: Instruments, Ideas, and Institutions of Warfare, 1445–1871*, edited by John A. Lynn. Urbana, IL: University of Chicago Press.

Levy, Jack S. 1998. "The Causes of War and the Conditions of Peace." *Annual Review of Political Science* 1 (1): 139–65. doi:10.1146/annurev.polisci.1.1.139.

Lifton, Robert Jay. 2003. *Superpower Syndrome: America's Apocalyptic Confrontation with the World.* New York: Thunder's Mouth Press/Nation Books.

Lindqvist, Sven. 2001. *A History of Bombing.* New York: New Press.

Lipsky, David. 2003. *Absolutely American: Four Years at West Point.* Boston: Houghton Mifflin.

Longerich, Peter. 2010. *Holocaust: The Nazi Persecution and Murder of the Jews.* New York: Oxford University Press.

Lorenz, Konrad. 1966. *On Aggression.* New York: Harcourt, Brace & World.

Lutsky, Neil. 1995. "When Is 'Obedience' Obedience? Conceptual and Historical Commentary." *Journal of Social Issues* 51 (3): 55–65. doi:10.1111/j.1540-4560.1995.tb01334.x.

Lynn, John A. 1993. *Feeding Mars: Logistics in Western Warfare from the Middle Ages to the Present.* Boulder, CO: Westview Press.

———. 2003. *Battle: A History of Combat and Culture.* Boulder, CO: Westview Press.

———. 2005. "States in Conflict." In *The Cambridge History of Warfare*, edited by Geoffrey Parker, 167–88. New York: Cambridge University Press.

McEllistrem, Joseph E. 2004. "Affective and Predatory Violence: A Bimodal Classification System of Human Aggression and Violence." *Aggression and Violent Behavior* 10 (1): 1–30. doi:10.1016/j.avb.2003.06.002.

McGrath, John J. 2007. *The Other End of the Spear: The Tooth-to-Tail Ratio (T3R) in Modern Military Operations.* The Long War Series, Occasional Paper 23. Fort Leavenworth, KS: Combat Studies Institute Press.

MacLean, Alair, and Glen H. Elder Jr. 2007. "Military Service in the Life Course." *Annual Review of Sociology* 33 (ArticleType: research-article / Full publication date: 2007 / Copyright © 2007 Annual Reviews): 175–96. doi:10.2307/29737759.

McMahan, Jeff. 2009. *Killing in War.* New York: Clarendon Press.

McMaster, H. R. 1997. *Dereliction of Duty: Lyndon Johnson, Robert*

References

McNamara, the Joint Chiefs of Staff, and the Lies That Led to Vietnam. New York: HarperCollins.

McNeill, William H. 1967. "The Draft in the Light of History." In *The Draft*, edited by Sol Tax. Chicago: University of Chicago Press.

_____. 1989. *The Age of Gunpowder Empires, 1450–1800*. Essays on Global and Comparative History. Washington, DC: American Historical Association.

McPherson, James M. 1988. *Battle Cry of Freedom: The Civil War Era*. New York: Oxford University Press.

McPherson, James M. 1997. *For Cause and Comrades: Why Men Fought in the Civil War*. New York: Oxford University Press.

Malešević, Siniša. 2010. *The Sociology of War and Violence*. New York: Cambridge University Press.

_____. 2011. "Nationalism, War and Social Cohesion." *Ethnic and Racial Studies* 34 (1): 142–61. doi:10.1080/01419870.2010.489647.

_____. 2015. "Where Does Group Solidarity Come from? Gellner and Ibn Khaldun Revisited." *Thesis Eleven* 128 (1): 85–99. doi:10.1177/0725513615587415.

Manchester, William. 1987. "The Bloodiest Battle of Them All." *New York Times*, June 14. http://www.nytimes.com/1987/06/14/magazine/the-bloodiest-battle-of-all.html.

Mann, Michael. 2012. *The Sources of Social Power: Volume 4, Globalizations, 1945–2011*. New York: Cambridge University Press.

Mansfield, Edward D., and Jack Snyder. 2010. "Does War Influence Democratization?" In *In War's Wake: International Conflict and the Fate of Liberal Democracy*, 23–49. New York: Cambridge University Press.

Mao, Zedong. 1961. *On Guerrilla Warfare*. New York: Praeger.

Marlantes, Karl. 2011. *What It Is like to Go to War*. New York: Atlantic Monthly Press.

Marshall, S. L. A. (1947) 2000. *Men against Fire: The Problem of Battle Command*. Norman, OK: University of Oklahoma Press.

Martines, Lauro. 2013. *Furies: War in Europe, 1450–1700*. New York: Bloomsbury Press.

Marvin, Carolyn, and David W Ingle. 1999. *Blood Sacrifice and the Nation: Totem Rituals and the American Flag*. New York: Cambridge University Press.

Massey, Douglas S. 2005. *Strangers in a Strange Land: Humans in an Urbanizing World*. New York: W. W. Norton & Co.

May, Ernest R. 2000. *Strange Victory: Hitler's Conquest of France*. New York: Hill and Wang.

Mazower, Mark. 2008. *Hitler's Empire: How the Nazis Ruled Europe*. New York: Penguin Press.

Mazur, Allan. 2005. "Testosterone." In *Encyclopedia of Human Development*, edited by Neil J. Salkind, 1259–60. Thousand Oaks, CA: SAGE Publications, Inc. http://dx.doi.org/10.4135/9781412952484.

References

Mehta, Pranjal, and Mehta Josephs. 2007. "Testosterone." In *Encyclopedia of Social Psychology*, edited by Roy F. Baumeister and Kathleen D. Vohs, 983–85. Thousand Oaks, CA: SAGE Publications, Inc. http://dx.doi.org/10.4135/9781412956253.

Milam, Ron. 2009. *Not a Gentleman's War: An Inside View of Junior Officers in the Vietnam War*. Chapel Hill, NC: University of North Carolina Press.

Milgram, Stanley. 1974. *Obedience to Authority: An Experimental View*. New York: Harper & Row.

"Military Health Services in the USSR." 1945. *Nature* 155 (3929): 198.

Miller, Jerry. 2010. *Stockpile: The Story behind 10,000 Strategic Nuclear Weapons*. Annapolis, MD: Naval Institute Press.

Miller, Rory, ed. 2010. *Britain, Palestine, and Empire: The Mandate Years*. Burlington, VT: Ashgate.

Miller, William Ian. 2000. *The Mystery of Courage*. Cambridge, MA: Harvard University Press.

Modell, John, and Timothy Haggerty. 1991. "The Social Impact of War." *Annual Review of Sociology* 17 (ArticleType: research-article/Full publication date: 1991 / Copyright © 1991 Annual Reviews): 205–24. doi:10.2307/2083341.

Moffett, Mark W. 2010. *Adventures among Ants: A Global Safari with a Cast of Trillions*. Berkeley: University of California Press.

Moor, Jaap de, and H. L Wesseling. 1989. *Imperialism and War: Essays on Colonial Wars in Asia and Africa*. Leiden: E. J. Brill.

Morris, Ian. 2014. *War! What Is It Good For?: Conflict and the Progress of Civilization from Primates to Robots*. New York: Farrar, Straus and Giroux.

Moses, A. Dirk, ed. 2008. *Empire, Colony, Genocide: Conquest, Occupation, and Subaltern Resistance in World History*. New York: Berghahn Books.

Mosse, George L. 1975. *The Nationalization of the Masses; Political Symbolism and Mass Movements in Germany from the Napoleonic Wars through the Third Reich*. 1st American edn. New York: H. Fertig.

Moyar, Mark. 2009. *A Question of Command: Counterinsurgency from the Civil War to Iraq*. New Haven: Yale University Press.

Mullaney, Craig M. 2009. *The Unforgiving Minute: A Soldier's Education*. New York: Penguin.

Muravchik, Joshua. 1991. "At Last, Pax Americana." *New York Times*, January 24, sec. Opinion. http://www.nytimes.com/1991/01/24/opinion/at-last-pax-americana.html.

Murphy, Bill. 2008. *In a Time of War: The Proud and Perilous Journey of West Point's Class of 2002*. New York: Henry Holt & Co.

Murray, Williamson, and Allan Reed Millett. 2000. *A War to Be Won: Fighting the Second World War*. Cambridge, MA: Belknap Press of Harvard University Press.

References

Murray, Williamson, and Robert H. Scales. 2003. *The Iraq War: A Military History*. Cambridge, MA: Belknap Press of Harvard University Press.

Nagl, John A. 2005. *Learning to Eat Soup with a Knife: Counterinsurgency Lessons from Malaya and Vietnam*. Chicago: University of Chicago Press.

Neff, Donald. 1981. *Warriors at Suez: Eisenhower Takes America into the Middle East*. New York: Linden Press/Simon & Schuster.

Nelson, Randy Joe, ed. 2006. *Biology of Aggression*. New York: Oxford University Press.

Nord, Philip G. 2015. *France 1940: Defending the Republic*. New Haven, CT: Yale University Press.

Nye, Joseph S. 1990. *Bound to Lead: The Changing Nature of American Power*. New York: Basic Books.

O'Brien, Phillips Payson. 2015. *How the War Was Won: Air–Sea Power and Allied Victory in World War II*. New York: Cambridge University Press.

O'Connell, Robert L. 1995. *Ride of the Second Horseman: The Birth and Death of War*. New York: Oxford University Press.

Oliver, Kendrick. 2006. *The My Lai Massacre in American History and Memory*. New York: Manchester University Press.

Overy, Richard. 1997. *Why the Allies Won*. New York: W. W. Norton & Co.

Pape, Robert A. 1993. "Why Japan Surrendered." *International Security* 18 (2): 154–201.

____. 1996. *Bombing to Win: Air Power and Coercion in War*. Ithaca, NY: Cornell University Press.

Paret, Peter. 1992. *Understanding War: Essays on Clausewitz and the History of Military Power*. Princeton, NJ: Princeton University Press.

____. 1997. *Imagined Battles: Reflections of War in European Art*. Chapel Hill: University of North Carolina Press.

____. 2009. *The Cognitive Challenge of War: Prussia 1806*. Princeton, NJ: Princeton University Press.

Parker, Geoffrey, ed. 1995. *The Cambridge Illustrated History of Warfare: The Triumph of the West*. New York: Cambridge University Press.

Parrott, David. 2012. *The Business of War: Military Enterprise and Military Revolution in Early Modern Europe*. 1st edn. Cambridge; New York: Cambridge University Press.

Patterson, Ian. 2007. *Guernica and Total War*. Cambridge, Mass.: Harvard University Press.

Pérez-Stable, Marifeli. 1993. *The Cuban Revolution: Origins, Course, and Legacy*. New York: Oxford University Press.

Pew Research Center. 2011. "War and Sacrifice in the Post-9/11 Era." The Military–Civilian Gap. Washington, DC.

Phillips, Joshua E. S. 2010. *None of Us Were Like This Before: American Soldiers and Torture*. New York: Verso.

References

Pinker, Steven. 2011. *The Better Angels of Our Nature: Why Violence Has Declined*. New York: Viking.

Plato. 2012. *Six Great Dialogues: Apology, Crito, Phaedo, Phaedrus, Symposium, The Republic*. New York: Dover Publications.

Pocock, Tom. 1986. *East and West of Suez: The Retreat from Empire*. London: Bodley Head.

Porch, Douglas. 1991. *The French Foreign Legion: A Complete History of the Legendary Fighting Force*. New York, NY: HarperCollins.

Potts, Malcolm, and Thomas Hayden. 2008. *Sex and War: How Biology Explains Warfare and Terrorism and Offers a Path to a Safer World*. Dallas, TX: BenBella Books.

Prakash, Om. 2008. "The Supremacy of the English East India Company, 1740–1800." In *The New Cambridge History of India: European Commercial Enterprise in Pre-Colonial India*, 268–314. New York: Cambridge University Press.

Prunier, Gérard. 1995. *The Rwanda Crisis: History of a Genocide*. New York: Columbia University Press.

"Punch Cartoons on WW1, The Great War | PUNCH Magazine Cartoon Archive." n.d. http://punch.photoshelter.com/gallery-image/World-War-1-Cartoons-WW1/G0000dASULVAdiAI/I0000712TyXiRNEU.

Rabb, Theodore K. 2011. *The Artist and the Warrior: Military History through the Eyes of the Masters*. New Haven, CT: Yale University Press.

Rahbek-Clemmensen, Jon, Emerald M. Archer, John Barr, Aaron Belkin, Mario Guerrero, Cameron Hall, and Katie E. O. Swain. 2012. "Conceptualizing the Civil–Military Gap: A Research Note." *Armed Forces and Society* 38 (4): 669–78. doi:10.1177/0095327X12456509.

Ralston, David B. 1996. *Importing the European Army: The Introduction of European Military Techniques and Institutions into the Extra-European World, 1600–1914*. Chicago: University of Chicago Press.

Raudzens, George. 2003. *Technology, Disease, and Colonial Conquests, Sixteenth to Eighteenth Centuries*. Boston, MA: Brill Academic Publishers.

Ray, Rajat Kanta. 1998. "Indian Society and the Establishment of British Supremacy, 1765–1818." In *The Oxford History of the British Empire: Volume II: The Eighteenth Century*, edited by P. J. Marshall, Alaine Low, and Wm. Roger Louis. New York: Oxford University Press.

Reed, Thomas C., and Danny B. Stillman. 2009. *The Nuclear Express: A Political History of the Bomb and Its Proliferation*. Minneapolis, MN: Zenith Press.

Reese, Roger R. 2011. *Why Stalin's Soldiers Fought: The Red Army's Military Effectiveness in World War II*. Lawrence, KS: University Press of Kansas.

Reichberg, Gregory M, Henrik Syse, and Endre Begby. 2006. *The Ethics of War: Classic and Contemporary Readings*. Malden, MA: Blackwell Publishing.

References

Reporting Vietnam, Part Two: American Journalism 1969–1975. 1998. New York: Library of America.

Rhodes, Richard. 1995. *Dark Sun: The Making of the Hydrogen Bomb*. New York: Simon & Schuster.

____. 1999. *Why They Kill: The Discoveries of a Maverick Criminologist*. New York: Alfred A. Knopf.

____. 2002. *Masters of Death: The SS-Einsatzgruppen and the Invention of the Holocaust*. New York: A. A. Knopf.

____. 2007. *Arsenals of Folly: The Making of the Nuclear Arms Race*. New York: Alfred A. Knopf.

Ricklefs, M. C. 2001. *A History of Modern Indonesia since C. 1200*. 3rd edn. Stanford, CA: Stanford University Press.

Ricks, Thomas E. 1997a. *Making the Corps*. New York: Scribner.

____. 1997b. "The Widening Gap Between Military and Society." *The Atlantic*, July. http://www.theatlantic.com/magazine/archive/1997/07/the-widening-gap-between-military-and-society/306158/.

____. 2006. *Fiasco: The American Military Adventure in Iraq*. New York: Penguin Press.

____. 2009. *The Gamble: General David Petraeus and the American Military Adventure in Iraq, 2006–2008*. New York: Penguin Press.

Rose, Alexander. 2015. *Men of War: The American Soldier in Combat at Bunker Hill, Gettysburg, and Iwo Jima*. New York: Random House.

Rosenbaum, Ron. 2011. *How the End Begins: The Road to a Nuclear World War III*. New York: Simon & Schuster.

Roth-Douquet, Kathy, and Frank Schaeffer. 2006. *AWOL: The Unexcused Absence of America's Upper Classes from the Military – and How It Hurts Our Country*. New York: Collins.

Rothenberg, Gunther E. 1980. *The Art of Warfare in the Age of Napoleon*. Bloomington, IN: Indiana University Press.

Roy, Kaushik. 2005. "Military Synthesis in South Asia: Armies, Warfare and Indian Society, C. 1740–1849." *Journal of Military History* 69 (3): 651–90. doi:10.1353/jmh.2005.0187.

Roy, Tirthankar. 2012. *The East India Company: The World's Most Powerful Corporation*. Story of Indian Business. New Delhi: Allen Lane.

Russell, Bertrand. 1917. *Political Ideals*. New York: The Century Co.

____. 2007. *Justice in War-Time*. New York: Cosimo Classics.

Rustow, Dankwart A. 1970. "Transitions to Democracy: Toward a Dynamic Model." *Comparative Politics* 2 (3): 337–63. doi:10.2307/421307.

Sala, Nohemi, Juan Luis Arsuaga, Ana Pantoja-Pérez, Adrián Pablos, Ignacio Martínez, Rolf M. Quam, Asier Gómez-Olivencia, José María Bermúdez de Castro, and Eudald Carbonell. 2015. "Lethal Interpersonal Violence in the Middle Pleistocene." *PLoS ONE* 10 (5): e0126589. doi:10.1371/journal.pone.0126589.

References

Samuel, Raphael. 1989. "Continuous National History." In *Patriotism: The Making and Unmaking of British National Identity*, edited by Raphael Samuel. New York: Routledge.

Sayer, Derek. 1991. "British Reaction to the Amritsar Massacre 1919–1920." *Past and Present*, no. 131 (May): 130–64. doi:10.2307/650872.

Scahill, Jeremy. 2008. *Blackwater: The Rise of the World's Most Powerful Mercenary Army*. Pbk. edn., fully rev. and updated. New York: Nation Books.

Schivelbusch, Wolfgang. 2003. *The Culture of Defeat: On National Trauma, Mourning, and Recovery*. New York: Metropolitan Books.

Sebald, W. G. 2003. *On the Natural History of Destruction*. New York: Random House.

Segal, David R., and Mady Wechsler Segal. 2004. "America's Military Population." *Population Bulletin* v 59, n 4. Population Reference Bureau. http://www.deomi. org/contribute/DiversityMgmt/documents/AmericasMilitaryPopulation2004. pdf.

Settersten, Richard A. 2006. "When Nations Call How War-Time Military Service Matters for the Life Course and Aging." *Research on Aging* 28 (1): 12–36. doi:10.1177/0164027505281577.

Shaw, Martin. 2005. *The New Western Way of War: Risk-Transfer War and Its Crisis in Iraq*. Cambridge: Polity.

Sheehan, James J. 2008. *Where Have All the Soldiers Gone?: The Transformation of Modern Europe*. Boston: Houghton Mifflin.

Sheehan, Neil. 1988. *A Bright Shining Lie: John Paul Vann and America in Vietnam*. New York: Random House.

____. 2009. *A Fiery Peace in a Cold War: Bernard Schriever and the Ultimate Weapon*. New York: Random House.

Sherman, Nancy. 2005. *Stoic Warriors: The Ancient Philosophy behind the Military Mind*. New York: Oxford University Press.

Sherry, Michael S. 1987. *The Rise of American Air Power: The Creation of Armageddon*. New Haven, CT: Yale University Press.

Sherwin, Martin J. 1975. *A World Destroyed: The Atomic Bomb and the Grand Alliance*. New York: Knopf: Distributed by Random House.

Shogan, Robert. 1991. *The Riddle of Power: Presidential Leadership from Truman to Bush*. New York: Dutton.

Siddle, Bruce K. 1995. *Sharpening the Warrior's Edge*. Belleville, IL: Distributed by PPCT Research Publications, PPCT Management Systems.

Sinclair, Robert R., and Thomas W. Britt. 2013. "Military Resilience: Remaining Questions and Concluding Comments." In *Building Psychological Resilience in Military Personnel*, edited by Robert R. Sinclair. Washington, DC: American Psychological Association.

Singer, P. W. 2009. *Wired for War: The Robotics Revolution and Conflict in the Twenty-First Century*. New York: Penguin Press.

Skocpol, Theda. 1992. *Protecting Soldiers and Mothers: The Politics of Social*

References

Provision in the United States, 1870s–1920s. Cambridge, MA: Belknap Press of Harvard University Press.

Sledge, E. B. 2007. *With the Old Breed: At Peleliu and Okinawa.* Reprint edn. New York: Presidio Press.

Small, Melvin, and Joel David Singer. 1982. *Resort to Arms: International and Civil Wars, 1816–1980.* Beverly Hills, CA: Sage Publications, Inc.

Smith, Dan. 2008. *The Penguin State of the World Atlas.* 8th edn. New York: Penguin Books.

Smith, David Livingstone. 2007. *The Most Dangerous Animal: Human Nature and the Origins of War.* New York: St. Martin's Press.

Smith, Tony. 1975. *The End of the European Empire: Decolonization after World War II.* Lexington, MA: Heath.

Smith, Tyler C., Isabel G. Jacobson, Tomoko I. Hooper, Cynthia A. LeardMann, Edward J. Boyko, Besa Smith, Gary D. Gackstetter, et al. 2011. "Health Impact of US Military Service in a Large Population-Based Military Cohort: Findings of the Millennium Cohort Study, 2001–2008." *BMC Public Health* 11: 69. doi:10.1186/1471-2458-11-69.

Snyder, Timothy. 2010. *Bloodlands: Europe between Hitler and Stalin.* New York: Basic Books.

Sommer, Doris. 1991. *Foundational Fictions: The National Romances of Latin America/Doris Sommer.* Latin American Literature and Culture (Berkeley, California) ; 7. Berkeley: University of California Press.

Spores, John C. 1988. *Running Amok: An Historical Inquiry.* Monographs in International Studies. Southeast Asia Series; No. 82. Athens, OH: Ohio University Center for International Studies, Center for Southeast Asian Studies.

Staub, Ervin. 1989. *The Roots of Evil: The Origins of Genocide and Other Group Violence.* New York: Cambridge University Press.

_____ . 2011. *Overcoming Evil: Genocide, Violent Conflict, and Terrorism.* New York: Oxford University Press.

Steinmetz, George. 2007. *The Devil's Handwriting: Precoloniality and the German Colonial State in Qingdao, Samoa, and Southwest Africa.* Chicago, IL: University of Chicago Press.

Stein, Lorenz von. (1885) 1964. "On Taxation." In *Classics in the Theory of Public Finance,* edited by Richard A. Musgrave and Alan T. Peacock, 28–36. New York: Macmillan.

Stephenson, Michael. 2012. *The Last Full Measure: How Soldiers Die in Battle.* New York: Crown Publishers.

Stockholm International Peace Research Institute. 2015. *SIPRI Yearbook 2015: Armaments, Disarmament and International Security.* New York: Oxford University Press. http://www.sipri.org/yearbook/2015.

Stora, Benjamin. 2001. *Algeria, 1830–2000: A Short History.* Ithaca, NY: Cornell University Press.

References

Strachan, Hew. 1983. *European Armies and the Conduct of War*. Boston, MA: Allen & Unwin.

Strauss, Barry. 2004. "The Dead of Arginusae and the Debate about the Athenian Navy." *Nautiki Epithewrisi [Naval Review]* 545 (160s): 40–67.

Symonds, Craig L. 2011. *The Battle of Midway*. New York: Oxford University Press.

"Syria: The Story of the Conflict." 2015. *BBC News*. Accessed July 7. http://www.bbc.com/news/world-middle-east-26116868.

Taber, Robert. 1965. *The War of the Flea: A Study of Guerrilla Warfare Theory and Practise*. New York: L. Stuart.

Tajfel, Henri. 1974. "Social Identity and Intergroup Behavior." *Social Science Information* 13: 65–93.

_____. 1981. *Human Groups and Social Categories: Studies in Social Psychology*. New York: Cambridge University Press.

_____. ed. 1982. *Social Identity and Intergroup Relations*, edited by Henri Tajfel. European Studies in Social Psychology. New York: Cambridge University Press.

Tanner, Stephen. 2009. *Afghanistan: A Military History from Alexander the Great to the War against the Taliban*. Updated version. Cambridge, MA: Da Capo Press.

Taylor, Fred. 2004. *Dresden, Tuesday, February 13, 1945*. New York: HarperCollins.

Teachman, Jay. 2005. "Military Service in the Vietnam Era and Educational Attainment." *Sociology of Education* 78 (1): 50–68.

_____. 2007. "Military Service and Educational Attainment in the All-Volunteer Era." *Sociology of Education* 80 (4): 359–74. doi:10.2307/20452717.

Teachman, Jay D., and Vaughn R. A. Call. 1996. "The Effect of Military Service on Educational, Occupational, and Income Attainment." *Social Science Research* 25 (1): 1–31.

The Big Picture: The Citizen Soldier. 1951. Army Pictorial Service. https://www.youtube.com/watch?v=_lvCuXW3mwI.

Thornton, John. 1999. "Warfare, Slave Trading, and European Influence: Atlantic Africa 1450–1800." In *War in the Early Modern World, 1450–1815*, edited by Jeremy Black, 129–46. London: UCL Press.

Tilly, Charles. 1975. "Conditions Favoring the Nation-State." In *The Formation of National States in Western Europe*, 1–5.

_____. 1985. "War Making and State Making as Organized Crime." In *Bringing the State Back In*, edited by Peter Evans, Dietrich Rueschemeyer, and Theda Skocpol, 169–92. New York: Cambridge University Press.

_____. 1992. *Coercion, Capital, and European States, AD 990–1992*. Cambridge, MA: Blackwell Publishing.

Tolstoy, Leo. (1869) 2007. *War and Peace*. Translated by Richard Pevear and Larissa Volokhonsky. 1st edn. New York: Alfred A. Knopf.

205

References

Tomsen, Peter. 2011. *The Wars of Afghanistan: Messianic Terrorism, Tribal Conflicts, and the Failures of Great Powers.* New York: PublicAffairs.

Tooby, John, and Leda Cosmides. 1988. "The Evolution of War and Its Cognitive Foundations." Technical Report 88–1. Ann Arbor, MI: Institute for Evolutionary Studies. http://www.cep.ucsb.edu/papers/EvolutionofWar.pdf.

———. 2010. "Groups in Mind: The Coalitional Roots of War and Morality." In *Morality and Sociality: Evolutionary and Comparative Perspectives,* edited by Henrik Høgh-Olesen, 91–234. New York: Palgrave Macmillan.

Trigger, Bruce G. 2003. *Understanding Early Civilizations: A Comparative Study.* New York: Cambridge University Press.

Tsouras, Peter. 2005. *The Book of Military Quotations.* St. Paul, MN: Zenith Press.

Tufte, Edward R. 2007. *The Visual Display of Quantitative Information.* 2nd edn., 5th printing. Cheshire, CT: Graphics Press.

Turchin, Peter. 2007. *War and Peace and War: The Rise and Fall of Empires.* New York: Penguin Group.

Turnbull, Stephen R. 2006. *The Samurai and the Sacred.* New York: Osprey.

Turner, Bryan S., and Peter Hamilton, eds. 1994. *Citizenship: Critical Concepts.* London; New York: Routledge.

Ucko, David H. 2013. "Clear-Hold-Build-Fail? Rethinking Local-Level Counterinsurgency." *War on the Rocks.* November 7. http://warontherocks.com/2013/11/clear-hold-build-fail-rethinking-local-level-counterinsurgency/.

Urben, Heidi A. 2010. "Civil–Military Relations in a Time of War: Party, Politics, and the Profession of Arms." PhD Dissertation, Washington, DC: Georgetown University. http://hdl.handle.net/10822/553111.

US Army Combined Arms Center. n.d. "Clear, Hold, Build." http:// usacac.army.mil/cac2/AIWFC/COIN/repository/LWAPRO9/8-Clear%20Hold%20Build.ppt.

US Department of Veterans Affairs. 2010. "Fact Sheet: America's Wars." Washington, DC: Office of Public Affairs, Media Relations. http://www.va.gov/opa/publications/factsheets/fs_americas_wars.pdf.

Van Creveld, Martin L. 2004. *Supplying War: Logistics from Wallenstein to Patton.* 2nd edn. New York: Cambridge University Press.

———. 2008. *The Changing Face of War: Combat from the Marne to Iraq.* New York: Presidio Press.

———. 2011. *The Age of Airpower.* New York: PublicAffairs.

Van Evera, Stephen. 1994. "Hypotheses on Nationalism and War." *International Security* 18 (4): 5–39.

Voltaire. 1757. *The History of the War of Seventeen Hundred and Forty One Translated from the French of M. de Voltaire. The Third Edition. In Which Is Now Added a Continuation of the Said History, from the Battle of Fontenoy to the Treaty of Aix-La-Chapelle. By the Same Hand.* London: printed for J. Nourse.

References

Walsh, Chris. 2014. *Cowardice: A Brief History.*

Walzer, Michael. (1977) 2000. *Just and Unjust Wars: A Moral Argument With Historical Illustrations.* 3rd edn. New York: Basic Books.

____. 2009. "Responsibility and Proportionality in State and Nonstate Wars." *Parameters* 39 (1): 40–52.

Wang, Lin, Glen H. Elder Jr., and Naomi J. Spence. 2012. "Status Configurations, Military Service and Higher Education." *Social Forces* 91 (2): 397–421.

Warden, A. A. 1914. "Compulsory Military Service and National Health." *The Lancet* 1 (4724): 787. doi:10.1016/S0140-6736(01)20571-6.

"Wars in the World." n.d. http://www.warsintheworld.com.

Watkins, Shanea J., and James Sherk. 2008. "Who Serves in the US Military?: Demographic Characteristics of Enlisted Troops and Officers." The Heritage Foundation.

Watson, Alexander. 2009. *Enduring the Great War: Combat, Morale and Collapse in the German and British Armies, 1914–1918.* New York: Cambridge University Press.

Weber, Eugen. 1976. *Peasants into Frenchmen: The Modernization of Rural France, 1870–1914.* Stanford, CA: Stanford University Press.

Weber, Max. 1946a. *From Max Weber: Essays in Sociology.* Edited by H. H. Gerth and C. Wright Mills. New York: Oxford University Press.

____. (1919b) 1946. "Politics as a Vocation." In *From Max Weber: Essays in Sociology,* edited by H. H. Gerth and C. Wright Mills, 47–76. New York: Oxford University Press.

____. (1922) 1978. *Economy and Society: An Outline of Interpretive Sociology.* Edited by Guenther Roth and Claus Wittich. Berkeley, CA: University of California Press.

____. (1927) 2003. *General Economic History.* New York: Dover Publications.

Weigley, Russell Frank. 1977. *The American Way of War: A History of United States Military Strategy and Policy.* Bloomington: Indiana University Press.

____. 1991. *The Age of Battles: The Quest for Decisive Warfare from Breitenfeld to Waterloo.* Bloomington: Indiana University Press.

Weinberg, Gerhard L. 2005. *A World at Arms: A Global History of World War II.* 2nd edn. New York: Cambridge University Press.

Weiss, Eugenia L., and David L. Albright. 2014. "Introduction to the Special Issue: Mental Health Care for Military Service Members, Veterans, and Their Families: Opportunities for Social Work." *Social Work in Mental Health* 12 (5–6): 387–90. doi:10.1080/15332985.2014.927408.

Wieviorka, Olivier. 2008. *Normandy: The Landings to the Liberation of Paris.* Cambridge, MA: Belknap Press of Harvard University Press.

Williams, Timothy. 2012. "Suicides Eclipse War Deaths for US Troops." *New York Times,* June 8. http://www.nytimes.com/2012/06/09/us/suicides-eclipse-war-deaths-for-us-troops.html.

References

Wilmoth, Janet M., Andrew S. London, and Wendy M. Parker. 2010. "Military Service and Men's Health Trajectories in Later Life." *Journals of Gerontology Series B: Psychological Sciences and Social Sciences* 65B (6): 744–55. doi:10.1093/geronb/gbq072.

Wilson, Edward O. (1978) 1982. *On Human Nature*. Bantam New Age Books. New York: Bantam Books.

____. (1975) 2000. *Sociobiology: The New Synthesis*. 25th Anniversary. Cambridge, MA: Belknap Press of Harvard University Press.

Wilson, Peter H. 2009. *The Thirty Years War: Europe's Tragedy*. Cambridge, Mass.: Belknap Press of Harvard University Press.

Wimmer, Andreas. 2002. *Nationalist Exclusion and Ethnic Conflict: Shadows of Modernity*. Cambridge University Press.

____. 2013. *Waves of War: Nationalism, State Formation, and Ethnic Exclusion in the Modern World*. Cambridge Studies in Comparative Politics. New York: Cambridge University Press.

____. 2014. "War." *Annual Review of Sociology* 40 (1): 173–97. doi:10.1146/annurev-soc-071913-043416.

Winerip, Michael. 2011. "Military Children Outdo Public School Students on NAEP Tests." *New York Times*, December 11. http://www.nytimes.com/2011/12/12/education/military-children-outdo-public-school-students-on-naep-tests.html.

Winik, Jay. 2001. *April 1865: The Month That Saved America*. New York: HarperCollins Publishers.

Winter, Jay. 2010. "Veterans, Human Rights, and the Transformation of European Democracy." In *In War's Wake: International Conflict and the Fate of Liberal Democracy*, edited by Elizabeth Kier and Ronald R. Krebs. New York: Cambridge University Press.

____. ed. 2014. *The Cambridge History of the First World War*. 1st edn. New York: Cambridge University Press.

Wrangham, Richard W. 1999. "Evolution of Coalitionary Killing." *American Journal of Physical Anthropology* 110 (S29): 1–30.

Wrangham, Richard W., and Luke Glowacki. 2012. "Intergroup Aggression in Chimpanzees and War in Nomadic Hunter-Gatherers." *Human Nature* 23 (1): 5–29. doi:10.1007/s12110-012-9132-1.

Wright, Evan. 2004. *Generation Kill: Devil Dogs, Iceman, Captain America and the New Face of American War*. 1st edn. New York: G. P. Putnam's Sons.

Wright, Quincy. 1964. *A Study of War*. Abridged edn. Chicago, IL: University of Chicago Press.

Zillman, Donald N. 2006. "Essay: Where Have All the Soldiers Gone II: Military Veterans in Congress and the State of Civil–Military Relations." *Maine Law Review* 58 (1): 135–55.

Index

Index

Index

Index

Colley, Linda 130
Collins, Randall
  on brutality 43
  forward panic 41
  violence and difference 26–7
Colombian civil war 147
colonialism *see* conquest; imperialism
combat
  religion and 51–2
  women and 166
communication
  development for war 2
  WWII networks 85
community, nationalism and 125–7
conquest 175
  acquisition and domination 92–4
  Africa 100–3
  Asia and 98–100
  end of European empires 3
  post-empire world 152–4
  Spanish in Americas 94–8
  threats of annihilation 2
conscription
  selective 171–2
  states and 128–32
  United States 129, 165–6
Constantinople, fall of 75
conventions of war
  legitimate/illegitimate targets 90–1
Cooper, Frederick 153
Cornell University 141
Cortes, Hernan 95
Cosmides, Leda 14–15
courage and heroism
  distinction from bravery 55
  faith in 52
  large armies and 78
  self-sacrifice 45
  virtue of 2
cowardice, fear of 36
Craig, Campbell 114
Crane, Stephen 48
Crassus, Marcus Licinius 72
Crawford, Neta 150
Croatia 24–5
Crusades, horses and 73
Cuba
  Missile Crisis 116
  Revolution of 158–9

culture
  "bellicosity" in 25
  as a cause of war 23–5, 27–8
  narcissism of small differences
  26

Daggett, Stephen 160–1
Dahomey (ancient Benin)
  female soldiers 15–16
Davis, Paul K. 50
death
  20th c. wars and 83–4
  bodies on battlefields 32–4
  classifying warfare and 8
  fear of post-death mutilation 36
  killing efficiency 34, 110
  long-term health of soldiers 138
  major risk of 139
  stoicism against gunpowder 77–8
  toll of conquests 175
DeBruyne, Nese F. 83
democracy 118
  conscription and 131–2
  deferring elections 134
  democratization of violence
  162–3
  inclusion/exclusion 125–6
  staged elections 134–5
  war and political order 175–6
desertion, soldiers' fear and 35
Dethloff, Henry C. 171
Diamond, Jared
  deaths in American conquest 95
  diseases to the New World 93
discipline
  binding warriors together 58
  coercing soldiers 46–8
  definition of 56–7
  gunpowder revolution 76
  large armies and 78
  obedience and 57–60
  stronger than devotion 129
disease
  Europeans in Africa 100–1
  Spanish in Americas 97
Douhet, Giulio 111
  The Command of the Air 109
Dower, John W.
  dehumanizing the enemy 115

Index

Index

214

Index

Index

Index

Index

Index

Index

Index

Index